Camus' Plague

Other Books of Interest from St. Augustine's Press

Joseph Bottum, *The Decline of the Novel*

David Ramsay Steele, *The Mystery of Fascism*

James V. Schall, *On the Principles of Taxing Beer:*
And Other Brief Philosophical Essays

Rémi Brague, *The Anchors in the Heavens*

Rémi Brague, *Moderately Modern*

Marvin R. O'Connell, *Telling Stories that Matter: Memoirs and Essays*

Josef Pieper, *Traditional Truth, Poetry, Sacrament:*
For My Mother, on her 70th Birthday

Peter Kreeft, *Socrates' Children: The 100 Greatest Philosophers*

Peter Kreeft, *Ethics for Beginners: Big Ideas from 32 Great Minds*

John von Heyking, *Comprehensive Judgment and Absolute Selflessness:*
Winston Churchill on Politics as Friendship

David Lowenthal, *Slave State: Rereading Orwell's 1984*

Nathan Lefler, *Tale of a Criminal Mind Gone Good*

Will Morrisey, *Herman Melville's Ship of State*

John Poch, *God's Poems: The Beauty of Poetry and the Christian Imagination*

Roger Scruton, *The Politics of Culture and Other Essays*

Roger Scruton, *The Meaning of Conservatism: Revised 3rd Edition*

Roger Scruton, *An Intelligent Person's Guide to Modern Culture*

Aristotle, *De Anima, or About the Soul*

Stanley Rosen, *The Language of Love: An Interpretation of Plato's Phaedrus*

Robert Greene, *The Death and Life of Philosophy*

Anne Drury Hall, *Where the Muses Still Haunt*

Giulio Maspero, *After Pandemic, After Modernity: The Relational Revolution*

Winston Churchill, *The River War*

Winston Churchill, *Savrola*

Camus' Plague
Myth for Our World

GENE FENDT

ST. AUGUSTINE'S PRESS
South Bend, Indiana

Copyright © 2022 by Gene Fendt

All rights reserved. No part of this book may be reproduced, stored in a retrieval
system, or transmitted, in any form or by any means,
electronic, mechanical, photocopying, recording, or
otherwise, without the prior permission of St. Augustine's Press.

Manufactured in the United States of America.

1 2 3 4 5 6   27 26 25 24 23 22

Library of Congress Control Number: 2021949314

Paperback ISBN: 978-1-58731-106-2
Ebook ISBN: 978-1-58731-107-9

∞ The paper used in this publication meets the minimum
requirements of the American National Standard for Information Sciences –
Permanence of Paper for Printed Materials, ANSI Z39.48-1984.

St. Augustine's Press
www.staugustine.net

FRONTISPIECE

Oran, 2020

One notices a syndrome;
it is noticed because it is fatal.

A little research shows
it's been here for a while,

but only rats and dogs
had died of it till now.

(Are these terms metaphors?)

Quarantines begin:
some sectors are more affected.

Many lose their jobs,
some get rich; both die.

Children suffer torture,
city squares empty,

a cough provokes suspicion,
bands and opera cease.

Doctors confabulate
with politicians; doors close;

the words that escape are all
quite technical.

It goes on. News
and opinion multiply,

replicate themselves,
mutate colorfully—

and not. It goes on.
Are these terms metaphors?

For Matt Formato,

and

thirty-some years of fellow students

TABLE OF CONTENTS

TOWARDS A PREFACE

> Solitudes unite those society separates…, and destinies tend to
> repeat each other.
> —Albert Camus, LCE 12–13

Camus has most often been read as an atheistic existentialist, an absurdist philosopher of revolt. It is rather queer, then, to be able to see that in *The Plague* he is working quite rigorously through a number of the most important thinkers and problems in the history of philosophy, using terms he would have known well thanks to his studies leading to the *diplôme d'études supérieures* in Philosophy. We should read him knowing he is not a man of the last 15 minutes—or less; he studied and was conversant with many of the most important primary sources among philosophers, and we should not be surprised to find he was particularly interested in their ethical and anthropological ideas, including particularly their conceptions of human community. We should also not be surprised to find philosophy shot through the entirety of his art, neither absent from some of it nor merely more or less well-camouflaged stalking horses in one or another character or novel. To be a philosophical thinker means to really have it in your bones; it should come out in everything—at least it meant that in a previous age, which Camus much admired.

Frequently the history given to these philosophical ideas makes them all seem quite contradictory, but nonetheless a great number of them still live in our world, side by side in our modern city, at least among those who have some self-reflection; the lack of this latter has always been a living option. Despite their seeming mutual contradictions, they coexist in our living—at least physically, and—in the sociological sense, socially. The real, then, is not the rational, as Hegel taught—and as might be proven by the fact that there are still Hegelians among us despite all these mutually contradictory ways of living. Camus' interest in human solidarity means he is interested in discovering what real human community is possible across these real diversities among people. He seems to wish to achieve this without death camps, or the noisy "de-ratization" vans available to modernity. Seeing such diverse people side by side, noting how they connect and fail to connect, is one contribution the novel can make to our own self-reflection about matters such as the nature of happiness and how, if ever, it may be achieved, to what extent, and with whom. If, as has been held for millennia, all human beings desire happiness, then there is no human version of solidarity that can be achieved without answering such questions, and we would all do well to reflect upon them with as much detail and finesse as we can manage. There are, of course, always inhuman versions of solidarity available. Since our modern world has versions of ancient, modern, absurdist, rebellious, Hegelian and Christian characters within it—alongside the inhuman, and Camus' great interest is in trying to see the possible grounds and extent of human solidarity among all these actual diversities, the novel itself—by presenting its many diverse characters and showing what and how they do accomplish significant forms of solidarity (and how they fail)—shows our world what it is made of, for the modern world is precisely this motley assortment. Thus reading the novel can begin the thought processes, and perhaps even some emotional catharses, which are necessary in order to allow that solidarity which is possible for us to gain some traction. One of the ways *The Plague* is the myth of our time is that in it Camus exhibits forms of solidarity among all these who are here with us now.[1] Thereby Camus' book shows itself to be, as he thought all art must be, "a gift to the future" (*MS* 151).

1   Thomas Merton says "*The Plague* is a modern myth about the destiny of man," and so "must be read not simply as a drama or as a psychological study, but as a myth of good and evil, of freedom and determinism, of love against what Hopkins called 'the death dance in our blood'" (181). In the course of his essays Merton suggests that the plague is "the presence in our world of a cynical unprincipled appetite for power which seeks to 'do with man what one wishes'" (183); contentment "to justify one's existence by reference to … automatically accepted norms" (198); the "plague of cerebration … [of] Cartesian man, the detached subject, who is because he thinks" (219); as well as the more usual French society and resistance under the Nazis (262); and "the ambiguous and false explanations, interpretations, conventions, justifications, legalizations, evasions which infect our struggling civilization" (268). This is probably not an entirely comprehensive list of what 'plague' stands for, but any reading of the novel will be able to find all these, and they aren't just in the novel.

Camus attempts this in full knowledge that "the order of the world is shaped by death" (*P* 117) and there are many ways of dealing it out—our science and technology are inventing new ones every day. The "machine gun rattle from [the] exhaust of the 'deratization' van" (*P* 52) that interrupts one of the doctor's conversations puts together several of the (at that time) newer ways: the machine guns which had been so wonderfully effective in WWI, and the vans of Jews driven around with, first, the exhaust pipes filling the cargo space with the exhaust, and later, the more efficient Xyklon-B gas substituted. In the novel's later development the rat poison is pumped into the sewers, which come up in the basement of every house. No doubt it was a gas heavier than air, so stayed in its place. In the war, which has long been taken as the prime referent of the novel's symbolism, more efficient solutions than small vans were invented for deratizizing society. Could we invent something new that enters every house, that would effectively deratizize our city? No doubt we have; the technological world does not stand still. But what if, as Tarrou says, "each of us has the plague within him" (*P* 229)?

Numerous people with whom I spoke of this project after January of 2019 commented on its appropriateness for the time. Of course, there is a point to that—we live in time of obvious plague now ourselves. But this point might make a person miss the point I think is more true, and which I think Camus' novel shows: modernity itself is a time of plague. Ah well, no doubt, so were ancient times, and the Middle Ages. But the modern city and its citizens do not see themselves this way: plague is not normal, "It's too stupid; it can't last long;" "it vanished from the temperate countries long ago" (*P* 34)—all those things characters in the novel think and say. But a reader of the novel learns to see that the particular plague named in the novel merely brings to the fore—for a reader—that there is a plague which has always been here, which was the normal, is the normal, and does last—in the books and in the bedclothes, under the modern carpet, in modern normal behaviors, patterns of thought—and of non-thought. Merton says that "the measure of Oran is the measure of modern man in his banality, his love of system, his routine practicality, his indifference to life in depth" (Merton, 187). That is a good start in describing the modern plague, though we have many more aids to superficiality than Merton or Camus could have dreamt of—and so we are more successful. Such things increase both the virulence and the transmissibility of spiritual plague; various citizens (in the novel) exhibit its sundry symptoms, but as Tarrou says, we all have it. And have had it: even Socrates could agree with Dr. Castel's evaluation that "these little brutes always have an air of originality. But, at bottom, it's always the same thing" (*P* 52). In his *Apology*, Socrates' calls the plague leading to his accusation a *diabolê*. It has passed from mouth to mouth, father to son, playwright to audience by breath.

One might consider that the originality of our modern plague is that many people admit of no symptoms; so, many think it doesn't exist. Really, however, even this was true in previous centuries, though not about bubonic plague. Socrates might have proposed that the problem was ignorance, perhaps a lack of self-knowledge, due to a lack of self-examination. He himself was a gadfly, given to Athens not to spread disease, but to wake the citizens up to it. Aristotle called those who did not know the end of human life and the ends of its various forms of association natural slaves, and he made no bones about there being many such. Several times the more gentle, Socratic theme is suggested in the novel, but as with Socrates's diagnosis, one has to wonder if this ignorance is accidental, natural, cultural, or perhaps due to ignoring the command of a god—whether the one at Delphi, or some other. And this last ignoring, too, might be accidental, natural, cultural, or perhaps even freely chosen. Perhaps Aristotle's condemnation is closer to the truth. One has heard of such a plague, but refuses to believe such things exist in the modern world: "It's unthinkable. Everyone knows it's ceased to appear in Western Europe" (*P* 33), as if only barbarian (or, as we used to say, "third world") countries could have plagues. What could spiritual plague even mean? All of these themes are suggested in the novel, but this is a work of art, and Camus is in no hurry to prove any of them conclusively. All of the characters, even the criminal, would seem relatively normal to the twenty-first century reader; absent a pre-existent ideological prejudice, the reader has a rather full world of plausible ways of life as well as character judgements available. Is only one "good faith"? Are any?

By contrast to Camus' work here, Roquentin, in Sartre's first novel, who is nauseated at the existence of a tree root, clearly "wins out" as holding the true faith—or at least "good faith"—as opposed to Ogier; though, of course, it is not supposed to involve faith in any ordinary sense at all.

Camus thought that the philosophical elements of Sartre's novel broke its balance as a work of art, but in *The Plague* it is not at all so clear, as we will see, which characters choose best, act most in "good faith," see most lucidly, or "win out"—if any can win out in our modern state of plague. But perhaps, as even in Socrates' time, some do. There is only one named character in the novel whose way of living seems conclusively to be abandoned. That is Cottard, who has no real connection with, much less friendship with or concern for, other people. To be sure, he seems to be "always trying to strike up friendships"—but to the end that one would "make a good witness" (*P* 50). Or, they can be useful in black market dealings or in more ordinary business, but there is no suggestion of pleasure or honest care. Any friendship he might have would easily be labelled a friendship of use by Aristotle, and Cottard fears that when his usefulness evaporates, so will his witnesses and "business" partners. He finds Tarrou easier to deal with than others, but he is puzzled and troubled by the latter's constant various invitations to join in the work of the quarantined community. It is unthinkable to him to risk one's life or health to aid others; every socially approvable thing he does needs to be seen—or what is it for? (cf. *P* 51)

Cottard is something more than merely an example of "bad faith"—of living so as to be seen in a certain way by his neighbors; he has committed a serious crime in the past—he hints that it may even be a capital offence—and though he may wish it, he does not for a moment believe that since God is dead everything is permitted. The crime, perhaps, is the root of his original "aloofness, not to say mistrust of everyone he met" (*P* 50). The first description of him, sounds rattish: "a plump little...was lying there, breathing heavily. He gazed at them with bloodshot eyes. Rieux stopped short. In the intervals of the man's breathing he seemed to hear the little squeals of rats. But he couldn't see anything moving" (*P* 18). Cottard seems almost to be outside the human condition; certainly he is outside the mundane citizenry, who still fund the police, and whom he fears will soon come knocking. They do, eventually. Still, even the very plain old Joseph Grand sees him as a neighbor. Tarrou keeps trying to bring him in. There are such people as Cottard in every modern city; do they make themselves so? What relation ought we to have with such a one? Cottard certainly refuses all efforts to bring him into human solidarity. In the end, he is clearly to be pitied, as Tarrou pitied "that poor blind owl" (*P* 226) he had seen his father condemn to death. He is the mark of the fact that human solidarity has its limits; since, like the world, "the social order ... [is] ... based on the death sentence" (*P* 226). Drawing the limit to human solidarity is a matter of life and death; Cottard seems to think every limit is mere prejudice. Certainly convenience, mutual pleasure, unexamined cultural habits should all seem inadequate bases for drawing such limits. Nonetheless, we will and do draw them, or there is no social order—but that answer will not decrease the death sentences either. Thus, writ small, we see that the problems of these characters are still living in every modern city.

An anecdote: One blue September morning, after preparing for a class in which we were reading *Civilization and its Discontents*, I was walking past a TV which had been pulled into the hallway and was on—something that I had never seen, though a TV might be in the hallway unplugged after use in a classroom. The sound was off; it was a live feed of New York and one of the towers was on fire; as I walked by a plane flew into the other tower. These lines ran through my mind as I took the remaining thirty steps to the classroom:

> He knew what those crowds did not know but could have learned from books: that the plague bacillus never dies or disappears for good; that it can lie dormant for years and years in furniture and linen-chests; that it bides its time in bedrooms, cellars, trunks, and bookshelves; and that perhaps the day would come when, for the bane and the enlightening of men, it would rouse up its rats again and send them forth to die in a happy city (*P* 278).

What I had seen walking by the TV was not something new, but a recrudescence—a raising to a higher level—of the usual sleepy infection: something we live with most of the time without thinking of. The rats had been roused again—"out of the blue" (*P* 15, 34), in a happy city. But a recrudescence of plague reminds us that "the hour has come for serious thought" (*P* 89). For a while, perhaps, we try that; then—being creatures of habit and having the habit of comfort—we seek to become as comfortable as possible in the new normal and fall into new habits which free us from thinking much. We are the citizens of Oran. The best thing to do, I told my class, is not to listen to the news, for what is going on is not new; the best thing is to study what might be the explanations of it, try to understand the nexus of human actions and social machinery in which such things happen—and each one's place and choices in that nexus. The only possible prophylactic against the real danger is spiritual preparation, for prophylactic measures don't just happen, they must be consciously taken up and used—all the time, for the plague is ever present. Freud had one way of trying to understand such matters, Plato's *Republic*, which we would read next in that class, another, but it was *The Plague* which came to mind, unbidden, in that stunning moment. One character in the novel—Tarrou—has come to the point in his own life where he no longer seeks political change—still less revolution, as he had worked for when younger—but sympathetic comprehension. He dies before the novel's final reflections, but the novel of which he is only one part allows us, the readers, such comprehension as he sought of the world in which we all live, whether under a recrudescence of the plague, or in the "normal" world—which is still shaped by death, and in which the plague only seems, at times, to be asleep.

For some years now most of my students have had no memory of that September event; they were unconscious, or born after it. They live in the normal world—not the normal world that existed before that particular recrudescence of plague, but a different normal, one equally conducive to sleepy happinesses and sudden, "unthinkable" evils—or, as we should learn to say, recrudescences of plague. What's normal is the level and sort of plague one is used to. Dr. Richard points this out when asked by Rieux whether he has seen any abnormal inflammations: "that depends on what you mean by 'normal'" (*P* 20). It's normal after particularly strong recrudescences to say "Never again." To put it on placards, all in caps, with exclamation points: "NEVER AGAIN!" One can say many things of plagues; one can even *say* that. It's the mark of a humanist, as the narrator says. But, my sweet lord, it is not the mark of comprehension, is it?

Plan of the Book

Our *Plague* itinerary will begin seemingly distant from the heart of the book's themes, but close to the artist's reasons for writing and the reasons for his way of writing. Camus considered that the work of the artist was essential for every worthwhile society, but that much of so-called art and many artists were either unaware of or had wrongly determined what the work of art is for. In his critical writing and interviews, he clearly outlines several errors of aim, as well as ways of failure even if one might have a right aim. Some of his stories, like "Jonas, or The Artist at Work" in *Exile and the Kingdom*, and characters, like Joseph Grand in *The Plague*, make us think, as well, of the why and the how of the artist—and of what is not an adequate why or how. Significant elements of Camus' view on these matters echo other masters, most particularly Aristotle, who held that a culture could destroy its citizens' capacity for virtue and happiness, and that one of the most important elements for every culture's education was music (which includes all of the arts). So we will start with the Aristotelian distinction between the barbaric and the civilized, and bring it up into Camus' more modern language, issues, and examples regarding art and culture.

Camus defines and criticizes art (implying art of every age) which has become nihilistic—it is not accomplishing the proper end of art; it is, in fact, destructive of such. He sees several versions of this in his day; they have not disappeared. His idea of nihilism is connected to Aristotle's terms for culture and art because the barbarian is defined as one who does not know the end or purpose of (particularly) human life, and its various partnerships. There is no natural end (that is a real natural end) in barbarian activity. This makes the barbarian a natural slave, for if one does not know his own end or the purpose of a partnership with others, any ends and purposes that person does set for himself or the partnership can only be right by accident and will be set by something other than the person himself: animal nature, inclinations and appetites, social practices organizing animal or social nature, another person or group—the masters (who may themselves also be slaves of nature). This is true of the partnership of society generally, and the partnership of artist and audience more particularly; about those partnerships Camus is very clear. The one who is ignorant of the end will merely be the living tool of whatever it is that moves him. Perhaps what Aristotle was pointing out was a settled habit of anti-Socratic ignorance. As the VIPs of Athens exhibited, much can be achieved this way—but its moral value is negative: it nihilates. Camus would seem not to want to believe that there are natural slaves, but Aristotle—who does believe there are such—considers that a culture which has them, will need a kind of relaxation appropriate to their souls, as well as the kind of art appropriate to the free (*Pol* 1342a15-30); two different kinds of art, for two different kinds of being (while yet admitting they are not different in biological species). Camus' criticism of several nihilistic forms of art echoes Aristotle's, now culturally unacceptable, claim that slaves have their own kind of music. The outline of Camus' criticism of art echoes his criticisms of culture, for the two go hand in hand—as Plato and Aristotle also held.

After this wide-angle view of Camus' thoughts on art and its more (and less) perfect production, the second part of the first chapter will consider the idea of myth as something that makes of the world and our experience a limited complete whole—an *opseôs kosmos*. Thus, myth can never be a fact in the world, or even a *fact* about the world. Rather, its myths are a culture's means of formation—moral, intellectual, emotional, and whatever we might mean by spiritual. The one who tells the myth—supposing there is one: Homer, Moses, Freud, Marx, Camus—has been formed by, as much as he is forming the story, unless you want to believe in the myth of the great man inventing his own culture. The aim of the book is to show that *The Plague* is the myth of our time; but a half step before we begin the examination of how that works we consider Camus' own myth about his artistic growth, and the development of what he saw as his main themes as an artist. While not considering this story the only one which could be told about his artistic development, we will use this self-preferred lens of understanding his work to begin talking about the characters in the novel who clearly instantiate distinct aspects of that autobi(bli)ography.

The developing layers which he saw in his life's work as an author he ordered as absurdity, revolt, and finally, love—which was to be the center of his next set of creative works, of which we seem only to have the posthumous and much belated novel, *The First Man* (1995). The traditional readings of Camus generally, and of *The Plague* particularly, get stuck almost entirely in what Camus called the first two levels, and not much new can be said about this work unless we take Camus at his word and look for what he claimed was coming to center stage through those first two movements and was in fact present from the beginning. As this book is attempting to read Camus as more deeply philosophically and theologically thoughtful about love, the last section of this first chapter—on love—is the most brief; the rest of the book will be clarifying his views on a variety of ways of understanding—and trying to live—love, through examination of the variety of characters and their choices, and the frameworks for those choices in the novel.

The second chapter opens explicitly the question of what happiness is, whether it can be achieved, and how. We begin with the opposition between the Aristotelian view of happiness and the usual modern definition of happiness as pleasure, or the satisfaction of the sum of inclinations—an idea shared by numerous moderns, but most precisely and problematically set against Aristotle by looking at Kant. Both modern Kantian and classical Aristotelian versions of happiness are at play in the novel—as well as several others, and through the characters we can see the philosophical issues aptly problematized. Within this discussion of happiness, the distinction between love based on inclination and that which Kant calls "practical love" helps us see most clearly how some characters are interacting, and the conditions under which human beings can really be happy together—as well as those ways of acting which inhibit (or destroy) such solidarity. It will turn out that what looks at first like the complete anti-podality between ancient and modern views relating happiness and the moral good does not play out so extremely in the real life represented in the novel. Both Aristotle and Kant would agree on their estimation of several of the characters' worth, and from the characters' own mouths we hear their evaluation not only of how the happiness they desire can be accomplished, but also their own estimation of their achievement of it and its worth.

To say that Camus was an atheist does not give much insight into either his character or how his art works. Despite the doctor's argument with Fr. Paneloux after the death of the child, which seems to many readers to be an anti-theistic argument from the existence of evil to the non-existence of God, Camus himself is hardly that. Nor is this work of art anti-religious, showing religion as only the source of problems rather than a plausible solution. Unlike many of our contemporaries, Camus himself—who was baptized and made his First Holy Communion in the Catholic church—does not even seem to think that belief in God is false, at least not Christianity: "Not feeling that I possess any absolute truth or any message, I shall never start from the supposition that Christian truth is illusory, but merely from the fact that I could not accept it.... The world of today needs Christians who remain Christians" (*RRD* 69–70). The third chapter will argue for the plausibility of Fr. Paneloux's sermons about the place and significance of suffering; it will show that one character in the novel lives up to the high demand of what the priest says love really is; that character is one who is all but completely overlooked in the scholarship—Rieux's mother. She is the quiet, living light in the center of the suffering city; that she is over-looked by most readers and scholars is perhaps symptomatic of both moder-nity and scholarship.

Father Paneloux, like Camus, is an Augustine scholar; we should prob-ably accept that Paneloux, "a learned Jesuit," is the better scholar (Camus was writing when being a learned scholar among the Jesuits would have been high praise indeed). But Camus himself is no tyro. Beside Paneloux's sermons, there are many details in the novel which play upon Augustinian themes. Augustine himself would recognize the world of this novel, which is a modern novel, but not novel: spiritually this world is still one we share with the saint. Even minor scholars, like myself or Camus, can recognize how we share that world, and a great artist can make that sharing visible in his work. Perhaps this novel is the work of an atheist, but what does it mean about your atheism when your work of art creates a world in which the one who lives the Catholic answer to the problem of our plague-stricken life, shares in all the dangers of human solidarity here with the rest of this world's citizens, and, perhaps, dies of that dedication is one plausible hero? Perhaps a "chronicle" which seeks to present only the facts is not capable of reaching far enough to make a judgment. Perhaps the choice of a "hidden narrator" as author of the chronicle is a defense mechanism, keeping the narrator/au-thor insulated from whatever might exceed impersonal, empirically verifi-able chronicle. And what measure should we give to Madame Rieux's love: is she the mimesis of divine love? Or is she divine love itself come, in person, into the world of the plague? The third chapter will consider these issues.

The fourth chapter is more esthetically oriented. We will take up certain half-erased equations (cf. *P* 191) which Camus creates between his work of art and a number of other works of art or recognizable scenes from West-ern culture. In this way Camus creates a depth of field within his work, which has been criticized by some as flat. Several of the scenes which are half-erased are religious or have considerable philosophical weight, and I leave them to this chapter, after the more direct depths of philosophical and theological understanding in the novel have been more exactly plumbed in chapters 2 and 3. I am, perhaps, missing details here, as we have not got all the same artistic and literary or cultural experiences, but Camus was writing a novel he meant not for scholars, but rather for the ordinary reader, and the half-erased equations I set out are matters of what would have been (and still might be) quite easily available experience in Western culture. What an artist can expect most of his audience to share in our present anomic, shattered, and—we should admit—barbaric and nihilistic, culture is probably much more of an artistic problem today, so perhaps such a construction as Camus' novel is cannot have the emotional power it once would have had; still, we might point out the connections, as it were, to older dynamos. I must, then, ask the modern reader to imagine the emotional experience Camus intended in these connections, as Henry Adams once asked his readers to imagine the Virgin who built the cathedrals as a dynamo, and to compare her real and emotional power with those dynamos which lit the first world's fair.[2]

The final chapter draws together what we have learned from these philosophical, theological and aesthetic *excursi* about the possibilities for love and solidarity from watching these highly diverse characters in the world Camus sets before us. We will return, at the start of that discussion to the sort of person who is a slave of nature, for even these have a certain sort of solidarity with one another. We will work through the characters in what can be seen as ascending and widening rings of solidarity and versions of love. Its central image (and some of its argument) is from a discussion Rambert and the doctor have under the statue of the Republic, which is in the center of town, dust-covered, and unremarked upon by any of the characters. It starts from Scipio's definition of a republic as Augustine discusses in *City of God* 19, and also ties in Kant's idea of the kingdom of ends originally broached in Chapter 2. Somewhere along the line, I think, every

2   See Henry Adams, *The Education of Henry Adams* (Boston: Houghton Mifflin, 2000), chapter 25, "The Dynamo and the Virgin." Adams' autobiography reads as a subtle, soft-spoken but sustained descent into the modern nightmare of what is taken as reality—the reduction to forces acting without order being finally, fully revealed. There are glimmers, glints, of love; but love is an inexplicable accident in this world, not even writable with in it. "The sunshine of life" (396): what was it?

reader will find herself. Should you find yourself wanting something more, or something other, you will perhaps find that as well, and something of a route to get there. A work of art might open us to something more than what we have thus far imagined—it may even do so for the artist, if that old story about the inspiration of the Muses has even a breeze of truth to it.

ACKNOWLEDGEMENTS

This book has benefitted greatly from over 30 years of discussing Camus' *Plague* next to Kant and Aristotle with students in my regular Introduction to Ethics course. Most recently, a series of long discussions with Matt Formato over the rougher drafts of this book have benefitted me (and the book) greatly, therefore this book is dedicated to him and both to those students I have had, and to those yet to come. Various versions of parts of this book have been presented and discussed at sundry conferences; among them the International Conference on Christianity and Literature at Harvard Divinity School in March, 2019, and several of the yearly European Studies Conferences at the University of Nebraska Omaha (2017–2019). I am grateful for all these discussions. Versions of several chapters or pieces thereof have also been previously published: "Barbarism and Modernity: Camus and Aristotle on the uses of the Arts," in *Saint Austin Review* 21:1 (Jan/Feb 2021), pp. 10–14; "Camus and Aristotle on the Art Community and its Errors," in *Labyrinth: An International Journal for Philosophy, Value Theory and Sociocultural Hermeneutics,* 2020/2: 40–59; "The Augustinianism of Albert Camus' *The Plague,*" in *The Heythrop Journal* 61:3 (May 2020):471–482; "Reason, Feeling and Happiness: Bridging an Ancient/modern Divide in *The Plague,*" in *Philosophy and Literature,* 43: 2 (Oct, 2019): 350–368.

ABBREVIATIONS

The following frequently quoted sources are noted in parentheses in the text according to the pagination of the edition/translation cited, or according to standard scholarly notation, e.g. Stephanus number for Plato, Bekker pagination for Aristotle, book–chapter–section for Augustine, etc.

Aristotle, *Nicomachean Ethics (NE)*, translated by Martin Ostwald. Upper Saddle River: Prentice-Hall, 1999.

_____. *Poetics (Po)*, translated by Stephen Halliwell. Cambridge, MA: Harvard University Press (Loeb), 1995.

_____. *Politics (Pol)*, translated by Benjamin Jowett. In *Basic Works of Aristotle*, edited by Richard McKeon. New York: Random House, 1941.

Augustine. *Confessions (Conf)*, translated by John K. Ryan. New York: Doubleday-Image, 1960.

_____. *City of God (DCD)*, translated by Marcus Dods. New York: Modern Library, 1950.

_____. *On the Freedom of the Will (DLA)*, translated by Anna S. Benjamin and L.H. Hackstaff. New York: Macmillan, 1964.

_____. *The Trinity (DT)*, translated by Stephen McKenna, C.SS.R. Washington DC: The Catholic University of America Press, 1963.

Camus, Albert. *The Plague (P)*, translated by Stuart Gilbert. New York: Random House, 1975.

_____. *The Rebel: An Essay on Man in Revolt (R)*. New York: Knopf, 1961.

_____. *Lyrical and Critical Essays (LCE)*, translated by Ellen Conroy Kennedy, edited by Philip Thody. New York: Vintage, 1970.

_____. *The Myth of Sisyphus and other essays, (MS)*, translated by Justin O'Brien. New York: Vintage, 1955.

_____. *Resistance, Rebellion and Death (RRD)*, translated by Justin O'Brien. New York: Vintage, 1988.

Immanuel Kant, *Critique of Pure Reason (A.../B...)*, translated by Norman Kemp Smith. London: St. Martin's Press, 1970.

_____. *The Critique of Judgment (KU)*, translated by Werner S. Pluhar. Indianapolis: Hackett, 1987.

_____. *Foundations of the Metaphysics of Morals (FMM)*, translated by Lewis White Beck. Upper Saddle River, NJ: Bobbs – Merrill, 1997.

_____. *Religion within the Limits of Reason Alone (Rel)*, translated by Theodore M. Greene and Hoyt H. Hudson. New York: Harper Torch, 1960.

Merton, Thomas. *The Literary Essays of Thomas Merton (Merton)*, edited by Brother Patrick Hart. New York: New Directions, 1981.

Plato. *Republic (Rep)*, translated by Allan Bloom. New York: Basic Books, 1968.

Sharpe, Matthew. *Camus, Philosophe: To Return to Our Beginnings (Camus, Philosophe)*. Leiden: Brill, 2017.

CHAPTER ONE
CAMUS' ART, THE PRESENT CULTURE, AND
THE ART OF *THE PLAGUE*

"Any authentic creation is a gift to the future."
Camus, "The artist and his time" (MS 151)

Since I am taking for granted that Albert Camus' novel, *The Plague*, is a great work of art, one that has been, is, and will be of permanent value to human beings, one good way into explication of its significance and value is to begin with what Camus himself thought about an artist's work, and the worth of artistic creation generally. Like his novel, Camus' view of art and what is and is not the artist's vocation has been frequently criticized, and—like the novel—often for contradictory reasons. For example, it is said that his novel—*The Plague*—and his view of art is idealistic or impersonal, and so out of touch with specifically named political and social realities which require distinct commitment both to enable one to see, and to make oneself part of the solution to, the present issues in human society.[1] The multiplication of post-colonial, racial and feminist criticisms since his death has considerably multiplied the details of (and responses to) these criticisms.[2] Or, he is romantic about nature, or about the ease of human

1   In reviews near the time of its first publication, Sartre, De Beauvoir, and Barthes all considered *The Plague* to be escaping from history and the real people who cause evil.
2   Among them see, e.g. Conor Cruise O'Brien, *Albert Camus: Of Europe and Africa* (New York: Viking Press, 1970), Edward Said, *Culture and Imperialism* (New York: Alfred A, Knopf, 1993), Christine Margerrison, *'Ces Forces Obscures De L'Âme': Women, Race and Origins in the Writings of Albert Camus* (Leiden: Brill-Rodopi, 2008); or less rancorously and with more balance, David Carroll, "The Colonial City and the Question of Borders: Albert Camus's Allegory of Oran," *L'Esprit Créateur*, Volume 41, Number 3, (Fall 2001): 88–

1

solidarity. His ethic is unclear and so unhelpful, or is inadequate to present day issues, or seems self-contradictory.[3]

Camus would think that such criticisms miss the point, for they arise out of a misunderstanding of what makes a work of art great and permanently meaningful to those who suffer the human condition. His own views on this matter are shaped by his study of tragedy, particularly that of ancient Greece, and what he names the classical French novel. To him, "revolutionary" or "committed" literature is either a misnomer, or a confession that one's vocation is not that of artist. As he says, "I know of only one revolution in art; it belongs to all ages, and consists of the exact adjustment of form to subject matter, of language to theme" (*LCE* 348). This itself might sound like an idealist emptying of the work of art from all of what might be called those gritty realities of history and contemporary life. In reality, he is defining his terms here. Art, like every other thing which we wish to distinguish from every other thing, has its limits; a whale, a giraffe and a human being, for example, may have several things in common, yet even among those things we have in common we can distinguish the whale from the giraffe, and both from the human. So too, art may have things in common with political tracts, ethical arguments and religious sermons, or historical accounts et al., yet it is something distinct—as, in fact, all those others are distinct. If it is "authentic" and "a gift to the future" it must be the sort of thing where new histories and problems may find themselves already well-limned and shown to have some ordered relation to the good—or not. This is a very particular virtue—the discipline of art, Camus often calls it—which, like courage, many may attempt and even accomplish something approximating, but those who really have it are exact, an exactness which arises only in patience.[4] If the great writer's (or authentic artist's) activity is

104 and Patricia M.E. Lorcin "Politics, Artistic Merit, and the Posthumous Reputation of Albert Camus," *South Central Review* 31.3 (Fall 2014): 9–26.

3   These last topics are given a much more adequate presentation than usual by Kevin Newmark, "Tongue-tied: What Camus's Fiction Couldn't Teach Us about Ethics and Politics," in Margerrison, Christine, Mark Orme, and Lissa Lincoln, eds., *Albert Camus in the 21st Century: A Reassessment of His Thinking at the Dawn of the New Millennium* (Amsterdam: Rodopi, 2008): 107–120.

4   Camus discusses these matters with regard to the classic French novel in "Intelligence and the Scaffold," *Lyrical and Critical Essays*, 210–218.

given here, the writer is the efficient cause of the work. The material cause would seem to be the subject matter or theme, which the artist shapes to the appropriate form; so, what of the final cause, or on what principle must we judge the value of the adjustment of form to subject matter, to speak like an ancient Greek—one concerned with the limits of things?[5] Literary art seems but one skill and practice by which a human being adjusts "form to subject matter, language to theme." Besides other arts like music or painting, other skills (political speeches, informational lectures, histories, etc.) also adjust form to subject matter, so judgement must not only be based on success at such adjustment, but at achieving the particular end of art as opposed to the ends of those other skills. As a first answer to this question of finality, here is Camus, directly: "The aim of art, the aim of a life can only be to increase the sum of freedom and responsibility to be found in every man" (*RRD* 240). In what follows, we should consider this direction true North. If we can become what we can imagine, literature is always a double-edged sword—it can lead us to imagine an evil we would not otherwise become (as characters in both Dante and *The Picture of Dorian Gray* complain), or introduce us through imagination to an unhappiness we

5   There is much philosophy behind this outline, starting with Camus' own (formally definitive, it seems to me) sentence. In *Either/Or I,* "A," the putative author, explains that "a classic work...is the absolute correlation of two forces" (49)—form and subject matter, which definition he uses to orient his impossible search for the most classic work of art of all classic works in all art forms. Camus is clearly echoing that classic definition, and focusing it on his particular art form—the novel. Camus has a classical notion of art as related to moral virtue and as an activity (so, not merely a *technê*, which is often translated as "art"). Like all virtues, the virtue of art must recognize and hold correctly to the limits of its operation; it is an activity of rational fittingness—*mesure*, a word which he pointedly appropriates and refers to in many essays and interviews. See particularly *Lyrical and Critical Essays*, 301–305, 353. For an excellent measure of the import of this term—*mesure*—for Camus see Matthew Sharpe, *Camus, Philosophe,* "Chapter 5: Excluding Nothing: Camus' Neo-Hellenic Philosophy of *Mesure*" and "Appendix Two: Camusian *Mesure*: Philosophic, Aesthetic, and Political." The idea that form, material, efficient, and final causes come together to show us the distinctiveness of a thing is also from Aristotle, visible, for instance, in his definition of tragedy (*Poetics* 1149b 22–28).

would otherwise embrace; and since every unhappy family is unhappy in its own way, there is a multitude of yet unwritten possibilities here; many of us live many of them. It might also accomplish something even more positive, traditionally labelled catharsis.[6]

In order to get a fuller picture of what Camus thinks of art, particularly literary art, and so an idea of that against which he is measuring himself, we will begin by cutting away what he thinks lies outside that realm of perfection in art—and life, and what cultural forces or personal inclinations may move the artist away from such virtue (section 1). This will lead us into a more centered investigation of what he thinks great art can and does accomplish, what its authentic work is in any culture (section 2). Many of those cultural forces are precisely those operating in the more severe ideologically and psychosexually motivated critics noted above; of course, some of the earliest critics were also motivated by personal animus, but as they are all dead, let us leave them each to their own peace. Finally, we will set out Camus' late born myth about his own work as an artist, which we will use as our directive in orientation to reading *The Plague* (section 3).

1. Barbarism, or Ways for Artists (And Cultures and Education) To Go Wrong

> The Barbarians are no longer at the city gates and beneath the ramparts; they are in positions of influence and in government. They shape the laws and public opinion... .
>
> Robert Cardinal Sarah

That the arts are the origin and center of a culture and universally employed in every culture's education is a staple of classical philosophy,[7] a point which

---

6 A much fraught term in literary aesthetics. My own thoughts on the matter can be found in *Love Song for the Life of the Mind: An Essay on the Purpose of Comedy* (Washington, DC: Catholic University of America Press, 2007), and "Aristotle and Tolkien: An Essay in Comparative Poetics," in *Christian Scholars Review* XLIX, 1 (Fall, 2019): 63–82.

7 See, for instance *Republic* 376e, *Laws* 643a–660b, *Politics* 1136a25–35 and Book 8.

Camus seems to accept as axiomatic. It is apparent, for instance, in Camus' parallelism (which we will be exhibiting shortly) of the kinds of nihilism between which his society was torn and under which same conditions, without playing for either side, "the artist, like everyone else, must bend to his oar" (*RRD* 250). Perhaps we should say that it is just a fact. We should at least note that the centrality of art for human culture is not merely an ancient view; Goethe's famous sentence that "who possesses science and art, possesses religion too"[8] summarizes the modern project of "culture" as a two-armed development (of science and art) through which the microcosm grows up to extend its reach through the entire macrocosm; the human no longer merely echoing the larger nature of the cosmos, but making the whole his own.[9] Thus 'culture' replaces religion, leaving nothing beyond the reach of man. Even for such moderns as Goethe and Freud, at least half of culture is the arm of art; if, in fact, it is not some art itself which (re-)draws this mythic picture. Whether we think of the human in the cosmos under the more limited classical picture (where he does not reach to the outer circles), or in the modern all-encompassing version (famously drawn in da Vinci's notebooks), it is clear that it is through their culture that human beings may be "said to be suckled with the same milk" (*Pol* 1252b 19) and so be united in their "village". The reach of the culture is the size of the village.

As is possible with every virtue, it is possible for those attempting to be artists to miss the mark in their work—and in many different ways; many of those ways may have dire consequences for their village. An

8   I first came across Goethe's oft-quoted line in Sigmund Freud's *Civilization and its Discontents (CD)*, translated by James Strachey (New York: W.W. Norton, 2010): 40.

9   The origin of the idea of the microcosm reflecting the macrocosm has been variously attributed to Pythagoras, Democritus, Plato and obscure unnamed sources from the east. Since at least the Renaissance, human culture—let us call it the reach of *anthropos*—has taken on the aspect of a *project*, not merely an *echo* of a smaller cosmos within the larger. So, in Leonardo's Vitruvian Man we see the human reach extends to the rim of the circle. We may now be at the point where this active working of the microcosm has completely replaced the idea of the smaller reality being a reflection both of and within the larger (divine) cosmos; now a more Promethean—or perhaps Samsonesque—interpretation of the idea and image is in play.

analogy is those who seem to act like the courageous, but don't really accomplish that virtuous activity in the way the virtuous do.[10] They might, for all that, be socially successful, be given medals, fêted. There certainly are those who Camus thinks are not oriented the right way at all, and lacking the appropriate orientation any "success" they do have can only be a bad thing for their society, which is, ideally, all human beings—including those of the future, to whom also the artist is giving his work. These may not be missing a mark they know and aim at; in many cases they do not even know what the mark is according to Camus, or they are placing something else in its stead; these are the barbarians. It will help us get clearer on Camus' view of art if we investigate such wider errors first. Aristotle's view about both barbarians and virtues is something Camus was familiar with,[11] and it is both interesting and worthwhile to begin with something of the ancient Greek's view to see how Camus' own analysis grows out of it, and is both relevant to and insightful about the present day and its issues.

To start with our first word, what is barbarism?

In his *Nicomachean Ethics*, Aristotle gives several colorful examples in speaking of particularly brutish characteristics, "rarely found among men" (and generally caused by disease there, 1145a29–31) but common among

10 Aristotle's exemplary discussion concerning courage and things like it can be found in *Nicomachean Ethics* 3.6–3.9.

11 I do not quite agree with some particulars of Sharpe's (*Camus, Philosophe*) chart relating Camusian *mesure* with Aristotelian virtue ("Appendix Two: Camusian *Mesure*: Philosophic, Aesthetic, and Political"). There it *looks* as if Camus is accepting one excess and denying the opposed, but saying "yes and no" to the middle position. For instance, considering his view on "reason's capacity to understand totality," I find Camus saying as loud a NO! to the (so-called) "negative" irrationalism of Kierkegaard as to the (real) "affirmative" totalizing rationalism (which Sharpe labels "YES!") of Hegel and Marx. Sharpe's discussion in the body of the book, however, shows that Camus does reject both extremes, and finds his *mesure* in "yes and no." Even so, defining negation as one extreme and affirmation as another, with the "yes and no" between them, Sharpe's explication seems to owe more to Hegelian logic than Aristotle's. Saying no to both extremes (as Sharpe shows Camus does) is perfect Aristotelianism; to the mean, however, one does not say "yes and no," but yes—which means "no" to motives on both sides which inhibit fulfillment of that yes.

barbarians (cf. also 1149a9–11), such as "that sort of human of whom it is said she rips open the pregnant womb to devour the child, or that sort around Pontus, which having become wild enjoys eating human flesh, and they lend each other children for feasting" (1148b). One might wonder what "lend" means in this context, but other than that these examples seem worthy of universal agreement as suitable ostensive definitions of "barbaric" as contrasted with "civilized," though not necessarily virtuous, characteristics. All of these—the brutishly barbaric, the civilized, the virtuous—are, to speak biologically, human possibilities. Like us, Aristotle expects that among the civilized there will be killing, some in anger, some for gain, some perhaps even justly, just as among the civilized there will be those who are excessive in their eating and drinking at a feast—but Aristotle's examples are of what is "beyond the pale"— meaning beyond the fortifications of the city, outside the polis of the civilized.

One of the marks of barbarian culture is that

> Among barbarians no distinction is made between women and
> slaves, because there is no natural ruler among them: they are a
> community of slaves, male and female. That is why the poets
> say, 'It is meet that Hellenes should rule over barbarians;' as if
> they thought that the barbarian and the slave were by nature
> one (*Pol* 1252b5–9).

And this remark ties into another important distinction, namely that the terms citizen and slave are correlatives for Aristotle; citizens cannot be slaves, and slaves do not have the completeness of nature to be citizens.[12] Citizen is, then, not merely what we consider citizen, which is more like a geographical designation. For the Greeks citizenship was an activity, a whole set of *praxeis*, in the engagement of which human nature found its fulfillment. It involved deliberating and acting together with other citizens in ordering the activity and ends of the polis, of which production was only one part—a part which slaves could accomplish and take part in, thus

12 What precisely natural slaves are lacking, how they are incomplete—lacking
    nous, logos generally, *thymos*, or some combination of these elements—is a
    matter of some debate, but not necessary to enter upon for our purposes.

becoming as human as possible for them. The fulness of practical activity of the citizen was what was lacking in barbarian peoples. They were slaves ruled by other slaves; they lacked the ability to grasp the true end of human beings as social; they were, rather, the incomplete ruling the incomplete to the natural incompletion of both. While Aristotle names certain peoples as being barbarians, what demands they be defined so is not necessarily their geographical place (though he does place them in *Pol* 7.7), nor their race, the color of their skin and hair, the distribution of vowels in their names, or any other such thing, but their cultural practices, and lacks—practices like eating their children, which could only exist as cultural phenomena among them.[13] The inadequacies of their culture feeds, if I may use the word, the continuing inadequacy of their souls: they have been ruined for human virtue. A successful constitution, on the other hand, prepares one for that virtuous life and encourages its practices (*NE* 1103b3–6).

But perhaps in our day even this conception of "barbarism" is questionable—is too culturally determinate—to have contemporary, not to say postmodern validity. After all, there are many people who think that ripping children out of the womb is a woman's right, and though they do not yet go so far as eating them, most of these people do think it a waste that such useful proteins as make up this meat cannot be used for research purposes and medicines in many states. These medicines, of course, would be taken internally, though perhaps more often by injection than by mouth. To be sure, our modern surgical techniques are cleaner than were available to the earlier barbarians—who did not even have forks—and if cleanliness is next to godliness, I suppose our culture must be more godly. Probably the same god, but we are higher on the worship ladder than such barbarians. Or maybe not; for as Camus, a self-confessed agnostic, wrote in his own post-Nietzschean time, "It is not certain that our time has lacked gods. Many have been proposed, usually stupid or cowardly ones" (*LCE* 228). At least the ancient pagans seem to have

---

13 Aristotle has frequently been held up as someone who is both racist and racialist; I do not think that reading of him is correct—it is certainly not necessary, but I cannot argue about that here. "Aristotle on the non-Greek Other," a recent paper (June 10, 2020) by Thornton Lockwood, given remotely to interested members of the Society for Ancient Greek Philosophy makes a quite reasonable case, as have other scholars previously.

avoided that, as did the Aztecs. And lest these remarks seem extreme or off the point, recall that Camus is not unclear about the connection between law, cultural practices, and the growth of horror in what he knew as recent history. "Bloodthirsty laws, it has been said, make bloodthirsty customs.... . One kills for a nation or a class that has been granted divine status." Sociology can pick these races, classes, ages, and even nations out; most sociologists, as most other academics, are from the divine class themselves. If certain groups are left out of consideration, they are not even ignored: they do not appear. Such clean, perhaps even surgical, killing has all the humanity of the plague bacillus. It is not new; only the methods are. In his own voice, Camus complains, "Without the death penalty, Europe would not be infected by the corpses accumulated for the last twenty years in its tired soil."[14] We now have different ways of accumulating corpses and infection. One of his characters—Tarrou—offers a more ambivalent phrasing: "the order of the world is shaped by death" (*P* 117). A more recent French philosopher has proposed this idea as a paradox: "We can no longer be sure that our civilization does not engender itself as barbarity."[15] Can we any longer make this distinction—barbaric/civilized? Chantal Delsol wondered, "at the end of the century, after so many disappointed hopes, man finally seems to be nothing more than a barbarian. Why then value him more than the trees?"[16] Or have I drawn the distinction wrongly? On which side is our general culture? It is clear that Camus did not put his own culture on the "civilized" side of the line. I would be surprised if he considered we have advanced—towards civilization.

---

14 This paragraph's last two quotes are from *Lyrical and Critical Essays*, 227f and 229. The essay was published in 1957.

15 Jean-Luc Nancy, *Adoration: The Deconstruction of Christianity II*, trans.by John McKeane (New York: Fordham University Press, 2013), 25. He is not alone: Zbigniew Herbert, in his book of essays, *Barbarian in the Garden*, translated by Michael March and Jaroslaw Anders (New York: Harcourt Brace Javanovich, 1986), and J.M. Coatzee's novel, *Waiting for the Barbarians* (New York: Penguin, 1980) also suggest that we have met the barbarian, and he is us. See also Robert Cardinal Sarah's remark at the head of this section, and several others in *The Day Is Now Far Spent*, translated by Michael J. Miller, (San Francisco: Ignatius Press, 2019).

16 Chantal Delsol, *Icarus Fallen*, translated by Robin Dick (Wilmington DE: ISI Books, 2003), 164.

Is it possible that a whole society could require its 'citizens' to materially participate in the killing of children through taxation to support such feasting? Could it make eating itself (with appropriate utensils, unlike Ugolino[17]) a necessity for 'citizenship' and a passport? Finding the proteins so helpful might it then not encourage breeding for the sake of the harvest—developing replaceable organs as well as medicines—and then we should be as gods and live forever. Some shall anyway. But I am daydreaming, as we see Dr. Rieux does when the word 'plague' is first mentioned. Good morning, fellow citizen! We should end this somewhat too detailed daydream engendered by a word (as is the doctor's) with a final point: the tribe which lends its children, as well as the woman Aristotle mentions are (unlike the good Greek wife, Agave, in *Bacchae*) unable to recognize what they do as horrifying. Ugolino is not horrified by what he is doing now either. Agave wakes up. I suppose that one of the things Camus' novel stands in place of is a time and a place when there was such a society—one that could not believe (later) what it did and what had happened in it—"And in Paris, too!" (*P* 34) Could there be so again? With a whole government organized on such principles, and the society accepting it? Obeying it? Are there natural slaves?

We have been led to this: The intellectual virtue Aristotle calls *technê* (art or skill, the root of our "technical" words) is that virtue which allows cleaner, faster and more regular and exactly measured results than just punting after what one desires; it is a rationally ordered practice pursuing a particular product or end, though the desire which sets the end may be as barbaric and wild as anything thought of in Pontus. Here the distinction we may develop is barbaric/modern, and by modern we would mean more technologically advanced, as the ICBM is a considerable technical advance over the ancient siege machines of Archimedes, machine guns more effective than bolt action rifles, and the fork cleaner than the finger, but likely not as clean as a new needle. Education is one excellent, and even ancient, means of developing such modernity further. Even since Camus' day we would have to confess that surgical techniques have advanced admirably. This is called progress, and it is not a myth. Almost all of the modern university's education aims at just such technical training and advancement. So, the modern university aims at overcoming barbarism in the sense opposed to modern, but this does not

17   See Dante's *Inferno*, cantos 32 and 33.

necessitate or imply that it, much less anything else in our culture, is attempting to overcome barbarism in the sense opposed to civilized. Of course, we all know that such a thing ceased to exist in the West long ago. The ancients considered that overcoming barbarism, in the sense of becoming civilized, was the main task of education. Education's main aim was not raising one into technological competence—which may very well produce merely a more efficient barbarism. Camus shows himself to agree with these ancients.

The central point of this set of distinctions is to show that in the world-view determined by *technê* (an intellectual, but not a moral virtue) the human being is merely another "resource" or tool; perhaps, on some occasions, advancing to the level of "capital." A living tool, by the way, is Aristotle's definition of a slave (*Pol* 1253b 28–54a18). That one can now get a college degree in Human Resources, or Human Resources Management is merely an indication that, as with forests and mines, there are more and less efficient ways to utilize these resources and arrange these toolings. The primary objects in ethics are individual human beings. Administrators— of quarantine camps, death camps, schools, economies, or what you will— consider efficiency the prime good (Cf. *P* 219). Under this determination, it is not essentially a *moral* problem that these resources are sometimes wasted, or tools broken, it is a problem of efficiency; that is the sort of problem every *technê* solves. These ways, of course, require constant study, as improvements in other technical areas require reconsideration of "best practices" of utilization of human resources. This is how slaves rule other slaves in our day. Unfortunately for many human beings, Camus' father included, military commanders were slow to discover the necessity for changing their utilization of the common soldier in the face of trenches with well-dug in machine guns and easily moveable mortars. Technical mastery over nature includes as a matter of course mastery in the use of human resources: obviously we need degrees in which people are trained in this technical virtue; our science is improving daily: that's modernity, not barbarism.[18]

---

18 In *The Fall*, Clamence notes that we are all against slavery—adamantly so: "That we should be forced to establish it at home or in our factories—well, that's natural; but boasting about it, that's the limit!" (44). A little later: "Just between us, slavery, preferably with a smile, is inevitable then. But we must not admit it" (46). Clamence is an elegant, well-spoken modern man—hardly a barbarian.

At any rate, since the barbarism with which Camus is concerned is that of our first distinction, not this last, let Aristotle's examples stand as our central image of barbarism, by which neither I, nor Aristotle, nor Camus mean to point out a certain temporal order, or even facility in Greek, but something possible at all times, in all places, in all languages. Perhaps, as I have suggested, we no longer feel like we can make such a distinction; as if calling any culture "barbaric" is barbaric. In that case neither Aristotle nor Camus has anything to say to us, for they presume this distinction, and are working to clarify it further—and show us that one side of the line is superior to the other. It would necessarily follow, if we abandon the distinction barbaric/civilized, that Camus is mistaken when he claims that the "poet for all times speaks accurately for our own" (*LCE* 323). For if the only distinction we can make among cultures is the temporal one—barbaric/modern, we should hardly expect art from one time should be able to speak to another; it can only be an example of "what they did back then". Let us be clear that Aristotle's criticism of barbarian culture does not presume the barbarian's complete irrationality or inability to organize the things of physical and social life—some invented and ran empires, after all. We have gone to the moon; Alexander only got to India; the Persians were stopped at Marathon. Barbarians are barbarians based on their non-cognizance of the end, the telos or final cause of human being, and, since we are social animals, of human society. At the beginning of *Politics* he criticizes barbarian cultures for not realizing the difference between a woman and a slave, for the end or telos of the partnership or community with a woman is a different thing than the end of partnership or community with the slave. The barbarians are slavish in that, like technology, they can accomplish great tasks, but (also like technology) are not capable of foreseeing and setting the proper ends; such beings need a master for even their own human good to be accomplished (*Pol* 1252a 32–b 8).

Let us illustrate by going back to Aristotle's examples of brutish barbarism. The end of nature in the community of man and woman is the production and raising of children into that human community and thus the continuing life of their "city." As natural social beings, the achievement of this continuation of the community is of itself a significant part of the natural human good. Therefore, destroying this "for the sake of which" sort of being (the child) and, by eating it, returning it to that of which it is a proper end is to turn what is an end in itself into a mere means to an end. Doing this is a backasswardizing of nature. It is a symptom of barbarian slavishness not to be able to see this. For a culture to celebrate it, as is said of the people of Pontus, is an indication that they ought to be ruled by more reasonable people, perhaps Greeks—in order that their own natural good might be achieved by them. Their sort of celebration is, rather, the destruction of a most significant aspect of the natural human and social good. The child is not the only human good, or even the highest human good, though it does have the potential for that according to Aristotle, but it is a natural good, an *end*, a "for the sake of which" sort of being; it is not merely a *means* useful for achieving some other "for the sake of which"— as was once considered true of money, forests, and mines.

These Aristotelian distinctions are not merely some intellectual artifact from a long forgotten day, for we find them also in the modern economist John Maynard Keynes, who places it in the future, as if "now"—at the time of his writing—it is not so. Fortuitously enough he refers to this distinction in an essay he titled "Economic Possibilities for our Grandchildren." There he voices the hope that "we shall once more value ends above means and prefer the good to the useful. We shall honour those who can teach us how to pluck the hour and the day virtuously and well."[19] It seems J.M.K. lived in a barbaric society—one that did not cognize the end, or place it above the means; he hoped for better for his grandchildren. He hoped to be led into a society which lived in proper accord with this distinction of ends and means and he also seems to know what proper and therefore better meant: recognizing ends and valuing them above means. He recognized the ability to do this as a virtue, and a higher virtue than rational ordering of means of production to any end whatsoever, which we have been calling *technê* after Aristotle, and at which J.M.K. apparently thought his particular society was expert, while being entirely ignorant of its proper ends. Mr. Keynes is confessing to living in a barbaric society. He seems unaware that the improvement of *technê* is a popular slave activity, and since the barbarian does not know the end of nature, that improvement becomes a "for its own sake"—an eternally progressing machine. Perhaps, it is merely a certain

19 John Maynard Keynes, "Economic Possibilities for our Grandchildren," in *Essays in Persuasion* (London: Macmillan and Co., 1931), 372.

residue of religion which imagines a difference between well-being and efficiency that disturbs Keynes here. A fully technologized systems approach
to problems will erase such conscientious disturbances.

A more comic example of this kind of mistake might be heard in the
contemporary honorific phrase "pushing the envelope." An envelope, for
those not up on history, was an element of a very old technology which allowed for the sending of private messages from one person to another
through public conveyance. I suppose the phrase does not literally mean
pushing the envelope along to its destination, but more like pushing out
the folds and seams of the envelope. One could, of course, still write a message on this, but it is no longer intelligible to call it an envelope. Flattening
the folds and breaking the seams makes it something else. It has been
evolved into a postcard perhaps. What has been destroyed is precisely that
for the sake of which the envelope was invented—to deliver a private message
by public conveyance. It is no longer the same species of thing; nor can *its*
end be accomplished. "Pushing the envelope" is, then, not a praiseworthy
end, nor a good to be aimed at; it is a process of destroying the end, a self-
contradictory activity. It could be considered a justification, or phrase of
commendation, only by a barbarian—someone who does not know the
end. But hey, it's different! It's new! That it is considered daring and high
praise in our culture is symptomatic.

These examples may seem extravagantly beside the point, as if the author has forgotten his end. Let us bring them back to the issue: call the barbarian denial or non-recognition or destruction of the existence of this sort
of ordering in nature or action—that some ends of human action are more
final than others by nature—nihilism, since what it does is reduce to nothing the ends implicit in nature or human action. Nihilism is a verb, then;
it is a sort of human action—upon nature and upon the human being itself.
We might call the imperative form of this verb methodological denial, as
in the methodological denial that there are any such ends in nature. Such
methodological denial is linked in modern thought to methodological atheism: the rigorous denial that god has any relation to the world or what goes
on in it. Such methodological atheism is, it is said, part of the purification
of science from everything not subject to those strictly limited modes recognized as "empirical." Further explication and argument of these relationships in the history of ideas would take us far away from our end, but echoes

of this sort of imperative, "purely methodological," limitation will appear later in our discussion, particularly in chapter 3.

In a couple of essays on art, Camus distinguishes two sorts of nihilism,[20] in which we may see the outline of two forms of cultural barbarism, of which, as we see through Aristotle's examples, the essence is not to know the end. These two forms of cultural barbarism or nihilism Camus calls totalitarian and bourgeois. They exemplify the active destruction of the ends of art, and his essays are the *cri de coeur* of an artist who feels himself crushed between them, and who must combat both of them at the same time.

Let us, then, take as the primary sense, or the focal meaning of barbarism, what is exhibited by Aristotle, and seconded by Keynes: not knowing, or destroying the natural end, perhaps through methodologically denying that there is one. Then, according to Camus, there are two opposing ways of barbaric or nihilistic operation in modern culture, both of which accomplish the same thing: deny the end of nature or destroy that "for the sake of which" an activity or partnership—in this case the activity of art—is undertaken. What we today call "the art community"—the community of artist and audience—is one sort of partnership, and Camus is intent upon showing how the purpose of that partnership is destroyed in two different ways. Since the "aim of art" is to "increase the sum of individual freedom and responsibility to be found in every man and in the world" we may already expect these nihilistic works of art to be those "that tend to make man conform and to convert him to some external rule. Others tend to subject him to what is worst in him" (RRD 240). Artists who aim thus are barbarians: they do not know the end; they aim at a wrong one. They are destroying that for the sake of which their partnership with their fellow citizens exists.

The second form of barbarism suggested in Camus' sentences ("subject him to what is worst in him") is bourgeois nihilism; Camus (writing in the 1950s) saw this sort developing and already powerful in the West; it makes art "a deceptive luxury." This nihilism develops in two ways: it can adapt itself "to what the majority of our society wants... [and so become] a

20 Actually, a lecture and an interview, both of which can be found in *RRD*: 235–272.

meaningless recreation" (*RRD* 253)—or, if the artist rejects this and refuses to become a manufacturer of the demanded titillations for the usual "art consumer," he embraces some form of "art for art's sake" which feeds on the affectations or abstractions preferred by the artist and his like-thinking coterie. This latter Camus calls "merely a voicing of irresponsibility." Such a one may "charm a few individuals" (*RRD* 255) or produce a larger coterie of like-minded sophisticates, but neither he nor the manufacturer of mass titillation are taking as their subject "reality as it is lived and endured by all" (*RRD* 257), and so none is able to achieve the universal communication among men concerning that lived reality at which art aims, for the sake of increasing freedom and responsibility.

The problem of bourgeois nihilism is not merely a problem for art, but is rooted in, and a symptom of, our society being what Camus calls "a society of merchants," that is, one in which "things disappear in favor of signs." We are not so much a "society of money (gold can arouse carnal passions) but one of abstract symbols of money" (*RRD* 253). The measure of wealth is not a reality or set of realities embodying various versions of worth—houses, farms, gold coins, cattle, works of art—but a set of figures which enumerate certain possibilities of exchange. This removal from reality carries into every-thing, not only the world of art, and has merely advanced further from re-ality since Camus' day, symbolized most effectively by the present next big thing—virtual reality. But before achieving this *contradictio in terminis* of the present age we might exhibit Camus' point by asking a couple of other questions, like what exactly *is* a derivative? What *real* thing is quantitative easing loosening the quantity of? We have, of course, a whole college dedi-cated to learning these terms and learning how to operate among such sym-bols. It is part of the *technê* of finance and modern economics. These are, without question, the *technai* of modernity, as Mr. Keynes understood. Keynes and Camus inhabit the same culture, and recognize it.

This further implication concerning the virtuality of society looks to be the *reductio ad absurdum* of Camus' position. For if the world has be-come even more virtual now, even more a life in mere signs rather than re-alities, Camus' complaint that inauthentic art, in giving itself over to such, misses "reality as it is lived and endured by all" is, in fact, false. For our ever more modern society has become precisely ever more artificial, ever more a matter of signs, ever more an unreality in which all share: That is real life!

A real plague might break the hold of this artificial plague, but, barring that, the world we all share *is* the screen in front of us. Of course, we may try to escape the real plague by faster fleeing into the virtual—zooming into it; as long as the power stations don't go down, we'll be ok—won't we?

The point of Camus' complaint here is that we are embodied beings; physical plagues and total wars, like that which Camus endured, remind us all of this natural fact. The day may come when we are reminded again. The sorts of wars America and the West have fought since that time, as any sociologist or historian can point out, have not approached making the fact of embodiment one in which *everyone* feels rooted. Certain races, classes, and peoples have felt it, because they have been the "sacrifice" made on the altar of the divinity of other races, classes, and peoples. Only some peoples are perpetual refugees; only some classes offer their children to the military—others join wine clubs. The Aztecs have won: we acclaim those slaves who have been killed as holy victims or honored heroes, and the sun continues to rise—for us.[21] Although reality is that we all live and die as embodied beings, our type of virtual society, as Camus says, sets "a certain kind of humbug at the center of its experience and its universe" (*RRD* 253). He figures this society in his description of life in Oran; we may see it most precisely in what the narrator describes as the difficulty of dying there: "think of what it must be for a dying man, trapped behind hundreds of walls all sizzling with heat, while the whole population, sitting in cafés or hanging on the telephone, is discussing shipments, bills of lading, discounts!" (*P* 5). In the world of production, exchange, and appropriation, loss of function in the system leaves merely a superfluous residue, evaporating in the heat.

All of our carnal embodied realities are treated as something artificial—or virtual, perhaps, these days—even sex, which used to be dependably physical. Now, fortunately, we will remain on social media even after our death! We will be just as really there as we are now. These accounts will not, of course, be so up to date—unless we set up an algorithmic bot to like, dislike,

---

21   I intend this remark to fit not only the discussion of barbarism above, but also with Georges Bataille's excellent analysis of the self-deception at the root of Aztec sacrifice in *The Accursed Share,* translated by Robert Hurley (New York: Zone Books, 1988): Vol 1: 45–62. The Aztec entered the deathless realm of the divine by sacrifice, we enter virtually.

remember, etc.—yes that's the ticket! But I suppose Google and Amazon have beaten me to the punch. This universal artificial making, quite naturally, leads many people—not just the artists—to think they can and do create their own reality. Virtually, they do. Nonetheless, for some queer reason, most continue to go out (when they really do go out) via the doors rather than the windows, particularly when they are above the second floor. The contemporary bourgeois world is one in which real relations have gone the way of the envelope. It is no surprise that most art, too, should be cut off from its living root and be merely one more deceptive luxury—in one way or the other. Does the person who dies posting a selfie on social media realize he or she has spent its life for titillation? Should we hope so? And speaking of titillation…; never mind—it is impossible even to make a representative list. Such is one sort of modern bourgeois barbarian. It might seem one's freedom is absolute, which it is—virtually absolute freedom. We must, however, hope someone keeps the electricity on; power tools are helpless without it.

The other, and first, sort of nihilism Camus suggested above, which "converts" the human being "to some external rule," was the totalitarian form. Writing about the movements of the 40s and 50s, what was in the forefront of his mind was socialist realism; but it would be false to think that totalitarian nihilism died with the USSR. If the bourgeois barbarian, growing up in the artificial, magnifies and practices the pursuit of unreal ends, then, according to the socialist realist, *et al.*, the trick must be to strive toward realism both in life and in art. So, Camus considers the problem of being realistic in art and, using the example of film, concludes "there is but one possible realistic film: the one that is constantly shown us by an invisible camera on the world's screen. The only realistic artist, then, is God, if he exists." So "the artists…who insist on speaking of reality and reality alone are caught in a painful dilemma. They must be realistic and yet cannot be" (*RRD* 259). Full realism is as impossible to fulfill as a dogma of *sola scriptura*. The first is impossible to achieve in human art, the second is impossible to begin. The artist, as well as the religious person, needs a principle of selection from among the elements God's realism offers. Just as there was a principle of selection for that bugaboo of the contemporary university formerly known as the canon, and a principle of selection for scripture, so there was for the socialist realist, who considered that "in order to reproduce properly what is, one must depict also what will be" (*RRD* 260)—namely

18

the happy socialist state. It is interesting to note that Camus might well have had, besides the usual suspects, J-P Sartre also in mind, for Sartre had claimed, in "Existentialism as Humanism" that "existentialism [would] never take man as an end, for a man is always in a state of formation."[22] Socialist realism is thus a version of Sartrean existentialism; this fits with the latter's long defense of Stalin.

Before continuing further, let us note that the "universalist" views Camus is expressing here, while echoing the ancients, are not out of touch with what other modern artists have said. For example, Mark Rothko—whose painting would hardly count as traditionalist—considers that art is a form of social action, but its aim is not to produce ornaments for leisure, "soothe the savage breast of the weary warrior," or function for the direct good of the state or corporation, but rather to "constantly adjust eternity, as it were, to all the specifications of the moment." The artist's aim is not to "create partial unities, but…always resolve his fragments in man's subjectivity," creating through his art a plastic or poetic generalization of what the human reality is, thereby giving "human beings direct contact with eternal verities through reduction of those verities to the realm of sensuality." By this last term Rothko means not our usual sense, but rather that the painter creates a world in which we can, as it were, feel the edges, which are the edges of *our* world. A work of art which brings a palpable unity of the eternal truth and present experience to a resolution in human subjectivity, would be one which "added to the inner freedom of each person who has known and loved it," as Camus extols every true work of art for doing" (*RRD* 241). To fail to do this is to be guilty of escapism according to both Rothko and Camus—which can also be accomplished by spending one's "entire life turning the wheels of industry so that he has neither time nor energy to occupy himself with any other needs of his human organism," —something Mr. Keynes apparently discovered, and which we will see is the preferred method of the citizens of Oran, a thoroughly modern city.[23]

---

22 Jean Paul Sartre, *Existentialism and Human Emotions*, translated by Bernard Frechtman (New York: Citadel Press, 1985): 50.

23 Mark Rothko, *The Artist's Reality*, edited with an introduction by Christopher Rothko (New Haven: Yale University Press, 2004). The unnoted quotations in this paragraph are from (in order) pages 12, 22, 31, 25, 10.

A similar dilemma, between titillation and socially defined grandeur can be heard in the Renaissance complaint of Michelangelo:

> Ill hath he chosen his part who seeks to please
> The worthless world—ill hath he chosen his part,
> For often he must wear the look of ease
>   When Grief is at his heart;
> And often in his hours of happier feeling
> With sorrow must his countenance be hung,
> And ever his own better thoughts concealing
> Must he in stupid Grandeur's praise be loud,
> And to the errors of the ignorant crowd
> Assent with lying tongue.[24]

At any rate, in both the socialist and the existentialist case—which latter is perhaps merely the general metaphysic underlying both totalitarian and bourgeois versions of barbarism—the end is defeated by the means again. In the latter case all ends are abandoned, so any at all may be set.[25] Man's freedom is the purest nothing for Sartre, and so, as Dostoevsky put it, "everything is permitted." Any ends may be set. Then, too, anything is art. In the socialist realist case, as Camus states it:

> the aesthetic that intended to be realistic therefore becomes a
> new idealism [for the new socialist man does not exist really],
> just as sterile for the true artist as bourgeois realism. Reality is
> ostensibly granted a sovereign position only to be more readily
> thrown out. Art is reduced to nothing. It serves (*RRD* 261).

What it serves is the imagined future, which has the distinct disadvantage of not being real. Or perhaps that is an advantage—for the revolutionary can now fill in the blank with whatever particular dream the day has given

24 Quoted in Rothko, p. 2. "To Luigi del Eiccio," available at https://archive.org
    /stream/selectedpoemsfro00michrich/selectedpoemsfro00michrich_djvu.txt.
25 A person envisages "a number of possibilities, and when they choose one, they
    realize that it has value only because it is chosen;" Sartre, *Existentialism*, 21.

her. Thus the anything that is art is corseted into that shape ordered by the political-economic futurist ideal. Futurism itself being one of those (now passé) ideals history seemed intent on realizing. These days such totalitarian barbarism is not so easily localizable as when Camus was writing. It can be found everywhere. Thus, "barbarism is never temporary" (*RRD* 262), and thanks to our wonderfully advancing technology it is not localizable in space either. In fact, we can see it breaking into nearly as many political coteries, with varying visions of the future, as there are coteries of art for art's sake academicisms, or, for that matter, Christian churches. Unlike the bourgeois 'artistic' coteries—which have their very select venues and journals, these totalitarian coteries are (thanks to social media) present everywhere. And those who disagree with them are now, as they were in Camus' day, "on the wrong side of history"—the history which is not yet real. Thus "the future authorizes every kind of humbug" (*RRD* 263).

In the academic world, I should say in the academic world of humanities and social sciences, whole departments have been known to jump on these sorts of totalitarian bandwagons. Those who don't jump.... . Well we have solutions to these problems, fortunately. They are easily cancelled. That this, too, is the exercise of barbarians should be obvious to anyone who understands the purpose or end of a university. Someone who considers that the purpose of the university is only to provide the tools for, and begin the practice of, the habits required for successful jobbing in the various markets of the day reduces the students to mere means; natural slaves, to speak like Aristotle. Requiring a little learning at numerous kinds of tooling, as most general studies programs do, probably makes the students *less* adequate as tools insofar as they must give some time and effort to eccentric and—for their job—useless practices. Why any time at all should be spent on such courses is not a mystery, but merely a meaningless deception which must find its purpose—if any—outside the stated end of the students' jobbing. The students themselves, most of whom enter as barbarians or natural slaves and merely wish to get better at it, recognize this fact about general studies programs. Perhaps the real reason for such courses is faculty jobbing. The rule for discovery of all truth in the marketplace is well-known: follow the money. This organization of the university is merely another—very clean—way of eating the children.

If the aim of the university is neither to help create this sort of natural slave or living tool, nor to feed the children to the honored faculty and even more honored administration, but rather precisely to help in the fashioning and direction of a being which can come to know what ends are and how to order and set ends for him and herself, "to increase the sum of freedom and responsibility" to which all his technology and science are but servants, then clearly a significant part of that university education must be consideration of, and practice at, just that sort of activity. No science or *technê* has this as its aim; no science or *technê* has this as its practice; no science or *technê* has this as its task or particular study. I leave the negative conclusion regarding required general studies at a university, which is demonstrably derivable from these facts, to the side in order to look for the positive one Camus seems to be driving at.

It is not that the arts are necessary and sufficient for a non-barbarian human culture, for clearly rafts of art and artists are expressions, symptoms, and (junk) food for the variety of barbarians we have been considering. Camus' explication of these phenomena and people has only become weightier and more accurate since he wrote. These should be encouraged to step closer to the cliff edge to take a selfie. Rather, there must be a kind of art, literature in Camus' particular case, which aims at and succeeds in awakening and aiding the person into precisely that sort of rigorous consideration and acknowledgement of ends which mark those who are civilized. It is this that a purposeful anti-barbarian university general studies program sets as its end. And it is something very like this that Camus thinks authentic art has as its end. Let us be clear before we go to that topic, however, that neither such a university program's existence, nor the existence of such art will guarantee its success in drawing students, much less a whole society, out of barbarism, though without it we can be certain what will succeed. That future is already here.

2. The Work of the Work of Art

In his review of Jean Paul Sartre's novel, *Nausea*, published when he was not yet 25, and some four years before his own first effort in the art form, Camus outlined the difficult depths and dangerous shallows for an artist attempting this particular kind of "fusion of experience and thought, of life and reflection on the meaning of life." He begins by saying, "a novel is never anything but a philosophy expressed in images. And in a good novel the philosophy has disappeared into the images. But the philosophy need only spill over into the characters and action for it to stick out like a sore thumb, the plot to lose its authenticity, and the novel its life" (*LCE* 199). But how can philosophy be expressed in the images of a novel and yet not spill over into the characters and action, for clearly, what the characters do will provide quite a few of the significant images? To say nothing of those characters speaking from some perhaps incipient or inchoate philosophical *point d'appui* themselves, or perhaps even a well-considered and developed philosophical worldview. And can that idea fit together with his later remark, written when planning the first version of *The Plague*, that the great novelists of the classical French tradition "refuse to carry messages, and their only concern seems to be to lead their characters imperturbably to the rendezvous awaiting them?" (*LCE* 210)

Camus thought that Sartre's novel, though it was perfect "in everything that concerns the mechanical side of existence" and contained as well profound ideas and reflections, broke the balance required in a great novel, thus becoming one of that sort of failure in which "the theories do damage to the life." He is not accusing Sartre of being one of those who is unaware of, or acting contrary to the end of art as discussed in the previous section, rather, despite its ideas and several perfections it doesn't "add up to a work of art.... [It fails] to evoke in the reader the deep conviction that makes an art of the novel."[26] Beside profound ideas and perfect descriptions, a great novel must evoke in the reader a conviction of life: that the world of the novel, and of the lives in it, is a world in which, or a life which, he and she too could be or are seen to live, and, more importantly, can feel themselves to be living. One might be tempted to argue that Camus would, then, perhaps not consider magical realism, or science fiction, or something like Tolkien's legendarium as possibilities for greatness in literature, at least not for a novel, though I do not think such an argument follows at all from either what he has said or his practice as a writer. But this matter is not to the point. What is to the point is trying to show how he thinks a great novel works, and what balance it aims to accomplish, for that can give us better insight into his own practices and aims.

26 *LCE* 200 and 199, respectively.

Camus' own reflections about the greatness of a novel does not touch upon any character's presentation of a philosophy (much less the author's philosophy, as we might think true of Sartre's Roquentin) *tout court*, but upon the way the novel as a whole is (or is not) a lucid living mimesis of the containment of human suffering—as distant from chatter as from despair and madness, as distinct from magical fairy tale as from the kind of realism we find in Upton Sinclair, or Zola, or the metaphysics we might find dressed up in Sartre. The authentic novelist's work "he characterizes as a tradition transcending historical periods."[27] Though Camus determines himself, and particularly his authorship of *The Plague* as the work of someone who does "not believe in realism in art" (*LCE* 340), he also describes that book, readable "on a number of levels," to be certainly "nothing less … than a chronicle of the Resistance" (*LCE* 339). His realism is clearly not a literalism then, and the evocation of conviction he aims at is not merely that of a 'this could happen' sort, though it is nothing less than that; rather, "the great problem is to translate what one feels into what one wants others to feel" (*LCE* 212). In the case of *The Plague*, those feelings include the enclosing miasma of the occupation/plague/evil, its strictly limiting boredom and evacuation of meaning from language, enhanced by administrative regulation which provides its own structured absurdity. But such feelings, and others we will explore later, are not limited to the past historical experience of the anti-Nazi resistance. As the novel can be read on many levels—literal plague, or occupation, or the persistence of evil, being but three—so the characters and events which instigate such feelings bring us to notice the ways in which we share in the sufferings of this "completely modern" city (*P* 4) and by sympathetically (or not) entering the characters' responses, the work of art might loosen "a tangle of obscure bonds within [us], free [us] from fetters whose hindrance [we] felt without being able to give them a name" (*LCE* 249), as Camus describes his own experience of a novel. The sort of catharsis he aims to bring about, then, depends partly on us, on our own ability to read, to recognize our own feelings and our willingness to feel our own experience, and through the novel's working through of those feelings effect a greater freedom in us. We will be both *in our* real occupied,

---

27   Edward J. Hughes in *The Cambridge Companion to Camus* (Cambridge: University Press, 2007), ed. by Hughes, p.7.

or plague, or evil-inscribed lives and *able to see and feel* that life and the lives of others with us *as a whole,* a sight and completeness of feeling which is only possible *from without,* from outside the walls of our particular reality—that is, *in the novel.* In such bifocality is freedom born and strengthened. Camus thinks that the great novel will have a sufficient variety of excellences that it will touch home in this way in everyone; that is how it carries "conviction of life," such as he found Sartre's first novel did not. That is how he can expect it to be of permanent value to all, as he holds is true of Greek tragedy, and the novels he calls classic.

Unfortunately, as a great artist, especially a novelist, becomes an icon, his work tends to become a mythologic expression of his openly expressed philosophy, his particular biography or place in his culture,[28] or his socioeconomic and racial history, depending on which church the priestly reader or critic belongs to. As Edward Dahlberg once wrote, "The citizen secures himself against genius by icon worship. By the touch of Circe's wand, the divine troublemakers are translated into porcine embroidery."[29] Certainly, the reason such a wide variety of critical churches exist is because such priests and priestesses can make considerable sense of the scripture (or other artistic work) that they are facing. As we might expect, and know from experience, some of these critics reveal the iconic author to be demonic,[30] while others defend the icon as a prophet and forerunner of their own.[31] As each church rises and falls in its popularity, so also does the icon and its significance. Tracing such fluctuations of interpretation and evaluation is the work of "reception theory:" a sort of history and sociology of religion,

---

28 These need not, of course, be simplistic *roman a clef* relations; cf. Ieme van der Poel, "Camus: A life lived in critical times" in *Cambridge Companion,* 13–25 at 23: "Clamence, the protagonist, is not to be identified with his creator, Albert Camus, of course, yet some of the reflections on his personal life seem close to Camus' own... ."

29 "Can These Bones Live?" in The Edward Dahlberg Reader (New Directions, 1957), as found in *Consider the Lobster,* by David Foster Wallace (London: Little, Brown Book Company, 2005): p. 255.

30 In the case of Camus, we might point to the work of Edward Said, *Culture and Imperialism* (London: Vintage, 1994).

31 See Debra Kelly, "*Le Premier Homme* and the literature of loss," in *Cambridge Companion* (191–202).

so understood. Iconography, as it were, becomes a separate field of study. This latter fact might bring us back to an older theory, one which I think Camus shares, about how great art works. In a phrase: "Such works are mirrors, when an ape looks in, no apostle can be seen looking out."[32] The problem is that now we have whole school groups traveling through the museum of icons, each group shepherded by its own deacon or deaconess; the result is so much more noise that it is difficult to find a quiet spot from which to consider the work, a place to let us feel our own way through it—by which I mean, what is really for us in it. Camus puts the artist's problem this way: the artist must "find out how, among the police forces of so many ideologies (how many churches, what solitude!), the strange liberty of creation is possible" (*RRD* 251). The reader, too, must solve the parallel problem.

Such churches, and the wealth of competing visitors and tour guides, insulate us from the genius, for to follow along in such a church disallows what the artist in his art aims to achieve—a "privileged moment" in which the work "acts on us like a great musician playing on a very ordinary instrument and truly *revealing* it to itself."[33] The instrument, in the case of the artist, is the subjectivity of the reader; what is to be revealed is ourself to ourself. Neither the making of art, nor the enjoyment of art is a work of explication, but rather both are an emotionally accurate and intellectually clarified grasping and holding of—or being grasped and held in—our place in the world, such as we seldom achieve, or rarely appears so perfectly to us while in the contradictions and heat of battle (including its boredom) which is our life in the world. So, for Camus, the work of art allows us to grasp and be grasped by, in that present heat and dryness, a completeness, finality and clarity which embattled life makes nearly impossible; it is this vision and passional driving *through* the smoke and alarums *to* a whole in which we have our part which grants such freedom and peace as art may grant.

If it accomplishes this, the work of art achieves its aim, which "can only be to increase the sum of freedom and responsibility to be found in every

---

32 The phrase is Lichtenberg's; I have it from the frontispiece of S. Kierkegaard's *Stages on Life's Way*.

33 This great image is from an essay by Camus' beloved teacher, Jean Grenier, quoted in Toby Garfitt, "Situating Camus: The formative influences" (*Cambridge Companion*, 26–38) at 30.

man" (*RRD* 240). The novel realizes this freeing work by making us more lucid in both intellect and feeling about the life we are ourselves living. Titillation, the honing of political, economic, psychosexual and societal knives, or the working out of a catechetical proof are Charybdis, Scylla, and islands of the Cyclops—each proving a different method of destruction upon the work of the artist. Each produces a different enslavement or tooling—and perhaps arises from such slavery and toolishness in the reader or critic. Many times it is also true of the author, but these are the barbarians, or at least those who lack the virtue of the art. More accurate reading and writing is an exercise in the "the growth of a personality" as Joseph Grand explains his own efforts in *The Plague* (40). In the novel itself we might be able to see many things at work, and hear them named, and understand how they have been moving us—in reality. Additionally, the works which survive the ever present—and increasingly enlarging—dangers Camus has been pointing out as belonging to art, will also allow us "to indulge without restraint in the supreme joy of the intelligence which we call 'admiration'" (*RRD* 272).

It is fitting that such a passion be aroused in us, as the virtue of the artist in the world we share is almost as difficult of achievement as the virtue of the human being. For *ars brevis, vita longa est*: the work is easier to perfect than the being. That Camus' *Plague* is such a work, and how, in detail, it achieves its end, is the topic of the rest of the book, but first, what about this reading of *The Plague*? What does it presume, what is its more particular *point d'appui*?

3. *The Plague* as Myth of the Modern World

The proper understanding of "myth" is not that it is an archaic first attempt at scientific or historical explanation, but that it originates a worldview within which all the actions, stories, explanations (including scientific explanations) and judgements of daily life can and do take place. It *is the objective framework* within which the society whose myth it is understands their lives; it is what defines and delimits "objective". The vast majority of mankind does not even think to give what Kant called a transcendental deduction for that framework within which all their world appears; myth ust is that framework. One connection between religion and a work of art is just this: each creates a spacing, an "aesthetic distance" from which and within which life and its experiences can be seen as something whole, and being see as a whole, life becomes understandable, we achieve some clarity of vision; it embodies not only what Wordsworth called emotion recollected in tranquility, but emotion and actions set within a clear vision of the whole—a cosmos—within which, in turn, we may understand ourselves and our existence, and experience the engendering of emotions like those of our life. The myth is that in which we are able to know and to feel our existence.[34] To put things in a more directly philosophical statement myths are the embodied transcendental rational ideal of those in it (the readers, co-religionists, or audience); it is the unconditioned "*totality* of the *conditions* for any given condition," the unconditioned ground within which thought and feeling take place and are understood. It is a mistake to consider what we might call the elements of myth as having "any suitable ... employment *in concreto*."[35] Without such myths however, "no coherent employment of the understanding" is possible.[36] A myth makes of the world a limited complete whole—an *opseôs kosmos*;[37] and this making so can never be a fact in the world, or even a *fact* about the world. Its myths are a culture's means of formation—moral, intellectual, emotional, and whatever we might mean by spiritual. As a rule, what lies outside the myth cannot be seen to have happened, cannot be seen to be going on. The one who tells the myth— supposing there is *one*: Homer, Moses, Freud, Marx, Hitler, Camus, Rothko—has been formed by, as much as he is forming the story, unless you want to believe in the myth of the great man inventing his own culture. This last has sometimes been called the myth of patriarchy, though

---

34 A similar sense of myth is used by Jacqueline Lévi-Valensi in "Le Temps et l'e-space dans l'oeuvre Romanesque de Camus: une mythologie du reel," in *Albert Camus 1980,* ed. Raymond Gay-Crosier (Gainesville: University Presses of Florida): 57–71.

35 Immanuel Kant, *Critique of Pure Reason* A322/B379–A323/B380. Kant considers some particular embodiments of the transcendental ideal in *Religion within the Limits of Reason Alone.*

36 *Critique of Pure Reason* A651/B679. See also Kant's discussion of the three transcendental ideas—self, world, God—and their mistaken employment, A672/B700–A703/B731.

37 Aristotle, *Poetics* 1449b32; cf. also *Love Song* 208, 258, 274.

autochthony would perhaps be the more adequate name of the general form of this myth, depending upon which of the two matriarchy is considered the alternative of, for matriarchy, too, is a myth. This sense of myth does not only apply to those stories, such as Homer's, which we usually intend, but it covers also Nietzsche's sense when he suggests that we still believe in the gods because we believe in grammar, for our grammar, because it has substantives and verbs, makes us still look for that mythical "subject" the self whenever there is a feeling or thought or action;[38] or as he suggests— perfectly in line with Kant's discussion—because we think "world" we must also think "God".[39] That he has myths is symptomatic of a being whose knowledge is limited. Thus, the critique of myth depends on a different spacing, that is, a *different* myth granting the aesthetic distance upon the "what is the form" or "what had been formed"—the myth—of the first culture or epoch. So, we might ask of someone like Sir James Frazer—"what is that cultural myth from which you investigate the myths of 'primitive' cultures?'" Seeing our point, he would confess that it is the myth of empirical science, and undoubtedly chuckle, for everyone here knows that empirical science is not a myth—right? And Nietzsche's point might not be the insane one of attempting to speak without any grammar whatsoever, but a warning about the wrong way to think about things, into which we are led by, let us call them, the *facts* of our grammar. In such a case we would find him aligned with Wittgenstein, who is a much less explosive, but no less insightful writer of German sentences.[40] In every such case we are taking the myths as if they refer and have meaning in the same way that all those things that appear in them (the whole world—material and social) refer or have meaning, mistaking that *through which* and *in which* we understand to be the same sort of thing as that *which* we understand (or wish to understand).

Sophie Bourgault reports such a myth which Camus told about himself and his work as an author while in Stockholm to receive the Nobel Prize.

---

38 Friedrich Nietzsche, *Beyond Good and Evil*, entries 17, 20, 54.
39 Ibid., entry 150.
40 As explicated, for example, by Marco Bastienelli, "Wittgenstein and the Mythology in the Forms of Language," in *The Darkness of this Time: Ethics, Politics and Religion in Wittgenstein*, edited by Luigi Perissinotto (Mimesis International, 2015): 87–114.

He said that he intended there to be three layers to his work: "absurdity, revolt, and love." The last was to be the center of his reflections in the coming works; thus, after his sudden death, we are left "with an unfinished trilogy."[41] In the preface to the second edition of his youthful (1937) book of essays, *The Wrong Side and the Right Side*, published the year after his visit to Stockholm (1958), Camus tells a story of his work which aligns with this layering, for he finds "more love in these awkward pages than in all those that have followed" (*LCE* 6). He hopes, in the near future "to construct the work I dream of… it will speak of a certain form of love" (*LCE* 15). These statements are the best sign that Camus is, near the time of this re-printing, taking a new, at least more clearly defined, aesthetic distance on himself and his work, framing it as a coherent life-story under the aegis of these three "stages". I propose taking it to be true, that is, the framework that allows us to see more truly; but it also seems quite clear that Camus has been learning from his own work, and one thing he has learned is that, seen truly, love seems to have been "the backdrop of everything."[42] Or perhaps the center sphere of several, growing like an onion, but written and read—and lived?—from the outside in; perhaps only having lived and written through what is already behind him does he see what the living, growing center has been all along. In the reading of Camus' own myths it is not evident, within the absurdity of Sisyphus, or within *The Rebel*, that love is "the backdrop to everything." Nor the center either. Indeed, love seems to have a different significance—if it has any, if we treat each of the previous stages as the expression of Camus' myth at the time of its writing. But perhaps "like great works, deep feelings always mean more than they are

41   Numerous critics make note of versions of this myth. Sophie Bourgault, "Affliction, Revolt, and Love: A conversation between Camus and Weil" in *The Originality and Complexity of Albert Camus' Writings*, ed. by Emmanuelle Anne Vanborne (New York: Palgrave Macmillan, 2012):125–142, at 125. Germaine Brée, *Camus: A Collection of Critical Essays*, (Englewood Cliffs, NJ: Prentice Hall, 1962), 9, lists the themes as "absurdity…revolt…measure…love"; Thomas Merton repeats Brée's four cycles in his "Camus: Journals of the Plague Years," 222, but uses Bergault's three "layer" view in a section of his "*The Plague* of Albert Camus: A Commentary and Introduction," 197–200, referencing his *Notebooks* from 1946.

42   Bourgault, 125.

conscious of saying" (*MS* 8). Perhaps, then, his late myth about his work is the true confession about his life, as well as his work. Absurdity, rebellion, love—it's a life trajectory Augustine would recognize, as well as many other sinners. How shall we ask if such a myth is true? From what mythic standpoint could we judge?

This latterly told myth of his writing life is the confession of that world within which he wished his work to be understood, within which he understood himself now to have always been working, within which he thought his work could best work—or did, does, and will do its best work—for us. Those earlier works, taken for themselves—as their own autochthonous myths—were partial, of severely limited focus. Lucidity about his own life and experience demanded that he be living in another myth, a framework distinct from those—each of which brought its own kind of fame and trouble in its day. For the sake of understanding this novel as myth of the modern world it is worth recalling Camus' earlier "stages"— those which led into "love."[43] Let us consider each of them in turn, given Camus' own late told myth, "stories that could be true," of characters who might instantiate them —but rightly seen only if oriented to this proper centering: love.

4. Stages of Camus' Myth of his Œuvre

Absurdity

"The absurd is born of [the] confrontation between the human need and the unreasonable silence of the world" (*MS* 21). Many critics point out what Camus himself says, that both poles—human and world—together produce the absurd. "The absurd depends as much on man as on the world" (*MS* 16). Recognition of the absurd requires a lucidity which knows its

---

43 It is not new to say that *The Plague* is a myth of our world. E.g., Adele King says that in it "Camus creates a myth about man's fate" (78). "The plague is not an exceptional phenomenon but the condition in which we live" (75). The way of reading this myth is what is important here: from within Camus' myth about himself. *The Plague* is not, in such a reading, a myth about absurdity, or rebellion, but one which leads on from there to love. That was his aim all along, he says.

own desires for happiness, and grants only "the few tangible certainties that his immediate experience yields: sense experience, his own existence, other human beings."[44] This way of gaining any certainties about the world engenders the further certainty that the world is not ordered to human happiness or understanding.[45] But the absurd is not merely the experience of finding the world against the heart of man, it is also the "direct confrontation with the gap between thought and actuality—a gap which is created and made absolute by attempts to 'explain' it" (Merton, 297). According to the usual teaching, one may escape this certain, absurd conjunction by destroying either the human self—by suicide (*MS* 3–8), or by less final forms of intellectual oblivion (sex, drugs, rock-n-roll), or by denying the unreasonable silence of the world—through a leap of faith,[46] or through some other projection of eventual or permanent meaning; for example, that offered by socialism, or another political finality—whichever one is the right side of history.[47] Today. In these ways both understanding and one's heart will be shaped—and shaping—one's experience and choices in line with the end thus happened upon. "Belief in the meaning of life always implies a scale of values, a choice, our preferences. Belief in the absurd, according to our definitions, teaches the contrary.... . Value judgments are discarded here in favor of factual judgments. I have merely to draw the conclusions from what I can see and to risk nothing that is hypothetical" (*MS* 44f).

The Plague is set forth as a story told from this mythic point of view: the absurd. That is to say, it risks nothing hypothetical; it aims to just tell the facts. In his first sentence, our narrator calls what is coming a "chronicle," and having summarized the geography of the city and the habits of the

---

44 James Woelfel, *Camus: A Theological Perspective*. Nashville: Abingdon Press, 1975: p. 57.

45 The experience of nature's utterly destructive power, when it is not actually destroying the person, is the root of Kantian judgments of the sublime; an experience he explains we can only have because of the existence within us of an independent *a priori* moral power (*KU* § 23, 24). If there is no such power in a person, or if it is distrusted, the absurd appears instead of the sublime.

46 Or "philosophical suicide," as, e.g., in Chestov and Kierkegaard according to *MS* 21, 24–31.

47 Discussed under the theme of "conquest," *MS* 64–67.

citizens, concludes that Oran "seems to be a town without intimations; in other words, completely modern" (*P* 4)—expressing precisely thereby that the modern city (and citizens) largely do not live within earlier worlds like that of the Romantic imagination or, despite its standing churches, an even earlier medieval religious sensibility. We are all good empiricists, who see things—even the value judgments of others—as mere facts, thereby risking nothing hypothetical but depending entirely on sense, which gives us our developing data; at least, the chronicle takes that as its modern methodological approach. The narrator will tell us the facts, for "chance put him in the way of gathering much information" besides being himself "closely involved in all he proposes to narrate" (*P* 6). He is careful in numerous places not to make value judgments, though he does report those of others. The last chapter of the final part begins by calling what has preceded a "chronicle" again, one in which Dr. Rieux wishes it to be known that "he expressly made a point of adopting the tone of an impartial observer…describing only such things as he was enabled to see for himself" and "used only such [documents] as chance, or mischance, put in his way," all the while exercising "the restraint that behooves a conscientious witness" (*P* 280). The characters are set into this world of (as it were) complete objectivity, each with their own loves, desires, particular embodied pasts, and variety of hopes and fears. Most of the townsfolk are blankly sure "that everything was still possible for them" (*P* 35), when the plague is first named by Rieux. The town is closed, and "from that day onward one had the impression that all cars were moving in circle" (*P* 70). Means are connected to means, but there is no end to be achieved or arrived at. Thus, the townsfolk begin to realize the absurdity of life; but the disease has not introduced the absurdity, for the endless circling of economy, habitual behavior (*P* 4–5), and dried peas (*P* 9, 56, cf. 107–8) have been well drawn by the objective narrator before (as well as during) this lockdown. The situation painted by the narrator during the plague was already the case in more "normal" circumstances, it was merely not noticed. Thus, the modern city of Oran is the representation of the absurdity of modern life precisely as seen through the eyes of a living exemplar of the myth of objective understanding: the chronicling doctor. It will turn out that our narrator is unreliable in several ways; perhaps this is not merely a choice of literary form (why choose that?), but a symptom or consequence of the myth he embodies. The citizens are faced with the absurdity of life when the plague closes their town, but the chronicle shows it has been their case for long before that.

Dr. Rieux, himself a scientist and, whether from the practice of his profession or native temperament, rather distant—as we see enacted in his farewell to his wife—is providing a chronicle which presents strictly factual matters. Paneloux's second sermon, after quoting another chronicler of an earlier plague, teaches something about reading: "It was not [the chronicler's] task to tell us more than the bare facts. But when he read that chronicle, Father Paneloux had found his thoughts fixed…" (*P* 204). They are fixed on the one monk who had made the correct moral decision; he is piercing through the chronicle to a moral world which the chronicler does not touch. Even the moral judgments we see made are merely the facts of the judgments individual characters made, with no auxiliary judgments added. The chronicler leaves emotions and imagination, to say nothing of religious sensibility, outside of his description; we will see he is also this way regarding himself. If the novel seems flat, as many readers complain, consider the source. We will see, however, that in not a few instances the mere description of circumstances and rehearsal of events builds a place for auxiliary judgments on the part of the reader (as the earlier chronicle did for Paneloux), unless of course the concatenation of characters, events, and judgments is merely that, and no art at all is being practiced by Camus. And of course nothing is expected of us, the audience—except acceptance of the facts. We are to take this fiction as merely a chronicle of observed facts.[48] That logic seems suspect. For it is, on the other hand, an *invented* chronicle… .

Thus, the *author* is inviting us into a fiction bounded by the supposed positivity and objectivity of historical chronicle opposed to the needs, desires, imaginations, and hopes of the people of the town (including the narrator). It is thus that the absurd appears as the natural state of the thoroughly modern city of man. However, knowing it is a fiction—an invitation to imagine within an artistic structure which opens to, and

---

48   Edwin Moses, in "Functional Complexity: The Narrative Techniques of *The Plague*," *Modern Fiction Studies* 28.3 (1974): 419–429, summarizes the paradox nicely: "Camus' novel must conceal art; Rieux's chronicle must reveal artlessness" (425).

sometimes suggests or intimates, other sorts of judgments than those factual ones presented by the self-limited *narrator*—we find ourselves in a situation epistemologically parallel to that of listening to a skeptic, who wishes to convince us that "nothing is really known." In both situations the positivity of the speaker very exactly opens up an un-closeable question: In the case of the skeptic—do you *know* that? How could you? In the case of the novel—is this the whole of our world? Does the novel not intimate? Insofar as the narrator's self-removed chronicle gives us merely the facts and connection of events, it provides one pole of the absurd—here is the way the world is; and it also gives the other—here is what it does to all personal relationships and planning. It differs from a philosophical analysis of the absurd in giving us particular characters with individualized, if not idiosyncratic hopes and happinesses. A doctrine of the absurd is not taught thereby, but a passionate experience of it may be built up in the reader. Such a work of art is not one to bring our minds to rest in some dogmatic comfort, or to provide some substitutive satisfaction to the passions, but to open an infinite within the finite world of the work, and exhibit to the unclosed world its closed world figures, which are our own. The work of art opens to an infinite that cannot be closed—the real cosmos, and thus it is and will be a work that lives—and can live in many different ways, with many different emphases *depending on the reader*. That the reader may be an ideologue of the absurd provides one possible corseting for the work of art. Dr. Rieux enacts this in *his* world.

That the doctor/narrator is a practitioner of a sort of distancing or abstraction, even self-abstracted observation, we see evidenced in many scenes and phrasings of the novel. Besides his choice to write a "chronicle," we find him not really even puzzled about the rats, or attentive to the stories about them, or even noticing that he has stepped on one in a landing on the way down the stairs until he gets out onto the street (*P* 7). Abstraction from his own emotional life is indicated in his farewell to his wife, during which the only non-chit-chat and seemingly deep remark, "Please dear… take great care of yourself" (*P* 10), is uttered when she is behind a closed train window and cannot hear him. Perhaps, as he says, "the narrator has aimed at objectivity. He has made hardly any changes for the sake of artistic effect, except those elementary adjustments needed to present his narrative in a more or less coherent form" (*P* 169). Perhaps it is this very aim which

sets his own vision and experience of the world. On the other hand, in a work of art it is plausible for description of a scene including a character's words to intimate something further than merely the incidental facts and what the character intends by his words and deeds. A later comment, in chronicling how the closure of the town has caused one group to develop "a sort of feverish objectivity," concerns "the case of parted lovers, who present the greatest interest and of whom the narrator is, perhaps, better qualified to speak" (*P* 70), certifies—objectively—his uncertainty about his own emotions. He does not know whether or not he is qualified to speak as a lover; perhaps he is uncertain about what love is. He seems to exemplify one side of the Oranian dilemma about love—mild conjugality. But the certification of facts as facts will not get to love. Rieux's behavior and speech corset us into his *modus operandi* while allowing us to see and feel its stays and buckles. Other characters beckon, and their experience, too, we are taken into. Rieux's limits are not the limits of the world; his limits as narrator allow us to feel this. And he is not the only narrator, for at times he lets Tarrou's notebooks speak for themselves, and Tarrou has a deeper vision than just for the facts; thus the doctor has within him something larger than himself—an empirical impossibility of course, unless the soul can be so. But how can the contained be larger than the container? Perhaps this is an intimation; perhaps love would require it be so.

Rieux is the character who introduces another favorite theme in Camus—namely, lucidity—which the narrator presents as what is necessary to bring the plague to an end. Writing a chronicle would seem to be the form of expression best suited to lucidity, or perhaps to its first two steps. The doctor describes the theme this way: "It was only a matter of [1] lucidly recognizing what had to be recognized; of [2] dispelling extraneous shadows and [3] doing what needed to be done. Then the plague would come to an end, because it was unthinkable, or, rather, because one thought of it on misleading lines" (*P* 39). Perhaps the sort of objectivity he valorizes is itself a misleading line of thought, or incomplete. It does not seem that, in fact, plagues are unthinkable, or that they are likely to disappear merely by thinking of them correctly; in any case, the doctor himself, at best, only intermittently achieves such lucidity. For example, just before he pulls himself up short to expound this matter to himself, he has clearly been multiplying shadows, rather than dispelling them. There have been at this moment in the novel perhaps half a dozen cases of plague—to chronicle matters exactly, and yet Rieux has just spent several pages imagining hundreds and thousands of deaths and revivifying numerous well-known plagues from across time and space. Six is not an epidemic; imagination must be cut off: He opens a window and the sound of a machine saw brings him back to his present place and time. Even his presentation of lucidity seems, probably, to be expecting too much, for it comes despite an opening recognition that while "people say: 'It's too stupid; it can't last long.'…Stupidity has a knack of getting its way; as we should see if we were not always so much wrapped up in ourselves" (*P* 35f). If we lucidly recognize that that is the case, we should expect the plague to continue forever. The first step of lucidity, we should see from that experience of stupidity, is not going to happen, given the kind of people most of us are. And it seems that plague does not come to an end just because we see it clearly—unless, of course, everyone sees it and is willing to stop being stupid. Even then…. The novel lucidly exhibits that we should not expect either stupidity to end or lucidity to be born—not even during obvious horrors. Rieux's objectivity, which seems a mask for lucidity, is like that of most people—it waxes and wanes; but his expectation that a consistent lucidity, "dispelling extraneous [i.e., emotional, emotion-causing] shadows" (39) could cure the plague, stop wars, end a pandemic or poverty, or resolve any other evil that flesh is heir to, seems at least questionable, though it is, perhaps, a good beginning. It is not at all clear that Rieux's "recognizing what needs to be recognized" means recognizing love or anything about it; love probably involves imagination and emotion and moral judgments, not mere facts. "His business is only to say: 'This is what happened,' when he knows it actually did happen" (6). Being abstracted from both imagination and love seems a fact about our narrator. Deeper consideration of the implications and possibilities of lucidity must be put off till later, but at any rate it does not follow from Rieux's exposition that lucidity requires our agreement that absurdity is the truth of life; for his idea of lucidity seems to begin by ruling some important matters out. Other judgments are available, even within his chronicle.

Tarrou seems more consistently lucid about the absurdity of the world; indeed lucidity seems to be for Tarrou, as for Camus himself perhaps, that intellectual virtue which recognizes and continually holds before it the absurdity of the world. Or rather, since "the Absurd is not in man … nor in the world, but in their presence together" (*MS* 23), lucidity is that virile state of soul which holds itself in this absurd situation without forgetting or attempting to escape where it at every moment is. Thus, such a one, "conscious of the absurd… [is] devoid of hope and conscious of being so" (*MS* 24). Thus, a town given over entirely to commerce, where even all pleasures "seemed to be dictated by considerations of business" (*P* 24) wins Tarrou's approval, precisely for holding no extra-curricular hopes or imaginations; this makes it easier to remain "on point." He makes a list of open absurdities in answer to his own query "How contrive not to waste one's time?" The list includes "spending one's days on an uneasy chair in a dentist's waiting room…listening to lectures in a language one doesn't know… lining up at the box-office of theatres and then not buying a seat" (*P* 25). These activities do not aim at any telos except consciousness of not having an end affirmed by the world.[49] He thinks of Rieux's asthma patient, who spends his days in bed transferring dried peas one by one from one pan to another, as quite possibly a saint; his are "an aggregate of habits" (*P* 112), which infect nobody, and depend, so far as possible on no one's death; so he is the image of "a saint without God" (*P* 237). He is the living example of one who has realized that the "important thing…is not to be cured, but to live with one's ailments" (*MS* 29). That ailment is the absurd—the asthma patient is not wasting his time, but aware of every waking moment as it passes, from the pan of the present to the pan of the past. He does not leave his bed. Tarrou's own chosen path in absurd living is what he calls "comprehension" (*P* 120), and later—sympathy (*P* 230). Knowing that the absurd is Everyman's situation, he knows the temptations to escape— through suicide, murder, pleasures, illusions, inattention. All of these increase the infection; Tarrou works consistently to bring even the

49 Suppose Thomas Pölzler is correct that the purpose of art for Camus is that it "cultivates traits and attitudes that are indispensable to developing and maintaining an awareness of the absurd and an attitude of revolt. Most importantly, creating is supposed to make one more disciplined, more lucid and more patient" in facing the absurdity of life. Then Tarrou (given his suggested contrivances above) should be considered a groundbreaking performance artist. "Camus on the Value of Art," in *Philosophia* 48, 1: 365–376; open access pub. online 23 April 2019, 6th unnumbered page, https://doi.org/10.1007/s11406-019-00078-4.

collaborator—Cottard—around to living in conscientious solidarity with all the other victims of plague. He regards this comprehensive solidarity as the proper state for a human being, and his organization of teams of sanitary squad co-workers for the doctors, inviting all to share in the dangers of their shared situation, is the perfect expression of the sympathy he once felt for "the little man in the dock" (*P* 224), who is to him a figure for us all. This equality of all in the face of the dangerous absurdity of death is what Tarrou considers incumbent upon free men to recognize without condemning others, he himself having been cured of his earlier ideological barbarianism precisely by not blinking in the examination of his participation in it. Sentencing others to death (to achieve a better world where we won't have to) goes beyond the notice of our real situation—the absurd—into the illusion of knowing the future—or dictating it to others. "For many years I've been ashamed, mortally ashamed, of having been, even with the best intentions, even at many removes, a murderer in my turn" (*P* 228).

There seems, then, to be something mistaken in a view which sees Camus to be splitting Dostoevsky's famous Ivan's character—brilliant intellect, intense pity, and inability to love—in such a way as to consider Tarrou "the abstract rebel" and Rieux "the active humble rebel."[50] Tarrou does seem to achieve his lucidity *through* the intellectual history he retraces for the doctor—so, sharing the intellectual gifts of Ivan, but his pity is neither abstract, nor so intense as to make him functionally useless—as Ivan—rather, he seems to be powered by his clear, detailed understanding of Everyman's circumstance to work consistently in sympathy with them in order to help them to a less infectious state. Even to Cottard he feels it his "job in life" to offer second chances (cf. *P* 138, 144–45). Less infectious means, besides the literal, less subject to and so less contributory to, any illusory escapes from recognition of the rule of death and thus absurdity; rather one should constantly order experience to awareness thereof. I am not sure he is a rebel at all; he tried that in his earlier life, and discovered such action could only be rigorously carried out by closing one's eyes to the fact of sentencing others to death. This he now refuses to do. We shall see in him a

50 Andrea Lešić-Thomas, "The Answer Job Did Not Give: Dostoevsky's *Brat'ia Karamazovy* and Camus's *La Peste*," *Modern Language Review* 101, 3 (July, 2006): 774–88; see 784–785.

growth in the recognition of love, a recognition which exceeds mere refusal to infect, or refusal to pass on infection.

Nor does the doctor seem a humble rebel; one of the reasons he thinks led him to become a doctor was that "it was particularly difficult for a workman's son"; that, and his outrage at "the whole scheme of things" (*P* 121) being his primary motivations. These do not seem expressions of humility. They are, rather, acts of rebellion against his particular social status as well as against the whole world as he sees it. But we are now already broaching our next section's topic. This is fitting, as the recognition of absurdity rouses rebellion: the rebel "opposes the principle of justice which he finds in himself to the principle of injustice which he sees being applied in the world" (*R* 24). Let us close this part by considering that the novel shows the plague imposing a terrible abstracting monotony, but that recognition of the absurd is also pictured the same way when we listen to Tarrou's pre-plague suggestions for ways not to waste our time, and in Rieux's description of the activities of the town before the plague. Tarrou is one who "does everything to keep before him that absurd brought to life by consciousness" (*MS* 53). It is not the plague which brings the absurd into the modern city of human life; it merely makes noticeable to a few more people—maybe only to us readers—what that life already is. As Tarrou says later, we all have plague; that plague is not the Nazis, disease, famine, war or death, though death is "the event that proves [him] right" (*P* 115)—at least it is not only those things. The plague is, then, as it is in Oran, part of the high-ceilinged sun-struck climate—a "climate that is common" to all of us moderns according to (the early) Camus: the absurd.[51]

Revolt

Though it often sounds otherwise, Camus allows that the recognition of the absurd does not necessarily lead to any clear trilemma or perhaps quadrilemma, such as revolt, suicide, philosophical suicide (such as he considers Kierkegaard and Husserl to have accomplished) or mere ignorance or

51 At *MS* 18, Camus says his aim in the essay is "to bring out the climate that is common to" all the philosophers he discusses in the essay: Heidegger, Kierkegaard, Jaspers, Chestov, *et al*. What he means by climate I earlier called myth: all these philosophers share the same myth: the absurd.

forgetfulness (such as the citizens of Oran bury themselves in), only one of which is lucid. Rather, "one of the only coherent philosophical positions is… revolt" (*MS* 54). Perhaps revolt is the natural first response to absurdity,[52] and "in it we discover something permanent in oneself worth preserving" and that "this something does not belong to him alone, but…is common ground where all men—even the one who insults and oppresses him" (*R* 16)—have a natural community. So, revolt makes us aware of something deeper, or that there is something more to be discovered in us. Perhaps, Camus says, it "leads at least to the suspicion that, contrary to the postulates of contemporary thought, a human nature does exist, as the Greeks believed" (*R* 16).

Revolt, then, allows that there might be some other source of natural solidarity—or a solidarity that can arise out of our nature—beyond itself which is also coherent. "Man's solidarity" may be "founded upon rebellion" (*R* 22) but revolt is only one of the coherent positions, and one character in the novel even makes that claim to coherence seem…unlikely: the doctor's mother. We will begin to speak of her in the next section. The doctor, however, is the clearest figure of one who acknowledges the absurd, and revolts against "the scheme of things." He enacts this revolt in the scene after the child's death, and states it starkly: "weariness is a kind of madness. And there are times when the only feeling I have is one of mad revolt" (*P* 196). He is weary of what he sees as the world's constant destruction of innocence and happiness; at times this weariness becomes so noxious that he wishes to revolt against it.[53] He recognizes, however, that this is madness—for the world is what it is, and his revolt against it is even less effectual than Sisyphus raising his fist to the gods. "He felt like shouting imprecations" (*P* 196), but Sisyphus knew there were gods to curse, who might, on occasion hear—and continue not to care; the world, on the other hand, cannot pay any attention

52 We might add to "natural first response to absurdity," "at least of those who are not lacking *thymos* or *nous*, or whatever it is that makes some human beings natural slaves," to make this sentence more Aristotelian.

53 Camus confesses that the killing of his Catholic friend and fellow member of the resistance, René Leynaud, by the Nazis in 1944 made his own "revolt more blind. The finest thing I can say in his favor is that he would not have followed me in that revolt" (*RRD*, 53). He recognizes the fine (*kalos*) in someone who does not revolt, someone who is killed working for justice and does not revolt against the scheme of things.

to our words, cannot even decide not to care. To be heard is a happier situation; Sisyphus may be happy, but the metaphysical rebel does not even have this. To imagine being heard is madness. Is rebellion, then, madness?

Most of the time the doctor is not in that conscious mad rebellion; he works extremely long hours, and he pays much more detailed attention to his patients than to his wife. There are poor patients whom he does not charge and whom he continues to see for chronic conditions that are far less deadly than plague even at the height of the disease. In all this, perhaps he illustrates his connection with the townspeople of Oran, despite being rather insulated from the real force of life and feeling: there is something in each of them to be stood up for. Tarrou calls him "absent minded" (*P* 27), and unlike the man who becomes his friend, the doctor is too busy to keep the absurd at the front of his attention. Thus, at most times he is calm; no one—including himself—would take him as suffering madness. But in these times, where he seems most abstracted from his feelings, he admits also to an ignorance which would seem to bring rebellion into question as one of the philosophically coherent responses to the world. It seems, in fact, philosophically dark: "I simply don't know.... . For nothing in the world is it worth turning one's back on what one loves. Yet that is what I am doing, though why I don't know" (*P* 189). Wouldn't a real rebel grasp what love he can achieve before it (absurdly) smashes into a tree? This would seem to be an admission that the doctor's position is at least of questionable philosophical coherence: why such dedication? He cannot explain his own work even to himself. That is a different picture of absurdity than our previous section discussed; this absurdity appears in the consciousness of his own consciousness, not his consciousness of the world. Perhaps, in writing *The Plague*, Camus is already breaking through this stage of revolt to the third, always present, living heart of his own life's work. The doctor, at any rate, seems not adequate to the world he is in, not adequate even to himself. His admitted lack of understanding of his own action requires that we readers wonder about the coherence of rebellion, which he instantiates. Other characters move into and in another realm:

Love

In that section of *The Rebel* entitled "Rebellion and Art" Camus says that in every rebellion there is "a metaphysical demand for unity, the impossibility of capturing it, and the construction of a substitute universe. Rebellion, from this point of view is a fabricator of universes" (*R* 255). Much of the scholarly work on *The Plague* points to this rebellion as the *raison d'être* of the novel and its putative heroes. According to Camus, however, his earlier works were aiming to come through to love. Is love then, an act of rebellion? Then love, too, is a fabricator of worlds. Is all love so? Or perhaps love begins in praises, and loves the world, as Camus confesses he does. And can this praising love pre-exist rebellion? Persist through it? Perhaps refuse it; keep it in check? Camus says his earlier essays had more love than all that had come afterward. Is it rebellion then which opens us to love and solidarity with our fellows, or is it love which pre-exists and perhaps in a way powers the rebellion? And the demand for solidarity. Or does rebellion cover up what is and should be the center and the leading edge of life? Could that praising love choose a different path than rebellion, as Camus says of Leynaud? We take as our task in this book showing how what Camus called the third layer his work embodies is able to be seen already shining through a story told by a rebel, in the absurd darkness of a city under quarantine. In *The Plague* several philosophically and theologically distinct uses of this term—love—are clearly in play, as will be shown in later chapters, but anyone who has read Camus' final, supposedly unfinished, novel, *The First Man*, cannot miss the depth of love that that novel not only represents to, but mimetically engenders in, the reader. It certifies something true of Camus' 'self-mythologization,' as I have called it, of his own life-work, and if readers have not paid attention to this theme before—as in *The Plague*—his last novel certainly gives good reason to go looking. A number of those works which come between *The Plague* (1947) and *The First Man* (1995), however, seem to make this self-told myth quite questionable as a chronicle. One wonders how love can be the center, or even a minor theme, in a novel like *The Fall* (1956), or the still later short story "The Renegade, or A Confused Mind," from *Exile and the Kingdom* (1957) to say nothing of the philosophy expressed in *The Rebel* (1951). Perhaps that the renegade is a confused mind, and *The Fall* a conversation with the devil himself gives an intimation of Camus' center by the absolute clarity of its absence in those works.

At any rate, one has good reason to agree with what looks to be a more empirical approach exemplified by Matthew Sharpe, who arranges Camus' work in an order moving through a four stage cycle of pagan myth paired to Biblical motifs.[54] Thus, in the period 1937–42 the myth of Sisyphus and the Biblical motif of alienation and exile are central; from 1943–52 Prometheus joins hands with Biblical rebellion and produces *The Plague*; 1952–58 lacks a pagan myth, but Biblical themes of fall and guilt and the figures of John the Baptist and Christ are central; and his career is cut short under the myth of Nemesis and the Biblical theme of the Kingdom, for which the only work we have is *The First Man*. It would seem that love, if it is to come to the center in the life-work of Camus, must wait for the unfinished novel or something even beyond that. Perhaps Sharpe's is an artist's exhibition of Nemesis working to show that he who abandons alienation for love… . Well, let us consider otherwise in the book that follows, in which I will argue that love is already the heart—though perhaps hidden— in *The Plague*; and in which love will be shown in several ways to be the light in the world, and in at least one way to be a great caster of extraneous shadows—though perhaps some of those shadows give evidence by their darkness of real truths standing in the light.

54 Or a five-stage cycle which he draws from *Carnets*. Matthew Sharpe, in *Camus, Philosophe* outlines several versions of Camus' thought about the unity and order of his works, pp. 41f; he offers a summary chart of 5 stages with myths, motifs, and themes organized against Camus' creative work and essays (44f). The three-layer outline this part of the chapter has been based on, from Camus' remarks in 1957, seems clearer, especially since Camus himself points out the importance of love in those first youthful essays. Love was always the center.

CHAPTER TWO

REASON, FEELING AND HAPPINESS:
BRIDGING AN ANCIENT/MODERN DIVIDE IN
THE PLAGUE

> 'But, damn it, Doctor, can't you see it's a matter of common human feeling?... You're using the language of abstraction, not of the heart; you live in a world of abstractions.'
>
> The doctor glanced up at the statue of the Republic... (*The Plague*, 82)

In that discussion between *Übermenschen* which Nietszche once imagined as taking place from one mountaintop across to another, and which is as good a figure as any for the history of philosophy, we hear what sound like many contradictions. Nonetheless, they continue to speak to us in ways we seem to understand. While many say that modern philosophy begins with Descartes, modern moral philosophy begins with Kant. Kant himself sets this story in motion by calling his work philosophy's Copernican revolution, and this critical revolution is consciously set to turn around his moral philosophy: it is the moral law of pure practical reason which is the condition for the possibility of the sublime, and in line with which all judgments of beauty are called symbolic. It is pure practical reason which generates the positive resolution of what is, for theoretical reason, merely a dialectically unanswerable antinomy by giving us the one, non-spatiotemporally intuited fact: freedom. The work of both theoretical reason and aesthetic judgment hang on the moral philosophy. From this moral philosophy is born the modern idea of the universal community of not only human beings, but of all rational beings: call it "The Republic of Conscience."[1] Camus

1   This phrase is the title of a poem by Seamus Heaney; it is not disconnected from Kant's ideas.

certainly was familiar with Kant's claims and place in the history of ideas; but whether the ancient world is dead, or its ideas thoroughly disproven by this enlightenment is quite an open question, for the beautiful ideas, as Diotima taught Socrates, participate in eternity.

Camus can be seen working rigorously through a well-known division between ancient (Aristotelian) and modern (Kantian) ethics concerning the relation of reason, feeling and happiness, using terms he would have known well thanks to his years of studying for an advanced degree in philosophy. Camus' novel, as suggested in the preface, is not only a way for him to work through these philosophical differences *in vivo*, so to speak, but also a way of contributing to modern solidarity among human beings, who live by a variety of ancient and modern ideas. Thus, the work of the artist is a contribution to the improvement of life, and to the understanding of it, in his own society, and that of the world after him. Plato could have no complaints against such poetry; Aristotle would see it as a work of lasting, perfecting, and perfect friendship; Kant would understand it as a work of practical love—the performance of an imperfect duty to others. In the course of this novel we are able to see that, despite their seemingly large differences on these topics, Kant and Aristotle would agree in their judgment of many of the characters and actions in *The Plague*: the novel provides realistic insights into a philosophical agreement between their supposed oppositions. In particular, both philosophers would agree concerning the relative goodness and relative happiness of Joseph Grand and Raymond Rambert. The illustration of this agreement goes far to prove that Camus is valorizing a traditional ethic, or perhaps that a traditional ethic is a valid "existential" choice, a life of "good faith," perhaps even a faith that can help make one good.

1. The Philosophical Problems

The relation of reason to feeling provides one of the great divisions between ancient and modern ethics. For example, for Aristotle, virtue is the measure of the moral worth of the person, and the virtues are stable dispositions which include both affective and intellectual aspects. For Kant, on the other hand, one's particular feelings seem to be either that from which we must abstract to judge the moral worth of an act—so feelings have no significance in making moral judgments—or they are a constant hindrance to a person's proper moral activity. That they have no significance seems implied when Kant says "a sympathetic temper…has no genuinely moral worth" (*FMM* 398). Some people are born with the temperament of a social worker, but being born with a helpful temperament is not a moral qualification insofar as it is not an act of the will (= pure practical reason) according to Kant. Aristotle would agree with part of Kant's analysis here; he believes that there are "natural virtues," which are exhibited from early on, but they are virtues by analogy—acts of real virtue must be chosen, and for their own sake (*NE* 1105a32–33).

Further, while Aristotle does agree with the modern Kant that feelings (particularly the desire for pleasure) *can* in many cases be a hindrance to proper moral activity, he would disagree that they are a constant hindrance or temptation as appears to be the case a little later when Kant says that "the will stands, so to speak, at a crossroads between its *a priori* principle, which is formal, and its *a posteriori* motive, which is material" (*FMM*, p. 400). Since the *a priori* motive is that of pure practical reason, emotions, feeling, and desires are, even when not precisely crossing reason, a differently *rooted* set of principles, not the moral one. In his later writings this differential sourcing of the will's possible principles seems to judge as amoral—at best—Aristotle's unity of intellectual and affective aspects in the person's disposition, since "habit belongs to the physical nature of the determination of the will."[2] By contrast, for Aristotle, choice following upon correct reasoning about one's moral situation is insufficient, even if one's feelings are, on a singular occasion, in accord with that correct reasoning and choice; neither the person nor the choice is fully virtuous until it flows from the disposition, which markedly is the flow of proper feeling and desire.

This contrast is connected to a second great division between Kant and Aristotle (and between most moderns and other ancients), namely on the relation between virtue and happiness; this difference, in turn, is closely connected to quite distinct views of what happiness is. For Kant, happiness is an ideal of the imagination, "a maximum of wellbeing in my present,

---

2   *Metaphysical Principles of Virtue*, trans. James Ellington (Indianapolis: LLA, 1964), p. 409 (Akademie pagination); hereafter *MPV*.

and in every future, state," all of the elements of which "are without exception empirical" (*FMM*, 418). Such a view of happiness is quintessentially modern, one which Kant shares not only with Hume, but with Freud and Mill, for whom happiness is "pleasure and the absence of pain," or, in the narrower sense only "the experiencing of strong feelings of pleasure."[3] This means that happiness, as the summation of all of our empirical desires, might look even more like the constant counterweight to moral action based on the *a priori* principle, except that this ideal is so indefinite—not only as to what must be included, but also to what extent, and when and how each element (some of which have not yet been invented) is to be included—that we can have no sure idea of the direction in which this summation of all our material motives actually points.[4] In popular culture it is the pirate, Jack Sparrow's, compass. There is no true north.

We all know perfectly well that many immediately possible ends contradict each other; such difficulties acknowledge part of the problem of happiness seen as fulfillment of empirical desires. Augustine's *reductio ad absurdum* of Manichean philosophy provides a humorous example: at the same time a person may have before him all of the following desirable options—going to the Manichean meeting, the theatre, the circus, or the Catholic church, "to the last I add…whether he should rob another man's house, if he has the chance. And I add…whether he should commit adultery if an opportunity opens up at the same time" (*Conf.* 8.10.24). So many pleasant, entertaining and desirable things, so little time. There is no clear idea by which we can accomplish all these desires; certainly they can't all be accomplished now, when they are all so achingly available. The idea of happiness which includes satisfaction of all our desires—extensively,

3   John Stuart Mill, *Utilitarianism*. ed. Oskar Piest (Indianapolis: Bobbs – Merrill, 1957), p. 10 (1st quote), which is exactly echoed and then added to by Sigmund Freud, *Civilization and its Discontents*, trans. James Strachey (New York: Norton, 1961), p. 25 (both first and second quote); hereafter *CD*.

4   As Camus wrote in *Christian Metaphysics and Neoplatonism* (University of Missouri Press. 2007), where Christianity is what he seems to mean by sentiment: "Intelligence is powerless…when sentiment endlessly varies its nuances" (64). This seems unlikely to be properly said to be Christianity, but it is properly said about the impossibility of practical reason directing any achievement when attempting to discover direction from such a cloud of unknowing happiness.

intensively, and protensively—as the end of our action can therefore give practical reason no direction in any case whatsoever. If practical reason, a practical reason which "is and ought to be the slave of the passions,"[5] as Hume famously held, is attempting to achieve this happiness as the final end of all our actions, it is a necessarily irrational slave. It *cannot* know the end; for reason to be the slave of such an all-encompassing and materially incomplete imaginary end is to reduce it to a tool for I know not what, or, as Kant says, "who knows what tutelary nature whispers to it" (*FMM* 425). Perhaps we have found the root of barbarism, for such a reason is the slave to something else in nature; this would go far to explain barbarism's strength and universality—especially among moderns, who by and large have this idea of happiness.

On the other hand, Kant suggests that happiness being so vague (not an empty, but rather an over-filled and self-contradictory) idea, we might even hope that, far from being counter to each other, following the moral law might always accord with real happiness. For, while we can be sure when a *particular desire* is being thwarted by morality's categorical imperative, we could never be sure that our imaginary *ideal* of happiness is being so thwarted. Kant's examples of the impossibility of knowing whether a particular empirical end (say, cheesecake, or wealth) fits in with the universal empirical end of happiness or runs counter to it (*FMM* 399, 418), can also be applied to the question of whether following the moral law in any particular situation fits in with our imagined universal empirical end of happiness or runs counter to it. Just as it is possible that this extra piece of dessert will not bring on the gout, or perhaps it won't be a bad case, or maybe there will be a car accident and I won't live until tomorrow, so it is counter to my overall happiness not to enjoy it today, similarly, we don't know what all is included in the imaginary end happiness, so we can't know whether morality contradicts its achievement in this particular case of, say, keeping my promises to my spouse, or not. It may even be that following the moral law leads to happiness, though one is not acting rightly (even

---

5   Thus Hume, one of the fathers of modern day empiricism, also thinks that happiness is pleasure, as this quote entails. David Hume, *A Treatise of Human Nature*, 2nd ed., ed. L.A. Selby-Bigge (Oxford: University Press, 1978), p. 415.

though in accord with the moral law) when that law is treated as a means to happiness. This Kant will later label impurity (*Rel* 25; cf. *FMM* 397–398).

Furthermore, Kant sees that this modern definition of happiness naturally leads to the affirmation of another modern passion as natural: the desire to be free from all constraints by others (even though this is impossible in any society). Thus, he concludes, "our condition is such that in certain respects we are necessarily unhappy."[6] It is notable that Freud agrees that "the programme of becoming happy, which the pleasure principle imposes on us, cannot be fulfilled" (*CD* 34); unlike Kant, however, Freud really has no other principle available to direct our action, since the reality principle is just the pleasure principle suitably chastened by punishment and fear, particularly the fear of loss of love which he calls social anxiety (*CD* 85). So, the human being really is a "useless passion" as Sartre put it.[7] The impossibility or indeterminacy of happiness is absolute; the desire for its completeness and totality[8] is inescapably permanent. Because we are finite rational beings—which entails a multitude of desires that exceed animal nature: a computer and a cell phone, if not a Tesla—the idea of happiness is the self-actuating motor of a being *functionally* delusional, as that idea's connection to any particular work of reason in directing moral action is perfectly indeterminable. We imagine otherwise, constantly; and we are wrong. The songs of the Sirens come to mind, though that is an ancient story; according to Kant these are not to be entertained, but we must bind ourselves to the mast and take our direction from pure practical reason. Kant could accept everything Hume, Freud and Mill might tell us about what happiness is, and it would all fit with his analysis that the strength of this function often makes it look to imagination as if the moral law stands athwart the desire for happiness, since in fact it does thwart some

6   Allen W. Wood, *Kant's Ethical Thought* (Cambridge: University Press, 1999), p. 254.

7   Jean-Paul Sartre, *Being and Nothingness*, trans. Hazel E. Barnes (New York: Philosophical Library, 1956): 615

8   In Sartre's less than pellucid construction, "Each human reality is at the same time a direct project to metamorphose its own For-itself into an In-itself-For-itself and a project of the appropriation of the world as a totality of being-in-itself" (Ibid.)

particular desires whose ends are imminently achievable, and which are imagined as requisite elements of happiness at the moment.

Aristotle has no such difficulties: happiness is "an activity of the soul in accord with virtue and, if there are several, with the best and most complete, in a complete life" (*NE* 1098a16–19). This happiness is the final end of all action and choice. The life of moral virtue wound up with practical reason, while second in happiness to the life of contemplation according to Aristotle, is that which allows one to make the best use of the particular gifts nature and fortune have bestowed; it alone can build and allow for the best and happiest life.[9] However limited they may be, the virtuous person knows how to best utilize and organize not only the external goods of life (*NE* 1101a3–7), but also her physical, mental and emotional particulars; in fact, her own achievement of virtue will differ from another's such achievement precisely in many of these, for each virtuous person is born into a personally particular socio-historical-familial nexus and must have become aware of those particular excessive (and deficient) desires to which she was most subject and must have aimed contrary to them (*NE* 1109b1–18) in order to achieve her more perfect disposition—a disposition in which her desires are no longer excessive or deficient, but are regularly at the mean which practical reason determines. Being so rightly ordered, the achievement of those desires is both properly pleasant and morally good. Just for the record, Augustine seems to agree with this notion, for he says of the citizens of the city of God that "because their love is rightly placed, all their affections are also right" (*DCD* 14.9), which implies that the passional disposition of the person is part of the essence of their moral perfection. The question among all of these thinkers is about where one's love is placed.

Despite these seemingly strong contrasts, we shall see that Kant and Aristotle would have significant agreement in their judgment of characters and actions which are good, as well as which persons are happy. Both the agreements and the difficulties will now be illustrated by examining some characters and actions from *The Plague*. Though some have considered *The Plague* mere allegory about resistance to a common evil, that Camus' contemplation of such allegorical bones exhibits his own consideration of these

9   For detailed explication of this view see Richard Kraut, *Aristotle on the Human Good* (Princeton: University Press, 1989).

well-known problematic relations of thinking to feeling and happiness to morality is patent. Moreover, the novelistic approach to these issues, which give us not vapid or otherworldly trolley experiments (in which we know much more about the people we are running over than any trolley driver ever could), but a picture of individual lives engaged in moral choices in a world they all share, allows us realistic insights into a philosophical agreement between these supposed oppositions. We will see that Camus is both considering and attempting to resolve these important philosophical differences, to show us the commonalities which cross these differences in outlook, and perhaps through such discovery enabling us to find grounds for human solidarity across such and such-like differences. In this exploration we must reconsider the common critical choices about who really is his novel's hero, and so the resolution of this ancient-modern quarrel requires we question the usual interpretation of Camus as the absurdist philosopher of revolt, and of the doctor or Tarrou as the hero.

2. Camus' Characters' Plights

That Camus has precisely this ancient/modern division in mind can be seen in his opening descriptions of Oran. The narrator notes the "completely modern" habits, passions and vices of the townspeople in a way that seems to echo how Aristotle might judge them. For example, their way of loving ranges from "consum[ing] one another rapidly in what is called 'the act of love' or else settl[ing] down to a mild habit of conjugality. We seldom find a mean between these extremes" (*P* 4). Though we do not need Aristotle to point out that these extremes of habitual feeling and action constitute opposed vices between which one might hope to find whatever constitutes the virtuous habits of stable conjugal love, it cannot be doubted that this wording calls up that famous ancient doctrine. It also reminds us of Aristotle's ideas of friendship: there is that based on pleasure and that based on use, but given that no one hits the mean, there can be no friendship of virtue, though that friendship is not itself merely a mean between the two other forms. The virtuous friendship, rather, will be both pleasant and useful precisely because the friends act virtuously toward one another (*NE* 8.3, 8.4): they love each other as ends in themselves (*NE* 1156b10–14), not for that pleasure or useful ease which they supply.

These ancient echoes quickly become complicated by the modern over-tones of Kant's later criticism of acting from disposition, without noticing or being moved by the command of reason: the narrator notes the town's busyness, adding that, "for lack of time and thinking, people have to love one another without knowing much about it." Altogether, the town is such that "you can get through the days there without trouble, once you have formed habits. And since habits are precisely what our town encourages, all is for the best…and, after a while, you go complacently to sleep there" (*P* 4–6). Such unthinking sleep-walking is precisely what Kant seems to have had in mind in his criticism of morality as dispositional: it is the ro-botic mechanism at work, following along the easy ruts of an individual's constitutional, regularly answerable desires, abrogating the activity of the principle of pure practical reason even if acting rightly.[10] The narrator's de-scription, even of those few who might hit the mean, seems to bring them as well under the shadow of Kant's critique: theirs is a zombie virtue; the modern city encourages such busy mindless activity. Thinking is saved for work, for making deals, getting discounts; economic reasoning—yes; moral reasoning—what's that? Reason serves. And what it serves for is to make more money for amusement. In modern life moral reasoning is just another form of cost-benefit analysis where we measure pleasures and pains rather than debits and credits. It is not thought that "each animal has its own proper pleasure," (*NE* 1176a4), so that, "consequently, happiness does not consist in amusement" (*NE* 1176b28) for the human being. Rather, every pleasure counts equally as pleasure. "On Sunday mornings, for instance, sea-bathing competes seriously with churchgoing" (*P* 85). Reason may be a means to satisfaction, but that it should order our satisfactions in accord with some rational hierarchy simply because that is reason's hierarchy (as Aristotle, for example, describes the relation between the political and the theoretical lives) seems unfair to all those satisfactions other than reason. The idea that happiness consists "in activities that conform with virtue" (*NE* 1177a10) is like one of those old statues that dot the town, marking a battle long-forgotten, and to which no one pays attention.

The narrator suggests an unlikely "hero" (*P* 126–27, 130) for the story

10   Camus had noticed this "mechanism" as what one had to be wakened from in *The Myth of Sisyphus*, 10.

of Oran: Joseph Grand, a poor temporary assistant municipal clerk with "constriction of the aorta" who lives "in rue Faidherbe" (*P* 17)—literally, "a street made of greenery" in the high desert.[11] We meet him after he has just saved Monsieur Cottard—"a man with something pretty serious on his conscience" (*P* 54)—from suicide. When Dr. Rieux says "somebody should watch Cottard tonight," Grand responds, "I can't say I really know him, but one's got to help a neighbor, hasn't one?" (*P* 19). It becomes clear that Grand does this despite the fact that while Cottard "always seemed to want to start a conversation," he really should have seen that Grand had "some private work" (*P* 32)—one "connected with 'the growth of a personality'" (*P* 41)—that involved considerable quiet study. The combination of these descriptions of Grand seem a perfect illustration of the will that "is good through its willing alone" (*FMM* 394). His activities precisely illustrate Kant's two examples of imperfect duties—the duty to cultivate our talents and the duty to come to the aid of others (*FMM* 423); he clearly chooses to watch over Cottard out of recognition of the moral law, not out of any particular knowledge of or liking for him, or any habitual inclination for such helpful activities. Clearly there are other activities he much prefers to, and habitually does, spend his evenings on. He seems to perfectly illustrate here what Kant calls "moral apathy," where "the feelings arising from sensible impressions lose their influence on moral feeling only because respect for law is more powerful than all those feelings together"(*MPV* 408).

Kant's use of the word apathy here is unusual. In fact, his further description of this state echoes in one way the Aristotelian principle of the mean. He explains that "lively sympathy with good," or "enthusiasm" is what must be moderated in the exercise of virtue, for an excess of such emotion "leaves one languid." Clearly the deficiency of this sympathy is also a bad thing, as it would be counter to "a deliberate and firm resolution" (*MPV* 409). Moral apathy, then, cannot mean lack of moral feeling or sympathy

11 Robert Solomon, in *Dark Feelings, Grim Thoughts: Experience and Reflection in Camus and Sartre* (Oxford: University Press, 2006), considers this heroic suggestion "ludicrous:...Dr Rieux is obviously trying to put one over on us (a point that several commentators seem not to notice)," p. 120; see also p. 127.

with the good. It means, rather, apathy to all sensibly or inclinationally aroused feelings in the face of—and in favor of—the moral good.

Grand attempts to fulfill both sorts of what Kant calls meritorious or imperfect duties (helping one's neighbor, developing one's own talents) despite having been disfavored by fate and having received but "niggardly provision" (*FMM* 394) both from nature and his civic paymasters. Though the work of his morally good heart is constricted both by his slender gifts of physical and intellectual nature as well as his impoverished early upbringing and continuing penury, throughout the novel he nonetheless fulfills even imperfect duties whenever they appear; and when they conflict, as in this case, Grand judges correctly that as aid to his neighbor is vitally needed immediately, so development of his talent should wait. Grand's work—exactingly tracing out the Latin roots of French words (like "Faidherbe")—develops his own personality, even as he aims it at describing and developing the person of the woman within his novel. We should recognize the beauty of his main character, and her movement through the beautiful world in his novel as a symbol of the moral (Cf. KU §59: 351–354). His good will in developing his linguistic talents—and thus the growth of *his* personality—is thus wound up with that beauty which he is attempting to create. His aim in this (now understood as double) work is perfection—both of the work and the life, as is clear from his description of the effect he hopes to achieve in it. He wants it to be "such that from the very first words it will be possible to say: 'Hats off!'" (*P* 99). While Grand is speaking of his novel, the way the work on the novel ties up with the growth of his own personality, clearly makes the perfection he hopes to be recognized a moral perfection. Significantly, when Rieux says the first sentence has "whetted his curiosity… Grand told him he'd got it all wrong" (*P* 99). That may be the way a thing like a novel works, but the activity of the good will raises awe, respect, or reverence, not curiosity or some other appetite. Further, the work of the good will does not need to wait for its conclusion in order to be evaluated, for "if even the greatest effort should not avail it to achieve anything of its end…it would sparkle as a jewel…as something that had its full worth in itself" (*FMM* 394). Rieux considers Grand's image of how his novel will be received rather unusual, but that is because the novel is, to the doctor, only a thing, not the work of freedom.

Despite Rieux's lack of clarity concerning morality and its principles, something in the narrator rightly calls him "our *worthy* fellow citizen" (*P* 43, cf. 97), even while admitting that the language of conventional sympathy is "incapable of describing" him (*P* 130–131). This last is true because his activity involves a source beyond the ken of such sympathetic feelings.[12] Every reader of Kant will recall that it is good will which makes a person "worthy of happiness," whether or not he achieves happiness or accomplishes the end that the good will sets and does everything in its power to bring to pass (*FMM* 393, 394). Grand seems to be, then, a man who has transformed his original desire for the unlimited freedom imaginary modern happiness entails into that more complex (and lucidly rational) desire for a freedom fulfilled (and really fulfillable) under moral laws, in his own much constricted life in Oran in 194__. His recognition as "worthy" and "hero" by the narrator does not imply that Dr. Rieux himself has a clear-headed Kantian understanding of morals or worthiness, for he never actually appeals to (or seems to recognize lucidly) the kind of reasoning Grand so simply sets forth, represents, and acts upon. Nor does Grand himself need to be a philosopher, for, as Kant himself understood it, the moral philosophy of his *Foundations* does not aim to teach anything new to moral reasoning, but merely to clarify moral reasoning and judgement's correct working (*FMM* 389–391). Thus it is possible even for a utilitarian to occasionally make a correct judgement in accord with this deep-rooted principle; in fact, Kant suggests any such empirical moral figuring—such as utility calculations—depends upon a pure practical principle by which those calculations are oriented to what is the highest good (*FMM* 408–409); without it, they do not know how to begin to measure.

Grand's work—connected as it is with "the growth of a personality"—is, it also becomes clear, his happiness.[13] So it is quite strange, if not totally

12　David Sherman, in his *Camus* (Malden, MA: Wiley – Blackwell, 2009), vaguely hints in the direction of some agreement with Kant, claiming Camus has a "two tiered" approach to ethics in which the "first tier, the primary one, is *in some sense* transcendental" (p. 164, cf. p. 165, italics Sherman). He offers no further details concerning this Kantian theme.

13　And so, deep in the plague, he can say, "Happily, I have my work" (*P* 96). Recently, Matthew Sharpe has also argued that for Camus the virtues "are necessary if a person…[is] to live happily, fulfilling their nature" as "a political and rational being." Matthew Sharpe, "Camus and the Virtues (with and be-

inexplicable, that precisely when the narrator names Grand the "hero," who has "to his credit only a little goodness of heart and a seemingly absurd ideal," he thinks he is rendering "to the truth its due…and to heroism the secondary place that rightly falls to it, just after, never before, the noble claim of happiness" (*P* 130). Our narrator's last claim here either makes nonsense of what Grand does—for he does, it seems, give up his happy activity of study, not only for Cottard, but also to help Tarrou and the doctor's volunteer forces later in the novel—thereby putting a modern happiness *second* to that which makes him the hero of the work: goodness of heart. Or, on the other hand, if we accept the narrator's nobility rating of first happiness and then heroism, we must regard Grand's choice of those helpful actions he does take up as less noble than staying happily at home. Thus, the putative hero would be a hero by virtue of a failure of moral judgment. Opposing the narrator's inconcinnity with a different one, John Krapp proposes rather that Grand's intellectual work is a distraction from the proper moral dedication: "His uncompromising devotion to his sentence, even while assisting the sanitation squads, continues to distract him…[and] prompts the question of whether Grand can adequately articulate a sustained, responsible moral engagement."[14] Nothing in the novel suggests Grand suffers such moral distraction, though Grand admits that his night work for the doctors has taken its toll on his day job at the city offices, which he, in good conscience, ought not allow it to do. He lives as sustained and responsible a moral engagement as his aged and chronically constricted natural powers allow.

The only other possibility for Rieux's description is that by "the noble claim of happiness" Rieux means precisely what Aristotle means by happiness: the life of virtue—but this is not in agreement with Rieux's other uses of the term, as we shall see. Further, if this last were the case, there could be no question about Grand's quiet moral heroism being second to the noble claim of happiness; rather, happiness is a noble claim in Grand's case

yond Sherman)," in *Philosophy Today*, (Summer 2017) 61, 3: 679–708, at p. 682–83.

14 John Krapp, "Time and Ethics in Albert Camus's *The Plague*," in *University of Toronto Quarterly: A Canadian Journal of the Humanities*, (Spring, 1999) 68, 2: 655–76 at p. 668; henceforth abbreviated *TEAC*.

precisely because it is found in his virtuous activities—both intellectual and political/social. We would see that the particular shape of Grand's happiness changes due to changes of circumstance and the concomitant changes in what is required by virtue—as his neighbor attempts suicide, or as the town enters the plague, but in all cases his heroism and his happiness would be one. Thus, the doctor's distinction between heroism—second—and happiness—first—collapses in his case, as Aristotle would have said: his happiness is of a piece with his "goodness of heart." "Happiness is an activity in accordance with virtue, and if there are several, with the best and most complete…in a complete life" (*NE* 1098a16–19). The narrator's inability to be clear on this matter is another indication of his peculiar unreliabilities, on which more is forthcoming.

The narrator's description here of Grand is not empty nonsense, but perfectly backward, if Grand is, as I have been arguing, the picture of the good will. He does not act as he does out of "goodness of heart" if we understand by that the usual love based on feeling or inclination (as we might suspect the doctor of thinking),[15] but it is true only if we mean "practical love"—a love "residing in the will" and the only love that "can be commanded" (*FMM* 399). Grand's work on his book—painting an ideal of perfection—also echoes the task of the development of the personality. His efforts are hardly absurd, but in fact illustrate Kant's later insight that we must be constantly renewing our affirmation to make the vagaries of the specific acts of our *Wilkür* (or free choice) subject to the pure *a priori* law of *Wille*, just as Grand is constantly re-beginning his book. Kant, for example, says this: "we must begin with the incessant counteraction against [the propensity to evil in *Willkür*]" (*Rel* 46, cf. 60). Because we must constantly renew our dedication to the moral law as first principle of our choice, we must understand "[the good disposition as a complete whole] stands in the place of this series of approximations carried on without end"

---

15 In the course of describing his "obscure hero" the doctor notes that in choosing Grand, he gives "this chronicle its character, which is intended to be that of a narrative made with good feelings—that is to say, feelings that are neither demonstrably bad nor overcharged with emotion in the ugly manner of a stage-play" (*P* 130). This is less than half of Aristotle's idea of virtuous feeling, while for Kant, goodness of heart is not a feeling at all, but the activity of pure practical reason.

(*Rel.*, 61n). We may hope that the divine judge and editor is merciful in his calculus as we approach infinity. And again, "virtue is always in progress and yet always begins at the beginning" (*MPV*, 409). Finally, the narrator's placement of happiness above "heroism," when by the latter term he seems to picture Kantian duty for the sake of duty[16] not only reverses Kant's ordering of what he calls our two unconditioned goods—happiness and good will, but also misses Grand's own self-understanding and action: he leaves his happy work because "one has to help one's neighbor." If this practical love is what Rieux's goodness of heart means, it is identical with Kant's moral apathy: a quite singular feeling, not on the same level as any other, and certainly not second place.

His absurd consideration of Grand's heroism is symptomatic—Rieux is "the absurd hero"; seeing the world this way he cannot but fail "to follow all the worthy man was saying" (*P* 94). But Grand does not experience his own life as absurd: he knows his purposes, he has chosen them, he sticks with them, and—as we have seen—they are morally correct, and correctly ordered, according to both Kant and Aristotle. If he is an example of bad faith, let the world be filled with it. Contrary to Grand, the narrator, later revealed to be Rieux, is obviously one we should call "unreliable"—in several senses. Perhaps, then, it is something less than accidental that he seems to be the image of another modern ethical theory, or perhaps several. He seems to consider reason's only function to be producing adequate hypothetical imperatives for purposes all of the ends of which are given by inclination. In this he would be a perfect scientist, for science is that system of hypothetical imperatives by which human beings can organize the laws of nature to achieve whatever ends they set—whether poisoning or health. In the meeting

16 For example, according to Rieux, the way to deal with the plague, or evil, "was to do your job as it should be done" (*P* 39); this would abrogate happiness for the time of plague. For Kant, everyone's job is to follow the moral law; that truly would be the end of the plague=moral evil, as the doctor is saying. We should add that the doctor is incorrect in thinking that this necessarily abrogates happiness for the time of plague; whether or not such action would achieve real happiness is an open question since we have no idea about which of our own imaginations are mutually realizable, to say nothing of considering the imaginary ideals of others—which is what we prefer to do: pay no attention to their ideals.

of the city health committee Rieux seems to want to meet all inclinations (which would indeed make everyone happy). Unfortunately, the parties include those who know it is the plague, say so, and want to take adequate measures to control it (Castel), and those who don't want to admit it is plague because the news would be upsetting to the populace—as would the measures required to control it (Richard), as well as the usual administrative type who just wants the issue—whatever it is—to quiet down to the usual paper-shuffling (the prefect). The compromise produced by the meeting results in "small official notices…put up…in places where they would not attract much attention" (P 48). It is as successful as one would expect.

Since each individual has different inclinations, Rieux attempts, as far as possible, not to interfere with anyone's processes of achievement, though he may say it is beyond his ability to aid them, as, later, he neither aids nor interferes with Cottard and Rambert conspiring to escape the quarantine. That he might have a duty to stop such breaches of universal lawfulness does not appear in his discussions with them; his duties are, rather, merely the particulars determined under the hypotheses of his station and tasks. He is, in this way "just following orders"—orders which devolve upon him and so are heteronomous even if the end aimed at and achieved is that which the moral law approves. The satisfaction of such inclinations as Rambert's he regards as happiness (P 83), which he hopes each one can achieve, and aims—so far as possible while doing "his job"—never to get in the way of. He is singularly unsuccessful in his efforts to allow or enable this greatest happiness possible for all, exhibiting that such is not a plausible principle for organizing one's actions, one of which turns out to make the child suffer longer (P 194).

Once the quarantine is declared, he fulfills the duties of his position, which include abstracting the sick from their families and quarantining those members who had been in immediate contact with the sick, despite the pain those acts inflict. In most of his thinking he appears to be reliably utilitarian, wishing to allow or produce as much happiness as possible for the whole community.[17] Such duties as he admits are those understood as

---

17 Besides his phrasings in the meeting of the health committee, there is his repeated question to Tarrou in their meeting concerning the new sanitary squads: "Have you weighed the consequences?" (P 115).

being set by his task, as the necessities of a hypothetical imperative which he has been given or undertaken: being a doctor during plague. Thus, he operates entirely on what Kant calls "either rules of skill or counsels of prudence" (*FMM* 416) rather than the unconditional commands of morality. These "duties" he fulfills rigorously, in a blind endurance that, far from being "practical love," he says ousts love (*P* 168), though he does not know why he chooses this way (*P* 189). In Kantian terms he seems, if not entirely heteronomously motivated, incognizant of the source of duty's attraction, and incapable of considering that there is another possibility for the will (besides happiness or some lesser inclination), which autonomously assigns itself its duties: thus his incapacity to see Grand as he is or to explain Grand's actions and feelings correctly.

This confusion is aptly limned when our narrator describes those who signed up for Tarrou's "sanitary squads"; he describes Tarrou's creation as making fighting the plague "some men's duty" (*P* 121). Kant explains that duty really entails in morals the same sort of lawfulness as is found in nature (*FMM* 421). It is not only my teapot, or some teapots, whose water boils at 100° C, at standard sea-level pressure, but everyone's. So, too, the duty to help one's neighbor in time of plague by aiding in the work of taking the new patients to hospital, sterilizing their clothing and bedding, driving corpses to the cemetery, or helping the doctors keep their records (as Grand does), does not just belong to Grand and some others, but is the imperfect duty of everyone in that same situation: everyone in town, or rather, everyone who is a citizen of the community, for a community can only really be understood as a moral enterprise, not as a geographical fact. It is not at all the case that "it was the only thing to do, and the unthinkable thing would then have been not to have brought themselves to do it" (*P* 121). It is not at all unthinkable that many people on many occasions do not do any of these things, nor is it, even when recognizing it as a duty, unthinkable not to go to work and do it. Our free choice (*Wilkür*) frequently neglects what practical reason's (*Wille's*) laws demand; Cottard can't seem to think of any good reason for following it. Concerning the rules for our own action—our maxims—no such things are unthinkable, though there are two kinds of "unthinkability" if we test those maxims by considering whether or not they can be universalized. It is, first of all, impossible *to consistently will* "no one helps the others" to be the rule of nature for all. For all are finite creatures with needs, and being so, when one is oneself the patient, or a family member is, he and she shall *will* that the rule of nature be otherwise than they are willing when they hold themselves out of the action. This points to the fact that it is *literally unthinkable* that a community should be made up of beings who, as if by a law of nature, follow the rule never to help another member of the community, for the word community thereby becomes a nonsense word. There would, under such a "universal law," be no such thing as a community—which perhaps is the truth about a modern city like Oran. Whether or not there would be human beings there is a merely empirical question. Aristotle would say there are not any human beings there, for human beings are the social animal, and friendship is essential to our kind of being (*NE* 1155a5, *Pol* 1253a25–30). It looks like a human city, but belongs to a lower being—and is not a city.

On the other hand, that second kind of unthinkability applies immediately in the case of the duty to keep the quarantine (which Rambert is attempting to escape, and Rieux is hoping succeeds). Such is unquestionably everyone's perfect duty, for a maxim like "when in time of quarantine in a foreign city, I do everything in my power to escape, in order to return to my happiness" cannot even be *thought* a law of nature, since "quarantine" becomes an empty word in the proposed universal law: "Whenever anyone is in quarantine in a foreign city, they escape, in order to return to happiness." "Quarantine" no longer means anything here, for it means contradictories. Under either kind of unthinkability, it is not true that duties belong only to "some men" as the doctor is thinking; and he does not give any indication of understanding the kind of contradiction of rational principles that Rambert's immoral maxim entails, or that there could be such a thing as perfect duties derived from non-hypothetical imperatives. As I suggested above, I suppose a utilitarian could hold such a fluctuating view of duties; and Kant would expect that, given the doctor's *modus operandi*—basing "everything on experience," he might "seriously doubt…that reason of itself and independently of all appearances command[s] what ought to be done" (*FMM* 408). Our narrator's unreliability is, then, not merely narratological. Rieux is neither Aristotelian nor Kantian in his moral principles; his rather less reliable method of solving moral problems is, however, popular in modern cities.

Grand seems also to capture some significant elements of Aristotle's ethics. By his own admission his happiness consists principally in a form of *theoria* (*NE* 1178b29–32); for this reason, he has less need of external goods, and worries less about them (*NE* 1179a1–9). Grand's intellectual efforts are engaged in for their own sake, and though he has not much in the line of intellectual gifts, he makes the best use of his constricted natural and social conditions precisely by always performing virtuous actions and contemplating excellence (*NE* 1101a5–10, 1100b18–20). His immediate and reliably regular responses regarding all such actions indicate that these activities are unhindered—and these unimpeded activities of the best natural state of a human being are pleasant to him (*NE* 1153a10–15); though of course, as Aristotle says while discussing courageous acts, such pleasure in the activity "is not found in all virtues, except as it attains to the end" (*NE* 1117b16). He does not come as close to the end of his project as he would like, however, his continual practices of meditation on the beautiful—*kalon*—life and personality in the construction of his novel, his continual efforts to perfect that vision, and perfectly to express it, are themselves activities of virtue.

In addition, these continuously virtuous actions have shaped his feelings in such a way that he grasps the fullness of a moral situation more quickly and more adequately than his intellectual superiors who are less virtuous. He is not a mere everyday schmuck or someone whose small intellectual efforts are "a distraction," which raises "the question of whether Grand can adequately articulate a sustained, responsible moral engagement with the contingencies generated by the disease."[18] While he seems to lack friends with whom to share much of his virtuous intellectual activities (though Tarrou and Rieux do listen to his attempts at perfect expression), these activities are not a distraction. He does sustain responsible moral engagement with his neighbors and fellow citizens, and he does so without letting go of the highest and happiest activity available to human nature—contemplation of the good and beautiful. "Hats off, gentlemen!" (*P* 96). Grand, both before and during the plague, does everything in his power to achieve the good in as sustained, responsible, and articulate a manner as nature and his circumstance allow him. Yes, he is the hero; one who can be living—incognito—in every modern city. No one pays him any attention in his city; nor, from the usual (barbaric? slavish?) crowd, does he desire it, though there is a group he hopes to be honored by—the virtuous among

18   Krapp, *TEAC*, p. 668, cf. 672.

the civilized. This is Aristotle's virtue of seeking proper honor: the right amount, from the right sources, in the right way (*NE* 4.4); the applause of the many is inconsequential.

Camus illustrates Grand's virtuous use of his capacities with brilliant counterpoint. One day, when our clerk brings Dr. Rieux the death figures from his city office, the following exchange takes place:

> "Well," [Rieux] said, "perhaps we'd better make up our minds to call this disease by its name... ."
>
> "Quite so, quite so," Grand said as he went down the stairs at the doctor's heels. "I, too, believe in calling things by their name. But what's the name in this case?"
>
> "That I shan't say, and anyhow you wouldn't gain anything by knowing."
>
> "You see," Grand smiled. "It's not so easy after all!" (*P* 40)[19]

One cannot imagine Grand, if he were the doctor, answering Rieux as he has been answered here. After describing Grand's difficulty finding his words, yet his continual dogged efforts to become more exact—where exacting clearly means making the hearer feel as well as understand the truth he is expressing (*P* 99, 127—29)—the doctor considers that "pestilence on the great scale could [not] befall a town where people like Grand were to be found, obscure functionaries cultivating harmless eccentricities" (*P* 45). But Grand's activity is not a mere eccentricity—except perhaps in the scientific sociological sense, which tells us nothing about the truth of human nature. In the very next scene, at the aforesaid meeting of the city health committee, Rieux, who had sent away for plague serum a few days earlier, explicitly refuses to use the word, but uses some very exacting medical

---

19 Colin Davis discusses this scene in "Camus's 'La Peste': Sanitation, Rats, and Messy Ethics," in *The Modern Language Review*, Vol. 102, No. 4 (October 2007): 1008–1020. He says Rieux's earlier dicta about telling the truth "come adrift," frustrating the novel's drive for "simplicity and clarity" (pp. 1016–1017), but he does not analyze what this might show about the differences between the two characters. Grand works at truthful precision and emotional rightness; Rieux...comes adrift—the passive voice is perfect here: he *is moved* by other considerations.

language which carefully leaves the question of whether it is exactly plague unanswered; it is a masterpiece of obfuscation by detailed exactness (*P* 47–49). Rieux's sympathy and dread, perhaps—or some feeling that he must remove anything which at all allows or expresses emotion in order to achieve perfect lucidity—obfuscates both his desire to be clear (with Grand), and his ability to be so (at the meeting of the city health committee).

Mistakes about both of these characters' concern with language are common. For instance, David Sherman claims Grand is "looking for words that function transparently as a sort of 'photograph,'"[20] but Grand clearly wants something much more; he throws out one version of his first sentence because the sibilants are disturbing, and another because the rhythm puts a hitch in the horse's trot. His concern is about feeling at least as much as intellectual clarity. Intellectual clarity alone is insufficient for excellence—in writing and in life. That kind of photography is like chronicling; it is not what Grand is after, just as it is insufficient for the fulness of human life: the completeness and perfection of a work of art aims at a greater completeness and perfection of life. Both the right emotion as well as an exacting intelligence are the excellences human life requires in the activities which are our happiness.

John Krapp says that Rieux "postpones using the word [plague] until he is fairly certain it accurately denotes…. He wants to use language responsibly."[21] But this is false; he had already called the district warehouse for serum and named the disease to Castel in the previous days. Rieux is not the moral hero, and if he "speaks for Camus"—a daring presumption about a literary work, which most of the scholarly literature on the novel accepts—so much the worse for Camus. Rieux is, partly precisely because of his inconcinnities regarding feelings, not a thoroughly trustworthy narrator. Grand clearly aims at the perfection of both truth and feeling with his words; to ask whether he has "much more to do?" is "not the point, Doctor; yes I can assure you that's not the point" (*P* 94). The growth of a personality indeed: the point is the next act or sentence must have a like perfection. To a chronicler, however, he can be quite adequately described as "having all the attributes of insignificance" (*P* 41).

20 Sherman, *Camus*, 118.
21 John Krapp, *TEAC*, 663.

Tarrou is somewhere in between these two. He says that "all our troubles spring from our failure to use plain, clear-cut language" (*P* 230), which puts him in agreement with the first part of the doctor's idea of what is necessary for lucidity,[22] but it seems a Cartesian version of true understanding. The doctor knows what lucidity is, and its importance, but does not always stick to it; Tarrou seems to rigorously practice what he says. But both Rieux (who seems at times to aim against it) and Tarrou (who does not aim particularly to express it) are at least somewhat lacking on the other side of French thought, which is figured in Pascal: one must speak to the heart as well. Grand has fewer natural gifts than either of these men, who come to be his friends through their shared suffering, but he lives a better balance between reason and the heart.

To return to the main point of this chapter: our argument shows that, in this minor civil servant, small in natural gifts and external means, Camus presents not only a happy man moved by the categorical imperative, but also a version of Aristotle's most happy virtuous human life, a version which exhibits its permanent availability, even under the inauspicious conditions of the thoroughly modern city (though Oran is without the additional sleep-inducing technologies we have since discovered to be indispensable—for thoughtlessness). He is one who, in every free moment, when the physical and moral demands of being a citizen in a human city allow him, turns to that activity which is most final, self-sufficient, and divine: thus the best, most pleasant, and happiest life for man (*NE* 1177b20–26, 11178a3–8, 1178b7–23). And he makes for himself more free moments of this sort than most because he does not work, as do the other citizens of Oran, "solely with the object of getting rich" (*P* 4), but only so much as is required for his needs. "Even if human happiness is not possible without external goods, we must not think that it will require many and great possessions. For self-sufficiency does not depend on superabundance—neither does judgment or action—and it is possible to do good deeds without ruling land and sea" (*NE* 1179a1–4). Such is Joseph Grand. This is all in his name: his is the common grandness—both Aristotle and Kant could see it. He is nothing like Aristotle's student, Alexander the Great, who is perhaps being mocked here by his teacher: he is both more grand and more human.

22 These include "lucidly recognizing what needs to be recognized" and "dispelling extraneous shadows"; discussed in chapter one above, page 37.

3. A Return to the Philosophical Problems

If Joe Grand illustrates in himself both Kantian and Aristotelian versions of the morally good person and his acts, perhaps we can begin to re-orient our philosophical distinctions so as to bring ancient and modern back together. Despite the differences we have pointed out, there is a friendship and solidarity among these philosophers; it is not merely the solidarity of bodily action, like marching together. Let us begin with Kant's idea of "the worthy purpose of existence, for which…reason is quite properly designed" (*FMM*, 396). Reason is given to certain finite creatures in order that they might produce in themselves a good will, and such a will, indeed the capacity to act under the determination of the categorical imperative—reason's own law—raises the creature which has such a capacity sublimely above what we might call mere nature, which has no capacity even to conceive of the law upon which it operates.[23] "Consciousness of this determination produces reverence" (*FMM*, 401–2n), and because of this reason-produced reverence "a rational impartial observer can never feel approval in contemplating the uninterrupted prosperity of a being graced by no touch of…a good will" (*FMM*, 393).

This means that as a complete human being—a hylomorphic composite in Aristotle's terms, a finite rational will in Kant's—no one can be fully content with himself except insofar as he knows himself to be acting in accord with the categorical imperative from a settled principle which makes that imperative superior to any hypothetical imperative reason may consider for the accomplishment of any of the person's empirical ends, or even that summation of all our desires which goes by the name of happiness. However, since when we analyze our "scheming and striving…we everywhere come upon the dear self" (*FMM* 407), we cannot ever be certain that we are acting from that moral motive, though we can and do know when we are acting contrary to its direction. This point, together with Kant's peculiarly modern definition of happiness—the satisfaction of all one's inclinations—entails

23 Cf. *Rel.*, p. 44: "Yet there is one thing in our soul which we cannot cease from regarding with the highest wonder, when we view it properly, and for which admiration is not only legitimate but even exalting, and that is the original moral predisposition itself in us."

we need another term for the more complete satisfaction of the *whole* modern person, a happy satisfaction which is *at the same time* not judged by one's own correctly operating reason to be unworthy, which would thereby cause rational discontent at one's own material and emotional fulfillment. Perhaps the best word for this combination of human ends, since it almost has good will embedded in it, is *eu-daimon-ia*.[24] Kant puts the matter this way: "No man who is not indifferent to morality can take pleasure in himself, can indeed escape a bitter dissatisfaction with himself, when he is conscious of maxims which do not agree with the moral law in him. One might call that *rational self-love* which prevents the adulteration of the incentives of the will (=free choice, *Willkür*) by other causes of happiness" (*Rel.,* 41n). Note that Kant's phrase, "*other* causes of happiness," besides rational self-love implies what I am saying about the more complete (Kantian) *eudaimonia* including both rational (*a priori*) and material elements.[25]

This complete good of Kantian *eudaimonia* depends upon and embodies a good will, for only so can we have that element of complete *eudaimonia* Kant calls rational self-love. In fact, this phrase—"rational self-love"—seems to both limit self-love to activities within the purview of the moral law and its concomitant self-respect, as well as fill pure practical reason's skeletal working (pure practical reason's principle of universalization) with material muscle and body (the appropriate, skeletally limited, self-love and fulfillment of desire). It summarizes, in a way, both form and content of Kantian *eudaimonia*; in it we see how practical reason gives the will its end (the highest good, which combines happiness and the good will), and fills in that true object as the "idea of the whole of all ends"—reason's vision of a *world* in which all those worthy to be happy are as happy as they deserve to be.[26] Thus, this rational self-love would not let us break quarantine in

---

24 This is, of course, the Greek word which is often translated as "happiness" in Aristotle; having, literally, a good (*eu*) spirit (*daimon*).

25 For the sake of exactness, Kant's words are "alle Vermischung anderer Ursachen der Zufriedenheit aus den Folgen seiner Handlungen (unter dem Namen einer dadurch sich zu verschaffenden Glückseligkeit) mit den Triebfedern der Willkür verhindert" (*Rel.* 694–95n).

26 Immanuel Kant, "On the Common Saying: That May Be Correct in Theory, But It Is of No Use in Practice," in *Practical Philosophy*, ed. Mary J. Gregor (New York: Cambridge University Press, 1996): 273–309 at 280n.

Oran, though our happiness seems to lie outside the city; rational self-love would have us fulfill our duty to aid those in need in the way that makes best use of whatever skills we have. Rational self-love would not sit idly by, nor expend all our efforts merely to become as rich as possible. And we would do all these because they are our duty, or, as Aristotle might say, "for their own sake" (*NE* 1105a32). And if we, as Joe Grand, shape our desires and recalibrate our needs in accord with such a will's understanding of both the changing circumstances of our material conditions, and the changing needs of those rational beings around us—our neighbors and fellow citizens—we will find that we have perhaps as much of that feeling of happiness at the satisfaction of our material ends as it is possible for someone with our particular limitations of nature and history to have, with our particular neighbors and fellow citizens.

Joe Grand is the instantiation of both that limited perfection, and, perhaps, the greatest capacity for human solidarity: by acting always in accord with maxims that can be universalized he agrees with every moral maxim any neighboring citizen acts upon. And if it happens that we do not achieve these ends at which we aim with our fellow citizens and neighbors—if things go badly for us, as they did, at the end, for Priam, and as they do for many during the time of plague—we still will hold on to the one element of an Aristotelian happiness, and one element of Kant's complete good, which even under bad fates *is* within our control, and *through which* we may again become more completely happy (cf. *NE* 1101a 7–14): virtue and good will. And even in that failure, is there not a kind of happiness in consciously acting in accord with what is best in us? Perhaps even Sisyphus would prefer that limited happiness to the one Camus said he grasped. Finally, for the sake of completeness, let us remember that St. Augustine joins in this agreement. For, while it may not be possible to attain the best life in this world, it *is* possible to continue in those goods without which no good life may be lived—namely the virtues (*DLA* 2.19.50). In those cases, that is the best life possible for us in our particular historical juncture, and it is good in and of itself, though it is not the highest that can be imagined.

Further, this now Kantianly determined *eudaimonia* is something that every finite rational will *must* be aiming at under the rubric of "the single and complete good" (*FMM* 396). For, being finite, we *must* will the fulfillment of many desires, indeed the *incapacity* of the finite will *not to do so* appears in Kant's argument for both of the imperfect duties he discusses—to develop our talents and to come to the aid of others when able (*FMM* 423). As finite wills we require such things as help and developed talents and so cannot consistently will against them. Rather, because of our neediness, our will would contradict itself in attempting to universalize a maxim against either sort of act. The happiness of others and the perfection of our own capacities to set and achieve many purposes (let us call these excellences *technê, epistemê, dianoia, sophia*—four of the intellectual virtues named by Aristotle) are therefore required aims of the good will. The heart of Kantian practical wisdom (Aristotle's fifth intellectual virtue) *is* that good will, which forms and judges categorical imperatives. We might then best think of happiness as the matter and the categorical imperative as the form which describes this complete human good of Kantian eudaimonia; this is the true single and complete, most final and self-sufficient good of all finite rational creatures. It includes both the intellectual and the moral virtues Aristotle laid out.[27] Joseph Grand exemplifies this; he is resurrected out of the plague.

In the *Critique of Practical Reason*, Kant says that virtue is not "the entire and perfect good as the object of the faculty of desire of rational finite beings. For this, happiness is also required…even in the judgment of an impartial reason, which impartially regards persons in the world as ends in themselves."[28] Every virtuous person, then, wills this complete good (happiness with virtue) for every other person. Recognition of others as ends in themselves entails our aid in their achievement of their morally licit happiness. This Grand sees, and acts upon. Things we imagine to be parts of our happiness that cannot be brought into complete order within this form cannot really be elements of our particular human *eudaimonia*, however pleased

27 Stephen Engstrom has called this connection of elements in the complete good "Kant's hylomorphic account of willing" in his article, "Virtue and Vice in Aristotle and Kant," in Pavlos Kontos, ed., *Evil in Aristotle* (Cambridge: Cambridge University Press, 2018), pp. 222-39. The phrase I quote occurs on p. 228. An earlier essay, "Happiness and the Highest Good," in *Aristotle, Kant and the Stoics*, ed. Engstrom and Whiting (Cambridge: University Press, 1996) had put it similarly: "Gluckseligkeit can be rationally conceived only *through* the idea of virtue" (p. 106).

28 Immanuel Kant, *Critique of Practical Reason*, trans. Lewis White Beck (Indianapolis: Bobbs – Merrill, 1956), p. 111.

their imagined achievement may make us. Clearly, according to Kant, imagination may (and does!) supply us with wildly divergent possibilities from those ends we have actually achieved or can achieve, particularly in a world of plague—but that is not a criticism of either his or Aristotle's moral position (who advises that the suggestions of pleasure are those we must generally aim against in becoming virtuous—*NE* 1109b7–13). And if we are made unhappy by comparing such imaginations with our actual situation, or the situation of some others, or with the situation we may make actual for ourselves in accord with the categorical imperative, who is it then who causes our unhappiness? And how, precisely, have we done so? Our larger imagination is an engine of delusions—among them, that we can be God and get everything we want. Joseph Grand, small as his life may be due to the constrictions of nature and circumstance, is, then, far from being eccentric, or one for whom we should feel sorry; his story is rather the story of a man who has hit the mark of human life under very inauspicious conditions; this is equally true whether we measure with Kant or with Aristotle. His moral heart is perfect, only his aorta is constricted. He is virtuous, and he is as happy as he can be in such circumstances as have devolved upon him, and these two facts are intimately connected. To imagine otherwise is to destroy his actuality as an embodied person; it is imagining him otherwise—not considering who he really is. To consider that his choices are somehow torn between his happiness and virtue is not to understand the way he is living, or the happiness he confesses (so eccentrically, for a modern Oranais) in his poverty. It is true that he knows himself not always to have been thinking and choosing in accord with these remarks. Like most Oranians, there was a time when he was not paying attention, and so not finding the right words to show his wife his love for her. She left him, and the deep sadness he carries within himself from these failures is undoubtedly part of his motivation in his work at "the growth of a personality" (*P* 40)—he aims never to fail in that way again, and works to make himself such a person, even though it is unlikely he will ever be given the opportunity. He might, for all that, be figuring the hope for an Editor who "makes good [his] inability to fulfill this requirement" and imputes perfection to the constancy of his re-beginning.[29] Hats off, Gentlemen!

---

29 *Rel.* 89 (quote); cf. 60f regarding the imputation of the Editor.

Let us remember here that the impersonality of nature, indeed its often seeming anti-personality, as symbolized by the plague—not a particularly modern phenomenon—and as practiced by the Nazis, who are understood as the first referent of Camus' allegory, does not make the world absurd for either Aristotle or Kant. It does not do so for Joe Grand either; his own life is worthwhile for the good he aims at, achieves, and contemplates. Suicide is not his essential question; it is not a question for him at all. He is shocked by Cottard's attempt. Nature is not created for the safety and well-being of the practically rational creature, as Kant says (*FMM* 395–96), or perhaps for any, as even Romantic poets, like Blake and Rilke see: The tiger's symmetry is fearful, the world wondrous, with a beauty which calmly disdains to destroy us—until it does. The irrational creature can see none of these things. The human life, like Grand's, is about those intellectual and moral excellences that I have pointed out—and for their own sake. Let us see what a being capable of practical love can do in such a world: he is not the tiger or the lamb. The doctor confesses that "there are times when the only feeling I have is one of mad revolt" (*P* 202), but the one who is named hero of the novel never falls to such a response—though he lives in the same world, with fewer natural gifts and social possibilities. If the doctor speaks for Camus, as many commentators imply or presume, then his narrator's choice of hero is a confession of the failure of his own absurdist philosophy, the madness of rebellion, and the continuing import and value of an ancient and rational philosophical tradition—perhaps even a Romantic one.[30] But absurdity and rebellion are not the whole story for Camus, nor do they provide the unity for his work as an author, or even the unity for this book, as we are seeing.

Considering further, we see that Camus is a vociferous critic of modern culture, including even (and as it must) aspects of himself. This, too, is implied in his opening descriptions of Oran as a "completely modern" city—one "without intimations" (*P* 4). The people, we have seen, form habits—seldom virtuous—which would seem to mean they are morally corrupt, except those

---

30   That Camus is an absurdist, that suicide is the one serious philosophical problem, that permanent rebellion is the answer required by the human condition are the standard tropes by which he is summarized. Many recent critics add that he romanticizes nature. See, for instance, the entry in the *Stanford Encyclopedia of Philosophy*.

few who hit the mean. On the other hand, it seems these habits are formed, perhaps even among those who hit the mean, without much moral knowledge (for example about love), and they are driven by their usual modern socio-economic dispositions without moral reasoning ever waking up. As the narrator has said, one can get through life that way. But to live in such a way, failing to activate what Kant called the principle of personality, is to fail at becoming a human person; one remains buried in his or her inclinational nature—a slave to it. So, one might consider, as does Kant, that the disposition is indeed a physical determination—grown so strong as to make reason's alternative determination unhearable—and it is aided in the modern (even pre-smart phone) city by the constant hurry of business and subsequent lack of time. The town as a social enterprise is built, as it is physically—to deny entrance to beauty and wonder.[31] Something else is always in the way.

If one's disposition is indeed physically determinative and needs nothing further, and if everything in modern culture stands in the way of reason obtaining hearing in the soul, we might consider all such citizens as acting in ignorance, not voluntarily, and so not blameworthy (*NE* 1110a1, 1110b18). Perhaps this is this kind of sociality Aristotle has in mind, rather than some more extreme barbarism, when he says that upbringing in a bad culture can ruin a person for virtue: "it makes a great difference—indeed all the difference—whether one becomes accustomed to good or evil actions from youth" (*NE* 1103b22–25). It is the practice of virtuous actions that is the aim of every legislator, and every good constitution (*NE* 1103b2–6). The upbringing of the modern city is symptomatic of a failed constitution because it produces such invincible ignorance—if that is what it is. This is all Aristotle needs to be attributing to slavish or barbarian cultures, when he claims that they do not know the end.[32] Their lack of *nous* is symptomatic of their upbringing—everything in it worked against the activation of this natural human power; it is now more dead than the eye of a statue. Camus' novel is not just an allegory for Nazism then; Nazism is merely an

---

31 "Oran is grafted on to a unique landscape...ringed with luminous hills and above a perfectly shaped bay. All we may regret is the town's being so disposed that it turns its back on the bay, with the result that it's impossible to see the sea, you always have to go look for it" (*P* 6).

32 Cf. Aristotle, *Politics* 1252a32-34, 1255a 20–22.

extreme symptomatic expression of modern culture. It places a determinate, but faulty end in the place where modern more democratic and liberal society has "I know not what" or "what you will." Expect the rats to loose themselves again "for the bane and the enlightening of men" (*P* 287). If it is indeed a bane, we must investigate the grounds which allow such a judgment; this entails thought about what the good of human life is that such things should truly be called a bane. And then, if it enlightens about the true end, then it is not merely a bane.

This story about the most complete and final good of human life unites Aristotle and Kant in a well-defined eudaimonia, or rational and successful (within the limits of one's own real life) self-love; one that is universally lawful. Now, within this happy unity, let us re-examine the issue of the moral status of the passions and acting from a rational-passional disposition formed through such choices as Kant has been presenting. Here we may be helped by a brief look at another character, Raymond Rambert. Rambert is a journalist from "one of the leading Paris dailies" (*P* 11). When he finds himself trapped in Oran by the quarantine, he seeks out the doctor to try to get a certificate of health allowing him an exit, since he doesn't "belong here" (*P* 80, 82). He is, at this point in the novel, a clear exemplification of one who imagines his happiness (in the modern sense) is opposed to the demand of the moral law, since his happiness, symbolized by "his wife.... Well, she wasn't exactly his wife but it came to the same thing" (*P* 79) is in Paris.

That Rambert's woman works as a symbol of Kantian happiness for Camus cannot be doubted. She is never given a definite description (just as we cannot do so for happiness), or even the definite article, by Rambert: "The truth is I wasn't brought into the world to write newspaper articles. But it's quite likely I was brought into the world to live with a woman. That's reasonable enough, isn't it?" (*P* 78). Aristotle would agree with the first part of this—work is not the meaning of life, certainly not the work-a-day *technê* of newspapering. The two distinguishing marks of eudaimonia according to Aristotle are that it is final and self-sufficient. Rambert seems here to be recognizing that newspaper writing is neither, but loving a woman might well be both. The plague is a bane to him, yet as a result of this bane he is reconsidering his work and life and already making better judgements. At least he has been awakened into questioning—the beginning of any enlightenment. He has not grasped the real moral principles, though they may be vaguely working in him. He continues, "the truth…is that she and I have been together only a short time, and we suit each other perfectly." What suits us perfectly is what answers every desire—that is one understanding of love and love's object: it neither binds nor chafes nor hangs too loosely (as Grand's clothes do); perhaps it even makes us look good in the greater social world. Love it! After their discussion, which includes the epigram concerning the Republic heading this chapter, the doctor muses "Yes, the journalist was right in refusing to be balked of happiness" (*P* 80–83). As the story continues, the narrator includes parts of "the long, heartrendingly monotonous struggle put up by some obstinate people like Rambert to recover their lost happiness" (*P* 131). Rambert is the quintessential modern man, who in another novel is described as "reading the newspapers and fornicating" (*The Fall*, 6–7); he is after happiness, an idea so vague he cannot name or describe her. The doctor wants him to succeed—whatever that means. The doctor judges the plague as a bane because it stands in the way of so many people's happiness—whatever that is. It is a thing clearly contrary to the greatest happiness principle, and so must be fought against. Rambert, on the other hand, sees that his own choices have put him in this unhappy situation—he has not been choosing correctly, and now investigates what might count as correct. Maybe loving a woman. But what does that mean? "We suit each other perfectly"? Such an idea Aristotle would recognize as *philia* based in pleasure, it is not at all the same thing as a relationship built on a promise, which the virtuous would require themselves to keep. Depending on the vagaries of suiting, another woman might come along to more perfectly do so—but that love wouldn't be about her either, rather about the shifting figure of his happiness, which needs a new suiting. Happiness being that shifting imaginary thing Kant said, I suppose we should have to try them all on—as each might try us.

At any rate, after being refused by the doctor, not on moral grounds, but on grounds Kant would call "technically rational,"[33] Rambert begins a

---

33 The doctor says, "I can't give you that certificate because I don't know whether you have the disease or not, and even if I did, how could I certify that between the moment of leaving my consulting room and your arrival at the prefect's office you wouldn't be infected? And even if I did—" (*P* 81). None of these reasons appeals to moral principles, but rather to a lack of practical knowledge

long, and oft re-started process, through some smugglers and black marke-teers, of attempting to escape the city and get back to "his wife"—or what comes to the same thing. After one such week-long process ends in a break-down Rambert realizes that "all this time he had practically forgotten the woman he loved, so absorbed had he been in trying to find a rift in the walls" (*P* 147). While figuring and acting on the long-linked chain of hypothetical imperatives (each with its own particular end) which he had hoped would end in the achievement his greater (imagined assertoric) end—happiness, or the unnamed woman—he had forgotten that more distant and encom-passing end entirely. Every particular end is more definite, more immediate, and more capable of ordering action, as well as more clearly kept in mind than his imagined complete and perfectly "suiting" happiness.

What Rambert confesses about the kind and quality of his passionate and rational concentration on his beloved, and what he says of her love for him ("we suit each other perfectly"), shows his disposition regarding her—and other people—is as means (perhaps mutual means—as is required in business transactions) to the satisfaction of desire. The business-like ex-change is one kind of human love, as is that of equal mutual pleasure, which both Kant and Aristotle recognize; Kant calls it pathological love (*FMM* 399) as it is based in feeling (*pathê*). But because this is his disposition, a passional disposition affirmed by his reason, which is set to finding means to its achievement—and re-set to the same end several times, so a *practiced* disposition—it is difficult for him to see any wrongness in what he is about. This love, based on use or pleasure according to Aristotle, based in inclina-tion according to Kant, is insufficient for the human good; and insufficient as recognition of the human person: "For each loved the other not for what he was, but for what he had to offer" (*NE* 1164a10). Suits me.

Nonetheless, numerous members of Rambert's circle encourage this blindness—what he is considering as the good they help affirm is the good; the doctor wishes him good luck in his efforts, and neither he nor Tarrou do anything to stand in the way; Cottard does everything in his power to get him out of Oran. Thus, society still works as Augustine, long ago, explicated

(of both Rambert's present and immediate future), with possible implications of the impossibility of proving utility even if such knowledge were available. So much for disease passports.

concerning himself and his pear-stealing friends: the smoke and wind of others' words blowing in agreement with our definition of the good encourages us in choosing that good: "O friendship too unfriendly" (*Conf* 2.9.17).

In their discussion beneath the statue of the Republic, set in a square in the middle of town (*P* 82, and epigram above), neither Rambert nor the doctor seem to note or understand the "common ground" (*P* 83) upon which, as rational beings or even as citizens of France, they already stand. The Republic is merely a statue under which they stand, and at which the doctor glances—it is not pointed out by the doctor, nor does his discussion with Rambert suggest that this statue has some connection either to an abstract ideal or even to the effects in the world of apparent facts, as is true in the cave. It is not possible that Camus, who earned what we would call both a BA and an MA in philosophy is unaware of the philosophical sources of the distinctions the doctor uses (and fails to use) to define himself under this statue. Following this glance up, Rieux says that he "did not know if he was using the language of reason, but he knew he was using the language of the facts as everybody could see them—which wasn't necessarily the same thing" (*P* 82). In the cave scene in the middle of *Republic*, we discover that statues cause the movements on the wall which every cave dweller takes as the real things—the facts; they do not know this relation between statue and "thing," having never turned to look; nor have they gone further in rational dialectic to discover what the statue is a statue of. If one of them would look up to see the statues, it is doubtful he would make the connection of it to his "facts." Neither does the doctor.

The Republic of France is a fact that may be taken as a shadowy outline on the wall of the world, but a republic is not such a fact, nor is it yet some more determinate statuary like a constitution, whose space and shape on the wall may seem to grow (as America's) or shrink (as France's). Rather a republic is a rational social activity; it only really exists *as* such rational interpersonal activity. One fact Rieux may be referring to is that the law has come to Oran from Paris: "*close the town*" (*P* 59). This fact is determinative, as everyone can see. This message comes to Oran because "they've got alarmed" (*P* 59). Members of a republic, however, are self-determining; let us add the modern Kantian requirement—by a law that can be universal. Slaves may merely live in a republic, they may wander around in one; free men make the republic be—or make themselves slaves, thinking they are living in a republic, when, in fact, they are only wandering around in something that is called so by those around them. Choosing the good one sees oneself and can rationally consider the weight of, as well as the means of achieving it in accord with universal law, would be using the language of reason. Thus, to do so with others with whom one has committed oneself to work in a republic is an entirely different way of being than merely standing beneath the statue of the Republic, or driving along its streets.

This ideal and ground Kant describes as the realm of ends, a realm in which each citizen is both legislator and subject to the legislation of every other rational being (*FMM*, 437–38): a universal republic then. It is only by acting in accord with maxims which can be universally legislated that Rambert (or anyone else) *can* be treating all other rational beings (including his "beloved") as ends, as mutual and equal legislators, rather than as mere means—for each, too, can freely affirm his legislation. Grand seems to expect this from everyone. He has been in his low-paid, "temporary" civic post for decades, but has "a particular aversion from talking about his 'rights'…[while] on the other hand, he refused to use expressions such as 'your kindness,' 'gratitude,' or even 'solicit'" (*P* 43);[34] the first seems to put him above his fellow legislators in the moral kingdom, the second puts him below them; neither is proper for members of the kingdom of ends. This would be practical love, a love which embodies respect rather than mutually suiting pleasures. The "language of the heart" (which Rambert accuses Rieux of not understanding, *P* 79) Rieux pointedly does not respond to; for Rambert this means his inclinations. Kant's ancient parallel here, Aristotelian concord, or *homonoia*—a *sameness of mind* in the realm of action and judgment of the good (*NE* 1167a22–67b8)—sounds literally to

---

34 It strikes me as plausible that Grand here is acting and thinking in accord with the opening of Simone Weil's *The Need for Roots*, translated by Arthur Wills (New York: Routledge, 2002), p. 3–4: "The notion of obligations comes before that of rights…. . Recognition of an obligation makes it effectual…. . A man, considered in isolation, only has duties…. . A man left alone in the universe would have no rights whatever, but he would have obligations." Grand, like Kant, considers every rational being recognizes these truths: first he has obligations. Camus, as editor of a series at Gallimard, was instrumental in the publication of Weil's work, and was thoroughly impressed by her. As counterpoint to Grand's recognition of duty, the character who speaks most about "rights" is Cottard (cf. *P* 52–53).

describe Kant's idea of such legislation as a Republic symbolizes. We see this puzzle finally become somewhat clearer to Rambert as he works alongside the other volunteer assistants, and, after setting up his escape, decides to stay: "I know that I belong here whether I want to or not. This business is everybody's business." His passions, however, are still not in line—as Grand's are—with the moral law which unites him to those fellow citizens. When asked about "her," he confesses that

> his views hadn't changed, but if he went away, he would
> feel ashamed of himself, and that would embarrass his relations
> with the woman he loved.
> Showing more animation Rieux told him that was sheer
> nonsense; there was nothing shameful in preferring happiness.
> "Certainly," Rambert replied. "But it may be shameful to
> be happy by oneself" (*P* 194).

Rambert's virtuous choice here is not entirely virtuous. Aristotle proposes just this sort of person as "bearing the closest resemblance" to virtue because he is "motivated by a sense of shame, and avoidance of reproach" (*NE* 1116a26–29). We might see him as the man of moral strength (*NE* 1150a33–1150b1). He does not yet have, as Aristotle says is required for virtue, "the right reason" for his action, namely that it be "chosen for its own sake...from a firm and unchangeable character" (*NE* 1105a30–35); he does not have quite the correct feeling regarding the choice before him, but he chooses correctly. Kant also recognizes this sort of disposition as imperfect. More specifically, Kant calls this case impurity, for "although the maxim is indeed good in respect of its object (the intended observance of the law)...it is not yet purely moral...it has not, as it should have, adopted the law *alone* as its *all-sufficient* incentive" (*Rel* 25, emphasis Kant's). Since the fullness of Kant's picture requires that we aim at the happiness of others in accord with the moral principle, we see that Rambert has also moved closer to perfection than he was earlier according to Kant's scheme: he is right to be ashamed of happiness by himself. His confession is a sign that practical reason is functioning in him, for pure practical reason, as we have seen, aims at the unity of happiness and good will in a whole world. When, as the plague is ending, Rieux tells Rambert, "It's up to you *now* to prove that you are right" (*P* 270) he clearly is voicing something Kant would think that we all must prove, in our own hope: that the life directed by the moral law can deliver the flower of happiness. But she is no longer merely a flower that suits him. He has recognized her as a being responsive to the moral law first; that is why he would have rightly felt ashamed before her if he broke the quarantine; she—a moral lawgiver herself—would know his immorality and necessarily disapprove. Now, however, there is something to prove—for both of them, together—about happiness.

Grand, on the other hand, gives every indication that can be given in the phenomenal world of operating on the moral law as his all-sufficient incentive; he is the more perfect member of the kingdom of ends, as Kant recognizes. He has so frequently chosen this that his feelings have been shaped into agreement with this incentive. Thus, the moral feeling of respect is his lead feeling—the lead passion, behind which all others line up; his choices flow from this disposition of the passions. And since the moral feeling can only be aroused by the work of pure reason, it is not possible that this more perfect disposition is merely the robotic machinery of nature, or, even less, be a zombie virtue. For one only has the feeling of respect under practical reason's *present action*. Grand also exhibits with his fellow citizens, from Cottard and Rambert to Rieux, that concord—*homonoia*—which Aristotle expects "in those matters in which it is possible for both partners or all to attain their goals" (*NE* 1167a28–30)—even when they are not fully ready to be such partners themselves, as none of those others are. Grand not only unites Kantian and Aristotelian principles of morality, he is the living-out of that way which alone can bring about any universal human solidarity. Both Kant and Aristotle agree that Grand's disposition is morally superior to that near approach to virtue illustrated, finally, by Rambert: Joseph Grand is "our worthy fellow citizen," he waits for us in that Republic to which all rational creatures by their nature should tend, and the achievement of which is our complete happiness as those individual, historically particular, embodied persons we are.[35]

---

35 Joe Grand waits for us there, having given us his horsewoman, "because the highest moral good cannot be achieved merely by the exertions of the single individual toward his own moral perfection, but requires rather a union of such individuals into a whole...a universal republic based on laws of virtue" (*Rel,* 89).

CHAPTER THREE
THE AUGUSTINIANISM OF *THE PLAGUE*

> A novel is never anything but a philosophy expressed in images. And in a good novel the philosophy has disappeared into the images. (LCE, 199)

> The rational creature…must struggle by conjecture about visible things toward an understanding of the invisible ones. (DLA, 3.10)

Camus' explication, in the first epigram, of how his art form works and so must be read, is on all fours with Augustine's view, in the second, of how God has worked, and can be seen to work, in the world. In both cases we must learn how to read the invisible through the visible, how to turn the flow of images into understanding of truth. While Camus is considered by most critics to be atheist, and his argument between Fr. Paneloux and Doctor Rieux after the death of the child one of the classics of the anti-theistic argument from evil,[1] this chapter will show that such a reading is inadequate.

---

1   Camus himself aids this interpretation, having said "*La Peste* is the most anti-Christian of my books" and "The physician is the enemy of God, he struggles against death," as quoted by Roger Quilliot, *The Sea and Prisons: A commentary on the life and thought of Albert Camus*, translated by Emmett Parker (Tuscaloosa: University of Alabama Press, 1970), p. 151. How struggling against death proves anti-Christian is questionable. Recently there has been some pushback against this view, e.g., Matthew Sharpe, "The Black Side of the Sun: Camus, Theology, and the Problem of Evil," *Political Theology*, 15.2 (March, 2014), pp. 151–174, and Tal Sessler, who, in *Levinas and Camus: Humanism for the Twenty-First Century* (London: Continuum, 2008) shows that "the later Camus articulates a very different position, one that makes room for an alliance between religious and secular modes of resistance" [to evil, I presume] (p. 58f).

It suffers from an incomplete evaluation of Paneloux's sermons and is blind
to the Augustinian substructure of the novel, which reveals that something
more divine is present and active.[2] In reading this way it should be clear that
Camus' own philosophy and beliefs are not my main interest; rather I am
reading *The Plague* as a work of art, about which Camus also may have ideas.
So, while agreeing with his conclusion, I am reading the work differently
than Matthew Sharpe, who argues "that it is deeply problematic to read
Camus as an atheistic, or simply anti-religious, thinker," for Sharpe is interested in showing "that *Camus' thought* brings together sceptical-agnostic and
openly pantheistic-pagan elements, to give a lyrical voice to what Camus
called a sense of the sacred without immortality, or a kind of Sainthood
without God."[3] While this has much truth in it, a work of art may be deeper
and more rich than its maker's conscious purposes, thought and knowledge.
Certainly, if it is to be a gift to the future, something new must ever find an
opening into it; perhaps something ancient is ever present as well. To exhibit
this deeper religious ground behind the skeptical-agnostic-pagan figures, we
will center our remarks on the sermons of Fr. Paneloux—like Camus, an
Augustine scholar—and a chapter in Part Two which suggests that the doctor's mother fulfills the Augustinian picture of love which the priest's sermons
set forth.

In order to see the argument between the priest and the doctor accurately, we should attune ourselves to several earlier descriptions and intimations concerning each character. We should begin by recalling that the
narrator (revealed to be Dr. Rieux) emphasizes that the town of Oran is
"without intimations" (*P* 4), and that the first section of Part One ends
with this narrator saying, "He also proposes…" (*P* 6), without finishing his
sentence. For a man who is unwilling to speak to a reporter who "couldn't

2   Perhaps I am taking more seriously than he meant Camus' remark in *Actuelles,*
     2, that "*La Peste* is a confession, and everything in it is calculated so that this
     confession might be as complete as its form is indirect," quoted by Quilliot,
     The Sea, p. 149. Ronald Srigley spends some effort comparing Clamence and
     Augustine in his *Albert Camus' Critique of Modernity* (Columbia: University
     of Missouri Press, 2011); see especially pp. 90–92, and pp. 98–99. In the latter
     of these he concludes that "Camus' critical assessment of modernity begins to
     sound remarkably Augustinian."
3   M. Sharpe, "The Black Side of the Sun," p. 162, emphasis mine.

state the facts without paltering with the truth" and has "no use for state-ments in which something is kept back" (*P* 11), this ellipsis is the first of several (ironizing? revealing? authorial?) intimations that the doctor is nei-ther entirely straightforward nor an entirely trustworthy narrator. Another intimation of his incapacity for the full truth is his remark to his wife, who is leaving for a sanatorium due to her TB, that "once you're back everything will be better. We'll make a fresh start... Now off you go! Everything will be all right" (*P* 10).[4] As Camus knew well, suffering from TB as he did, this result is highly unlikely in the novel's time frame; there was no effective medicine for consumption. Rieux also does not want to say the word plague in public, even among other doctors—except Castel—who won't let him palter. At the end of the book, Dr. Rieux admits that he set himself not to report more than he had seen, nor attribute to his companions in the plague thoughts which they did not necessarily think (*P* 272). *The narrator* has a tendency to a quite positivist "chronicle," to quote what the first sentence of the novel describes as forthcoming; *the author*, on the other hand, does more: he shows us many things that the putative narrator misses and cer-tainly gives no intimation of understanding.[5]

Fr. Paneloux, the doctor's opposite number, is "a learned and militant Jesuit...who was very highly thought of in our town, even in circles quite indifferent to religion" (*P* 16). We first meet him helping Michel—the concierge of Rieux's building and first victim of the plague—back to his bed. By this we know he is not merely the intellectual powerhouse one might expect of such a Jesuit, but one who helps the sick man he meets on

4   It is surprising how reasonable critics miss what is going on here and so accept Rambert's later accusation about Rieux (that he is like St. Just) rather than what the chronicle, in fact, gives them. In the sentence after describing how Rieux sends his wife away, "knowing he will probably never see her again," Merton says he holds to "an uncompromising refusal of what he considers dishonest" (203). Except with his wife? Brother Thomas! Not even there.

5   Conor Cruise O'Brien, while discussing the inconsistent pretense of Rieux as narrator, argues that "This is not a novel. It is an allegorical sermon," and notes that Camus himself called it "a tract." *Albert Camus: Of Europe and Africa* (New York: Viking, 1970), p. 49, cf. p.58. The untrustworthy narrator form flows, I argue in both chapter 2 and chapter 4, from Rieux's character. Perhaps this tract allegorically presents the limits of empirical chronicles.

the road.[6] When we first meet him, "the Father's eyes were smiling behind his big round glasses." Love of his neighbor is not a cold duty, but a happy carrying out of gospel ethics. Rieux asks him what he makes of the rats and he answers with the truth, which he is the first to see: "I suppose it's an epidemic they've been having" (*P* 16). Fr. Paneloux's name means bread and light; or perhaps, thinking in Greek, "to show mercy (or pity) on all."[7] Perhaps he is both—or none of them; perhaps the name is satiric.[8]

We first meet Dr. Bernard Rieux "on the morning of April 16" (*P* 7)—the feast day of the almost rhyming St. Bernadette Soubirous, whose shrine at Lourdes is the most noted in the world for its healing powers. The mother of God, it is taught by the Catholic Church, appeared there, over the period of half a year in 1858. I mention this because Dr. Bernard Rieux's mother makes an important appearance in Oran just as the plague begins; she remains—unperturbed, it seems—through the end of the novel. Rieux is clearly neither God nor God's son; we might wonder if he is any kind of healer, his mother, however, well, let us see. "It was a fact," the narrator writes, "that everything seemed easy when she was there" (*P* 13). We must discern, in the course of our reading, whether these names and connections

6 Merton says "Paneloux has knowledge, discipline, will power, determination, sacrifice, even a bizarre kind of grace. But he is without love" (213); "his heart is sealed off from other men" (212). "His affectivity has been channeled into will-to-power and rigid authoritarianism" (215). It is disappointing that Merton should miss the import of this first episode; he really ought to recognize the gospel.

7 Adele King suggests his name means "praise of all things" in *Camus* (New York: Capricorn Books, 1971), p. 70; she does not present an etymology.

8 Wayne Cristaudo, "The Johannine Christianity of Albert Camus," *Culture, Theory and Critique* 52.2–3 (2011): 145–161, at pp. 148–9, says Paneloux is the "sad example of a lost soul who is a priest wanting to tell others of the nature of God, but whose love for and understanding of God is blocked by the absolutist preoccupation with the future, which involves forgetting the here and now." However, in his second sermon, Paneloux, resolutely refuses to say he knows what is over the wall of the present plague in a possible future state. Cristaudo also neglects that we meet Paneloux helping an unknown neighbor who is ill. We might be tempted to ask who has proven to be the neighbor, here and now; or later, who worked tirelessly, "in the forefront of the fight" (*P* 198) against his city's plague?

are truthful, antipodal to the truth of the person, or in some other way ironic—perhaps they are merely accidental, or personal-historical-acciden-tal.[9] Of course, if Camus is half as careful as his character, Joseph Grand, in picking his words, it is unlikely that the names and dates he chooses are all mere happenstance, or have only personal significance. Among other questions, this beginning makes us wonder which, if either, of these two men can be a true healer.

Most critics remark upon the fact that Paneloux opens his first sermon with the line "Calamity has come upon you my brethren, and my brethren, you deserved it" (*P* 86f), but they fail to connect it with what follows: "yet this calamity was not willed by God" (*P* 87).[10] Regarding merely the first part, one might correctly say that Paneloux "interprets the pain and devas-tation that the epidemic has brought as God's punishment for the town's sins, the chief one being its people's neglect of God and their duty to the Church."[11] No one attempts to connect the calamity and God's not willing it to what Paneloux says in speaking of God's love as one which demands more than some "mere Sunday bendings of the knee." For God wants "to

---

9   That the names of main characters are perhaps linked to people Camus knew during his wartime "exile" near Le Chambon-sur-Lignon during WWII is sug-gested by Patrick Henry, "Albert Camus, Panelier, and *La Peste*," *Literary Imag-ination: The Review of the Association of Literary Scholars and Critics*, 5.3 (2003): 383–404 at p. 391.

10   M. Sharpe, *Camus, Philosophe*, 119 notably skips precisely this line. Sreedharan Thoyakkat, "The World Is What Was Given, The World Is What We Make: Albert Camus' Bifocal Credo in *The Plague*," *IUP Journal of English Studies*, Vol. 4 Issue 3/4 (September 2009), 7–27 at p. 16 calls this second phrase "a dialectical somersault." Robert Solomon, in *Dark Feelings, Grim Thoughts: Ex-perience and Reflection in Camus and Sartre* (Oxford: University Press, 2006), ends up concluding that Paneloux is "a joke"—he probably means one of a theological nature, p. 127. John Robert Maze, in *Albert Camus: Plague and Terror, Priest and Atheist* (Bern: Peter Lang, 2010), says that "what Camus means here is that although God did send the plague he did so sadly" (p. 58). These are confessions, not analyses. Perhaps that is one purpose of Camus' art: to instigate each reader's confession.

11   Andrea Lešić-Thomas, "The Answer Job Did Not Give: Dostoevsky's *Brat'ia Karamazovy* and Camus's *La Peste*," in *Modern Language Review* 101. 3 (July 2006): 774–88, at p. 777.

see you longer and more often; that is his manner of loving, and, indeed it is the only manner of loving" (*P* 89). Let us suppose that Paneloux means all of these things, and is possibly correct. How may this be understood?

We see something of this divine manner of loving in Madame Rieux, who comes into Oran as the plague begins, the day after Rieux's wife leaves for the sanatorium. Jean Tarrou's first description of her concludes that "a gaze revealing so much goodness of heart would always triumph over the plague" (*P* 107).[12] Let us remember whenever our discussion turns to her that according *to l'évangile de Jean* the light came into the world, into the darkness, and the darkness did not overcome it; perhaps this Jean—who wishes to be a saint, though without God—sees something his namesake testified to. Shortly after that there is a scene in which she is the only light in the darkening city and the house, except for a desk lamp between Tarrou and Rieux as they have a private discussion. Just before that discussion his mother tells him that though he is gone from her most of the day, "I don't mind waiting, if I know you're going to come back. And when you aren't here, I think of what you are doing" (*P* 113). I suppose that this might have been true even before she came to town. She is the "small still flame in the dark core of human suffering" (*P* 90), which is this world of plague; and she practices the constant conscious presence of her beloved son. Augustine teaches us that all that is said by, and symbolized in, Madame Rieux has been true of God: "Behold, you were within me, while I was outside: it was there that I sought you, and, a deformed creature, rushed headlong upon

12 Except for Merton, who says that Mme Rieux is the "silent incarnation of the 'comprehension' about which Tarrou talks" (209), Solomon (*Dark Feelings*, p. 119), is one of the few critics who even mentions Rieux's mother. E.g., Domnica Radulescu, "L'amour dans *La peste*," in *Dalhousie French Studies*, Vol. 33 (Winter 1995): pp. 83–95 fails to mention her at all, as does Danielle Marx-Scouras, "Portraits of women, visions of Algeria," *Cambridge Companion to Camus* (pp. 131–144). Solomon says, "she is a surprisingly poignant presence.... If one did not know anything about Camus' personal life, she might not make any sense in the novel at all." We shall see that she *is* a quite important presence, perhaps even the sense of the novel. Maze adds that the description of Dr. Rieux given by Tarrou looks like Camus' own (verbal) self-portraits (p. 61). These last (see also note 9), like many other historical connections which may be found in a work of art, hardly explain how the work of art itself works. Suppose we had only the work—what might it still mean?

those things of beauty which you have made. You were with me, but I was not with you" (*Conf* 10.27.38).

It is very strange that even readers who notice Madame Rieux's presence in the novel do not see how perfectly she lives the love Paneloux said is owed to God, and which also is God's love for us. Merton, for example, insists that the "God of Paneloux may be adorned by Christian terminology, but he is not the God of Christian revelation.... . He is anything but the living God of the prophets, of the New Testament, and of the saints. Indeed, the most awful thing about Paneloux is that he is fanatically loyal to a God who is stone dead" (Merton 213). Perhaps readings like this are shaped by the deep influence of seeing Camus' work through the lenses of absurdism and revolt rather than love, which he says has been present throughout his work, and which this book takes as its directive for interpretation of *The Plague*. So, if the world is created by a God who is love, and in such a way as to allow our constant conscious presence, through that world, to his constant conscious presence, and if it is true that, since God is the good, we ought to prefer nothing above him, as the first commandment says, then Madame Rieux just is that living love Paneloux describes, present in Oran; she is not stone dead, however much critics may ignore her. Tarrou recognizes her light not because her love is the exhibition of his ideal "comprehension," but because she holds his comprehension in her light, that is, in her love, as we will see in his death. Her light is the condition for the possibility of his comprehension, as perhaps he himself comprehends at the end.[13] Dr. Rieux, of course, is not with his mother most of most days—he is too busy with the world, which is to him only a *res* or a series *in rebus*, which he chronicles; and then, more often than not, we find him sitting in the dark.

Augustine's *Confessions* enacts the proper response of the beloved to such a divine lover, and by doing so rouses up the thought and heart of the reader to do likewise. What Augustine is attempting, "too late" (*Conf* 10.27.38), is to make his entire life into a prayer of praise and thanksgiving. What he performs in *Confessions*, he confesses in *City of God*: "for us it is good to adore Him by means of justice, chastity and other virtues, and thus *to make life itself a prayer to Him*" (*DCD* 19.23, my italics); "Witness the

13 We discuss this matter in detail in chapter four.

prayer of the whole city of God in its pilgrim state...'forgive us our debts as we forgive our debtors.' And this prayer is efficacious...for those whose faith 'worketh by love.' For as reason, though subjected to God, is yet 'pressed down by the corruptible body,' so long as it is in this mortal condition, it has not perfect authority over vice, and therefore this prayer is needed by the righteous" (*DCD* 19.27). He was not conscious, before his conversion, that this is what he wanted, yet it was, and is, what every human being wants:

> You are great, oh Lord, and greatly to be praised; great is your power and to your wisdom there is no limit. And man, who is part of your creation, wishes to praise you, man who bears about within himself his mortality, who bears about within himself testimony to his sin and testimony that you resist the proud. Yet man, this part of your creation, wishes to praise you. You rouse him to take joy in praising you, for you have made us for yourself, and our heart is restless until it rests in you (*Conf* 1.1.1).

The Oranais assuredly are not approaching this response: "plague had induced in them a curious frame of mind, as remote from indifference as from fervor; the best name to give it, perhaps, might be 'objectivity'" (*P* 85–86). In this, too, it is a "completely modern" city (*P* 4).

While reading Augustine's prayer, on the other hand, we achieve what we were made for. The love Augustine practices in the *Confessions,* and in which he requires us to participate through his mimetic creation (or not be reading his *Confessions*), is a love that desires, and aims to achieve ("too late") the constant conscious presence of the beloved, which we see Madame Rieux's love practices. God, of course, is, and has been, doing his part—if he forgets us, we would cease to be. But God also makes it possible for us to do our part in that he has made the world out of nothing by his Word; therefore, each thing reminds us, "We are not your God; seek higher" (*Conf* 10.6.9, cf. 9.10.25, 5.1.1). This is why Augustine, in order to confess his own story adequately, which he can do only because God holds him stably even as he himself wanders far away (*Conf* 11.8.10), must, before the end, speak in detail of the Creation of the world. For by this divine act, every thing (*res*) in the natural world becomes a sign (*signum*). In the modern world of Oran—the world "without intimations"—no such reading through things is practiced. Every thing is just a thing, and then comes another; Rieux chronicles them.

The doctor's outlook is thoroughly contemporary, just as the town is "completely modern" (4).[14] Perhaps we may go a step further. For the chronicling doctor the world is there, and any attempt to attach further meaning to it—or read meaning in it or through it—is not only a failure to experience and consider the things themselves, as an existential phenomenologist might say it, but deceitful—and first of all, deceiving oneself. There are no intimations. It seems to me that this too is a confession, perhaps a confession of method: let us call it "methodological asigneity." According to this modern teaching, there are no signs, there are only things. This method seems to entail methodological as well as metaphysical atheism—unless of course God is a thing like other things. It is plausible to consider that a scientist could be committed to methodological atheism as a scientist without being committed to metaphysical atheism. This would mean that God is not used as part of the explanation of what is going on in any of her scientific explanations or in the equations of her science, but there may yet be a God who created, sustains and redeems the universe in which those equations work, and are true. Creating, sustaining and redeeming are not matters of scientific investigation. Methodological asigneity, however, determinately closes off any search for meaning at the thing itself and is thereby as anti-metaphysical as the positivists, who are a good example of such asigneity—if I were merely chronicling modern philosophy. For Augustine, on the other hand, it is precisely by reading the world as a sign, rather than taking it all as mere thing, that we may be freed from "piercing ourselves through" with love of the world and its various beauties for their own sake,[15] and are freed to love the world rather for the sake of

14 These matters of modernity are well explicated by Aurélie Palud in "The Complexity and Modernity of *The Plague*" in *The Originality and Complexity of Albert Camus's Writings*, Emmanuelle Anne Vanborne, ed. (New York: Palgrave Macmillan, 2012): 19–33.

15 Augustine uses this image of piercing ourselves (from 1 Tim 6:10) or relatives of it in numerous places; e.g., *DCD* 1.10, *DLA* 1.15. The point comes to this: "The good you love is from him, but only insofar as it is used for him is it

our beloved, who may be thus present through it to us always.[16] This is the love Paneloux's sermon refers to, this is the "something more than mere Sunday bendings of the knee" which love entails: constant conscious presence. Suppose you don't want the constant conscious presence of your beloved; what would that mean about your love? Or your beloved? It would seem to mean that your love is untrustworthy, or perhaps only that this beloved isn't sufficient. Augustine would agree on both counts; certainly, of every finite beloved it is necessarily true that he, she, or it is insufficient. As for oneself as a lover...let us here each make his and her own confession.

Augustine's original picture of "ordered affection" confesses these truths. For the baby, the breast is just a breast—a *res*, a mere physical good; for Augustine reflecting on the matter—as also, we might think, for Monica at the time—the baby's desire for milk and the mother's ability to produce it, as well as her (physical and moral) desire to feed him, are all not "their own," but God's gifts to them through which each is able to do good for the other, even though one (the infant Augustine) is unknowing (*Conf* 1.6.7). Monica might well be meditating on this glory as she feeds her infant son: aware of the physical, moral and theological truth of her act: "It was good for them that my good should come from them; yet it was not from them but through them. For from you O God come all good things" (*Conf* 1.6.7).[17] Her breast is, rightly understood, a *res et signum gloriae*. A chronicler would merely say Monica fed Augustine from her body. Fr. Paneloux—the Augustine scholar—says that this constant conscious presence

good and sweet. With justice will it become bitter, if you, as a deserter from him, unjustly love what comes from him" (*Conf* 4.12.18). Thus do we nail ourselves to the crosses of this world.

16 In the course of *Confessions* Augustine several times takes us through the entire world, including our own powers, in ways which read through it (and them) to God who makes them be and makes them good. A few examples are 1.6.7, 7.17, 9.10.24-25, 10.6, 10.25, 11.4.

17 Jean Onimus, *Albert Camus and Christianity*, translated by Emmett Parker (University, AL: University of Alabama Press, 1970), says that by reading Augustine, Pascal, and Kierkegaard Camus discovered "it is impossible to go to God *by way of* the world, through attempting to spiritualize the temporal" (p.53). That seems a very inadequate reading of Augustine, at least; perhaps not so wrong of Pascal, whose Jansenism was too extreme for the Catholic Church, who claimed Augustine as her own.

of the beloved (as is available to Monica in feeding her infant, or in walking properly through the world for any of us) is what every love wants, for every real love, as Augustine explains, gets its name from the divine exemplar who is that love, and engenders it in us; thus we may participate even now in the divine love. As John's first letter says, "In this is love, not that we have loved God, but that he has first loved us.... . And his love is perfected in us" (1 Jn 4:10–12). The lover who denies that such love is what he wants to accomplish, would not deserve the beloved, for he does not truly love. This is most particularly the case with God, who is all good. Recognizing this, Augustine is rightly "struck with terror at my sins and at the burden of my misery" (*Conf* 10.43.70), not only for his many years of wrongly loving many diverse things and people, but because even still "in my greed, I did not want to lose you, but together with you I wanted to possess a lie... . Thus did I lose you, because you disdain to be possessed together with a lie" (*Conf* 10.41.66).

Paneloux's sermon, Madame Rieux's act, and Augustine's prayer all seem related to, but oppose, the love of the newspaper man, Rambert, who is described as waking at four in the morning to think of his beloved— "Well, she wasn't actually his wife, but it came to the same thing" (*P* 77)— far away from the quarantined city, "for the great longing of an unquiet heart is to possess constantly and consciously the loved one, or, failing that, to be able to plunge the loved one, when a time of absence intervenes, into a dreamless sleep timed to last unbroken until the day they meet again" (*P* 102). The change of verb here, from "presence" to "possession," and the addition of the alternative "dreamless sleep"—which signifies desiring that the beloved suffer an unconscious absence from everything when the lover himself is absent—is clear: Rambert prefers his beloved not be allowed to be a free rational being who acts according to her own conceptions, as Kant would define all members of the kingdom of ends, but rather be more like a thing (*res*) which has no will or even conscious existence without the lover. My coffee cup sleeps, dreamlessly, from our last kiss till the next morning when I pick her up—she warms to my touch. On the contrary, though we have neither existence, nor consciousness, nor free will except because of God, they are God's free gift to us and we may live—as do other sorts of free conscious beings—awake and willingly apart from our lover, though we should prefer not to.

Let us pause here to explicate further the considerable difference between Rambert's relation to his mistress (and hers to him) when compared to the human being's relation to God. Without replaying the previous chapter's Kantian distinction between pathological love and the practical love which treats rational beings always as ends in themselves and never as means only, we might consider the premises that every lover wants both (1) the beloved's good and (2) to be together with the beloved. In the divine relation to the human, the second is the guarantee of, indeed efficiently and immediately produces, the first; God's being together with the human being just is the good for the beloved human being. Both elements are true of God's love without any loss of freedom for the beloved, or, as Kant would put it, without any loss or destruction of the beloved as end in herself who can make her own maxims. Between human beings, on the other hand, neither the first nor the second guarantees or necessarily produces or entails the other for the beloved. Rambert's day-dream at four a.m. is that he is God. Unfortunately, only if he is, in fact, God can this daydream be an expression of true love—that is, a love that wants both elements, really. Every human love, of itself, fails here.

It is depressing to read that Camus himself shared Rambert's dream, about Maria Cesares—not his wife. When on a speaking tour of South America he writes in his journal, "Whoever has not dreamed of a perpetual prison for the woman he loves, has never really loved."[18] It is apparent that none of his many women were able to do that to him; his life would have been considerably different had that dream been his wife, Francine's, reality. Hers would have been different too. Given this idea of love, one wonders how it could ever be compatible with justice. Clearly Camus would (and did) not accept anything like this imprisonment in dreamless sleep regarding any of his mistresses; yet he wished it upon them.[19] Rambert, perhaps, comes near to considering this problem as the novel goes on, as we saw in the previous chapter, though his worry seems to be not so much concerning his respect for her as her respect for him. Does he want her respect even as he puts her into a dreamless sleep? I suppose she must wake up forgetting that.

18 Olivier Todd, *Albert Camus: A Life*, trans. Benjamin Ivry (New York: Knopf, 1997): 276.
19 See, e.g., Todd, 417.

Clamence describes his similar "loves" with more exacting detail:

> I kept all my affections within reach to make use of them when
> I wanted. On my own admission, I could live happily only on
> condition that all the individuals on earth, or the greatest num-
> ber possible, were turned toward me, eternally in suspense, de-
> void of independent life and ready to answer my call at any
> moment, doomed in short to sterility until the day I should
> deign to favor them. In short, for me to live happily it was es-
> sential for the creatures I chose not to live at all. They must re-
> ceive their life, sporadically, only at my bidding.[20]

Clamence is demonic, where Rambert is merely an ordinary sinner; the former wants the whole world to require his present love in order to live; the
latter, only one. Camus had outlined the philosophical bones of this sort
of character (and "love") in his discussion of Sade in *The Rebel*: "enjoyment
must be prevented from degenerating into attachment" and "objects of enjoyment must also never be allowed to appear as persons" (*R* 43). Rambert
suffers attachment—perhaps only to his own suiting, though perhaps to
hers as well; Clamence does not.

To all of these we should prefer—and Augustine's *Confessions* begins
this practice in we who read—that we see through each *res* as *signum* of
God's gift and love. Reflecting on that original picture of ordered affection
(himself a baby being fed at Monica's breast), Augustine says,

> All these things are the gifts of my God: I did not give them to
> myself. These things are good, and they all made up my being.
> Therefore, he who made me is good, and he is my good. Before
> him I rejoice for all these goods out of which I had my being
> even as a child (*Conf* 1.20.31).

20 Albert Camus, *The Fall*, trans. Justin O'Brien (New York: Vintage, 1991): 68.
    Camus' epigraphic headnote for this book is from Lermontov, the end of
    which runs thus: "*A Hero for Our Time*, gentlemen, is in fact a portrait, but
    not of an individual; it is the aggregate of the vices of our whole generation in
    their fullest expression" (unnumbered page).

Thus do we "make life itself a prayer to Him, by inquiring into and imitating His nature" (*DCD* 19.23). Love only can exist in the realm of freedom, and real freedom of an embodied temporal creature entails real temporal consequences—as does the failure to love properly. Rambert eventually comes to realize there is something deeply wrong with his manner of loving: Kant's double view of love explains the battle in Rambert's heart from his original version of love—which is purely pathological—to his conversion to something superior. Clamence has no such struggle. Though Kant thought that a demonic free being cannot really be imagined,[21] Camus manages to place him before us. Augustine allows that even what Kant calls our pathological love can be a sign, and if we notice it is such, it is not merely pathological.

The entire scene of Tarrou's discussion with Dr. Rieux strengthens these Augustinian resonances. Let us begin our explication of this scene with Augustine, who understands that what he knows of the truth he knows by divine illumination: even when someone teaches us, "a man does not teach us, even though he speaks.... Who teaches us now, unless it be stable Truth? Even when we are admonished by a changeable creature, we are led to stable Truth, where we truly learn" (*Conf* 11.8.10). The truth does not belong even to the person who speaks truly, nor is it seen by his light, rather the Truth, who is God, gives light to each mind, by which each sees whatever truth he sees, or speaks of. When we see the truth, we all see it in the same light.

At the start of this chapter, in which Tarrou and Rieux discuss a new response to the plague and Madame Rieux confesses how she spends her day, Rieux had noticed that his mother's face "seemed to light up with a sudden glow...when he came in" (*P* 112). He then leaves this figure "of that radiant eternal light which glows, a small still flame, in the dark core of human suffering," to make his plan with Tarrou. These two hold themselves back from such illumination—as they both remain outside the light cast by the desk lamp between them—except once: Tarrou moves his head

21 *Rel*, 23: Kant holds that the predisposition to personality by which we may make respect for the moral law in itself a sufficient incentive for the will is original and inextirpable in human nature; Clamence seems not to have it; the laughter he hears comes from outside himself.

into the light only to ask "Do you believe in God, doctor?" and Rieux only to answer that "more or less" his idea of his profession was to fight against creation as he found it (*P* 116). Is it an accident of authorship that the light which the doctor and his friend share is a technological one, in an office separate from that room where the natural light of evening and his mother glow? Or are there rooms, perhaps mansions, which the light of science and technology cannot enlighten, for those rooms are themselves light, and in their greater light the lesser is swallowed up? They *choose* to leave for a room in which the only light is of human artifice, and they are frequently in shadow each to the other; they do not see each other wholly, or clearly. Can they then love wholly or clearly? After this scene, when they go back down into the world, the artificial light fails them. These pictures are a parable: "The eye is the lamp of the body, so if your eye is sound, your whole body will be full of light... . But if the light in you is darkness, how great is the darkness!" (Mt 6: 22–23).

The interaction of Tarrou and Rieux here presents a sort of inversion of what is known in philosophy as Augustinian illuminationism, though perhaps philosophical naming hides as much as it reveals. These two see themselves as fighting against creation as something that is evil, but they do not see how it is that they agree that it *is* evil (at least the plague they are fighting is), and are seeing it as it truly is—for it is only by the light of the Truth itself (or the light of the Good in *Republic*) which enlightens everyone that such an agreement can be something other than merely "the rubbing together of guilty minds" (*Conf* 2.8.16) to which each exclaims "'Well done! well done!'"(*Conf* 1.13.21, 10.36.59). They move into the light by asking, but they do not notice the light's work in their answers; they do not see the light's work on them in their agreement concerning whatever truth each sees. Their question and answer in relation to the light reveal these things about them to us, though they do not know that they are being made manifest by it. We see that they keep themselves out of the light, we see that each wishes to know the truth about the other, and that—by fits and starts—they come to see some of the truth about each other and the world. But the light by which *we* see these things are true about them is not from the desk lamp. The characters, of course, do not notice us noting these things about them. The picture this scene presents thus illustrates Augustine's point about the light of truth: "They hate the truth for the sake of the very thing which they have loved instead of the truth. They love the truth because it brings light to them; they hate it in as much as it reproves them... . Thus does it repay them, so that those who do not desire to be made manifest by it, it makes manifest as unwilling" (*Conf* 10.23.34). After this discussion, as they are going down the stairs in the dark (Rieux flips the switch, which pointedly does not work), the following interaction occurs: just after Tarrou affirms the doctor's statements with "You are perfectly right,"

> The doctor merely gave a little shrug, unseen in the darkness.
> "To tell the truth, all that's outside my range. But you—what do *you* know about it?"
> "Ah," Tarrou replied quite coolly, "I've little left to learn."
> Rieux paused and, behind him, Tarrou's foot slipped on a step. He steadied himself by gripping the doctor's shoulder.
> "Do you really imagine you know everything about life?"
> The answer came through the darkness in the same cool, confident tone.
> "Yes" (*P* 119).

That they lean together in the darkness to affirm each other, and that Tarrou is so confident that he knows the world completely—a certainty beyond the limits of reason—is an indication that however authentic and sincere his response, Tarrou must be missing something—he slips on the step. Perhaps he is missing precisely that lucidity which he saw in the gaze of Madame Rieux before this discussion began, a chaplet which ends as they go down the staircase in the dark. It is interesting that the source of the light gets smaller, and then does not work at all, as they move farther away from her.

Somewhat later the narrator says that "the most incorrigible vice [is] that of an ignorance that fancies that it knows everything and therefore claims for itself the right to kill" (*P* 120–121). While Tarrou no longer goes so far as to claim that right, he certainly did so earlier; but does this now mean he would have favored only non-violent resistance to the Nazis? And let us remember that this solidarity of men leaning together in the dark against what they agree is evil, against what they feel their very being threatened by, is a solidarity the

Brownshirts shared as well, and the communists—whom Tarrou abandoned.[22] Rebellion against presumed injustice may be a universal human response, but it does not join us all together. It goes without saying that many other kinds of political agreement operate this way: "Let's go; let's do it." Guilty minds rubbing together, needing agreement in order to stand in the dark hallways of history. Of course, it could be that this slip in the darkness, connected so closely to the impossible certainty of two men who are discussing in the dark, is merely—like the world—an accident of authorship, signifying nothing. And Rieux's mother's love is impossible too. She can't really be doing what she says; no one could. Tarrou, at least, thinks so: "for really to think about someone means thinking about that person every minute of the day, without letting one's thoughts be diverted by anything—by meals, by a fly that settles on one's cheek.... But there are always flies.... That's why life is difficult to live" (*P* 217). But the fly too, they say, is God's creation.

Paneloux's first sermon, then, had as its center these Augustinian presumptions about love—both the love of God, and our proper response to so great a lover as could make the world a thing through which we could be constantly and consciously in his presence. But the people of Oran have chosen to live differently; or should I say we moderns have done so? And to do so is not to be reading the world correctly; perhaps it is a refusal to believe the world is a sign at all. The world is just things, connected chronologically: metaphysical, not merely methodological, asigneity. But how

22 Maze (*Albert Camus*, p. 55) rightly points out what seems "a common error, namely, the assumption that there can be no political or social action if it is not based on moral choice. On the contrary, such action can derive simply from a person's feelings of attraction or repulsion, which come from basic motives and need not be disguised by moral rationalization." Somewhat later he points out as well the questionable nature of such solidarity: "Solidarity with one's fellows, or at least with those groups in society who find themselves faced with a common threat [isn't much].... Unfortunately, the perpetrators of history's worst excesses of violence and cruelty almost certainly managed to believe that they were on the side of virtue, and that in crushing their victims they were making the world a better place" (pp. 64–65). Being on the right side of history is pamphilic claim; see Stalin. We discuss this matter further in chapter five.

could one tell whether this empirical asigneity is seeing the world for what it truly is—or not? and so entails, as a matter of course, not acting in the world correctly? From what point of view could we make this judgment, and pretend even to its empirical truth? Pretend to *know* its truth at all? To see the world as it is, is to see it as a sign of love; that, at least, is Augustine's thought, one he gets from John and the testimony of many others; these do not suffer from modern asigneity (whether methodical or otherwise). Perhaps that is part of the significance of the description of Oran as "thoroughly modern," a city turned in upon itself, and away from the sea—the source of all life and symbol of freedom—turned away such that "you always have to go to look for it" (*P* 6). But instead of looking for it, we disorder the goods of the world after our own fashion: they are all things, they suit us—or not; plague is both result and cause, as sin is both cause and result.

While Camus, in his thesis, seems to consider natural and moral evil merely distinct, and implies that the first is resolved in accord with what has sometimes been called the "aesthetic defense" of the existence of evil—that evil provides the contrasting shading necessary for the most beautiful picture,[23] Augustine does not think these two "problems of evil" can be resolved separately. For according to Augustine, natural evil and moral evil are not merely distinct, but the latter is the cause of the former. Thus this sin, this plague, is not willed by God; it is enacted upon the world *by us*. We may choose to go out by the door or the window, but our choice will have no effect on the laws of the world which has been created good, which laws will be accomplished upon the body—both private and social—following that choice. We may choose to see and act upon a person or thing (even our own person) as it relates to our particular desires (as Rambert does) rather than as it is truly in the order of created goods—a free being to be loved for God's sake. The thing or person will continue to carry forth into the world the destruction of the good we have thereby accomplished upon it or her. Thus the evil men do lives after them—certainly after their acts— yet the good remains whose work it was originally. So says Augustine. Our freedom has consequences. It is real and so effects reality. Yet it is a good thing, a better kind of thing than an apple, or a pear.

23 *Christian Metaphysics,* 119.

Camus may not have understood Augustine with this precise fulness. In his thesis, which traces the development of the gospel of Incarnation through and against Gnosticism and Neoplatonism to Augustine's philosophical and theological synthesis, Ronald Srigley points out that Camus' remark, "In this world, in which the desire for God is getting stronger, the problem of the Good loses ground," is "stunning."[24] It certainly is that, but moreover, if one takes it as outlining a philosophical argument that as the desire for God increases the idea of the Good loses ground, it is entirely mistaken about Augustine's journey through the goods of creation, as we have been showing. There is, in fact, nothing in the Jewish or Christian Scriptures that could go this way, since Creation is made, through the Logos, to be "very good" precisely because it is created by the all-Good, from whom nothing comes defective. For the Christian, as for the Greek, awe is the mother of justice in men.

Camus, however, may mean his statement in its application to *the story* his thesis is telling—namely, that Augustinian Christianity arises *out of* the Gnostic-Neoplatonic matrix he traces. In this case, the remark is much less stunning, and it is true: for Gnosticism, desire of the world *is* evil, and in Plotinus "Desire is…frustrated by the world. 'So we must 'fly from here' and 'separate' ourselves from what has been added to us.'"[25] So, Camus may well mean "this world" then, to be merely the historical cultural world in which early Christianity is growing up—a world of Gnosticism and Neoplatonism—which development Camus is tracing, and which does have the problem he points out. It is certainly true of that historical-cultural world's understanding and practices that the growing desire for God loses track of the Good and its presence and activity in the world. This is precisely because in Gnosticism the Good is a stranger in this world. Christianity, however, still under persecution, stands apart from that historical-cultural world: it stands out of it and against it. For Christianity, Gnosticism—including the Manicheanism Augustine followed for so long—is a heresy, however popular it may have been among the elite, and Augustine himself

---

24 Albert Camus, *Christian Metaphysics and Neoplatonism*, translated with an introduction by Ronald D. Srigley (Columbia: University of Missouri Press, 2007). Camus text is p. 42, Srigley's discussion of it on p. 30.
25 *Christian Metaphysics*, 103; Camus is quoting *Ennead* II, 3, 9.

produces a famous summary of the distinctions between "the Platonists" like Plotinus and Christianity in *Confessions* 7.9.13–15.[26] It does not, then, follow that Augustinian Christianity must lose track of the good in the desire for God. That is, in fact, one thing Augustine clearly argues that Christianity keeps against the Gnostics: the world is good, and beautiful, and being in love with the world we misuse it for our own ends, rather than seeing through and with the help of that love to what is most worthy of love.[27] His *Confessions*, in fact, find *the world* teaching him about the absolute superiority of the goodness of God as evidenced *through* the goodness of creation. Camus' later remark that, "as for evil, Plotinianism teaches Augustine that it is tied to matter and that its reality is entirely negative (*Conf* VII,12, VIII, 13),"[28] is only partly true in its second half. According to Christianity, matter is not evil, nor is its reality entirely negative, but that lowest "nothing-something" with "a capacity for all forms" is given existence, *out of nothing*, and existence is always a good (*Conf* 12.6.6, 7.12.18). Evil's reality *is* entirely negative, but the sections Camus notes do not exhibit that matter is necessarily connected to evil for Augustine. They argue, rather, that all that is, is good. If evil were connected to matter necessarily, there could be no spiritual evil being. The narrator seems to get this right; he tells us at one point that "you had to look closely and take thought to realize that plague was here. For it betrayed its presence only by negative signs. Thus Cottard, who had affinities to it, drew Rambert's attention to the absence of dogs" (*P* 129). Dogs are a good; we notice an absence.

In fact, something of Camus' own idea of the absurd as that which has no metaphysical standing of its own, but exists only between man and the world finds purchase in Augustine's explication of evil as having no real

26   Camus quotes this passage himself, *Christian Metaphysics*, 116.
27   Camus is famous for his confessions of love for the natural world; here is one: "the sun taught me that history is not everything. I wanted to change lives, yes, but not the world which I worshipped as divine" (*Lyrical and Critical Essays*, p. 7).
28   *Christian Metaphysics*, 118. The note to *Confessions* must be mistaken, as there is no VIII, 13; it must have been a reference to VII, 13, which only makes half the point Camus claims. One of us minor Augustine scholars is mistaken about him here. Camus' notes to Augustinian texts have several errors pointed out by Srigley; this one is not.

existence. Augustine questions whether the way the natural man (as he himself in his long youth) looks at the world is the correct way to be looking,
or seeing. As he says, we frequently "long for better things," and "certain
things are thought to be evil because they do not agree with certain others.
Yet these same beings agree with others still, and thus they are good, and
they are also good in themselves" (*Conf* 7.13.19). This shows what it would
be to love the world both deeply (as Camus confessed) and correctly. It
would not be seen as absurd. The harmoniousness of God's picture does
not depend on there being evil, for there isn't any evil in it. If our way of
looking—as natural men—is not correct, the judgment "absurd"—which
seems to arise naturally from this face-off of human desire with the world
according to Camus, is not as trustworthy or foundational as Camus had
argued in *The Rebel*. Augustine's realization is that his own way of seeing
and loving is the root of his further difficulties; his desire for a happiness
which is not real happiness leads him not only into, but to become to himself "a land of want" (*Conf* 3.10.18). It is, then, not the contradiction between the human soul and the world which produces the absurd, but the
human mind itself, which, disordered in its choices, "should be its own
punishment" (*Conf* 1.12.19). Such an explication ought to make one doubt
that the "hermeneutics of suspicion" is such a modern invention as critical
theory considers. We find Augustine, however, practicing it upon himself;
would that Freud had been so honest.

Be that as it may about Camus' own understanding—of himself or Augustine, Paneloux's second sermon lays out the deeper implications of the
human love for God.[29] In it he says a number of things that are difficult to understand, to say nothing of accepting them. Among them are these: 1) that in
the plague "God had vouchsafed to His creatures an ordeal such that they must
acquire and practice the greatest of all virtues: that of the All or Nothing" (*P*
202); 2) that "the sufferings of children were our bread of affliction, but without

29 Sharpe thinks that Paneloux shifts "from his initial, strident Augustinian
    claims that the plague was justified punishment ... [to fall] back upon Au-
    gustine's conception of Predestination" (*Camus, Philosophe*, 122). I do not see
    this turn; rather, as Sharpe himself subsequently quotes, Paneloux returns to
    his original topic: "the love of God is a hard love" (*P* 205). The question, for
    Paneloux, is about love; that is what is at stake—he does not look away.

this bread our souls would die of spiritual hunger" (*P* 203); and 3) that by the total acceptance of God's will he is "not thinking of mere resignation or even of that harder virtue, humility. It involved humiliation, but a humiliation to which the person humiliated gave full assent" (*P* 203).

The middle sentence (2) is explained by Augustine in the *City of God*, as he attempts to explain the shared suffering of the good and Christian alongside the wicked and pagan during Rome's recent sacking: if God gave good things "to all who sought them, we should suppose that such were the only rewards of his service; and such service would make us not godly, but greedy rather, and covetous" (*DCD* 1.8). If all and only good things came directly to the just and good, and all evil only and directly befell the unjust and evil, we would be just and good out of a prudence which is mere covetousness, and our natural fear of suffering. Our souls would die; we would become things of nature merely; we would not be able to love the good or God for his own sake, but only for bodily life's sake and for the goods of time, as the Tempter once proposed was true of Job. The suffering of the innocent is thus the staff of the soul's life, allowing us a freely given love, a love neither bought by all good things nor insurance against bad things happening, but one that is person to person in absolute trust, in sickness and in health, which is what the human love for God is called to be—and our love for each other as well.[30] For that is what love is, says Paneloux, the Augustine scholar. It is, it seems to me, the just response to a world given to us from nothing, a world given for nothing, to us who were once nothing. Such love is the resonance of attunement coming from that nothing which we are: You are great, oh Lord, and greatly to be praised...

Regarding Paneloux's third point, it seems we may take this bread in three distinct ways. The resigned say, "there is nothing to be done but accept the suffering of children"; those who have the higher virtue of humility say,

---

30 In his *Expositions on the Book of Psalms*, edited and condensed from the Oxford translations by A. Cleveland Coxe for *The Nicene and Post-Nicene Fathers*, Vol. 8 (Grand Rapids: Eerdmans, 1983), p. 143 (on Ps. 44), Augustine re-iterates this point; between the original leading out of Egypt, and the leading out of our present Egypt, "'What is to be our lot?' Tribulations! 'Why so?' That it may be seen with respect to the soul that worships God, to what extent it worships God; that it may be seen whether it worships Him 'freely' from whom it received salvation 'freely.'"

"God knows best, not me." But there is something higher available: "My beloved has given this to me, therefore it is good for me to accept it, to love even to my destruction, even to the seeming destruction of what else I love, for my beloved is the highest good." Thus, God has vouchsafed to his creatures an ordeal (sentence 1)—he has given us a gift, granted us this favor: we may love unto death. God apparently considers courage a primary virtue, one without which no real love can exist. Even the pagan Aristotle understood something of this; when beginning his discussion of the virtues he says "*kai prôton, peri andreias*—and first, about courage" (*NE* 1115a). I do not think this "first" is accidental; I doubt that Camus, who considered himself more like an ancient pagan than anything else, would think it accidental either. Would you wish to be a different kind of being? A slave perhaps?

It is not the case that the value of courage to Aristotle requires him to consider war and its destruction a good thing; neither, then, does Paneloux or Augustine have to say that the death of the innocent is a good thing when saying that our love for God must accept such evil as that through which love proves itself to be true. Paneloux does not, as Thomas Hanna says he does, "accept this evil as finally good even though it is beyond his understanding how God will, in the end, transform it in accordance with his purposes." The Father says, "What we'd been seeing was as unbearable to me as it was to you" (*P* 196). Fr. Paneloux does believe God will transform it; but that very fact means he recognizes the death itself as evil, he is not accepting it as good; it needs transforming. Curiously, just after the previous remark, Hanna seems to hit upon at least part of the truth:

> The paradoxical greatness of this faith is that it poses the "should" against the "is" of this world but yet cannot bring itself to despise the "is." …As long as these conflicting attitudes are held together, Christianity can attain to a love of the good which is of this world…yet be able at the same time to accept the evil that arises in the world…

He then quotes Camus:

> I would think twice before saying…that the Christian faith is a resignation. Can one put down this word for a St. Augustine or

a Pascal? Honesty requires that we judge a doctrine by its summits, not by its sub-products. And in the final analysis, little though I know about these matters, I have the impression that faith is not so much a peace as a tragic hope. (*Actuelles*).[31]

Nor does Augustine anywhere suggest that death is a good—it is always an evil, the total destruction of the good creature. To love into death is what Christ does, as all our testimonies agree. In this way, then, we should understand what Paneloux says he means to do and not do: he will not "have recourse to simple devices enabling him to scale the wall" that plague has built around them, for he knows nothing about that; he will keep faith with "the Master who knew all the pangs of suffering in his body and his soul" (*P* 201f). And this is not heresy: no human being knows what is beyond the wall; faith is required here.[32] Among those pangs of soul Paneloux mentioned there was, at last, this one: "My God, My God, why have you abandoned me?" Of these lines Augustine says, "He uttered from the cross not His own cry, but ours;" for "our old man was nailed together with Him to the cross.... . For these are not the words of righteousness, but of my sins."[33] So, then, such complaints are what is prophesied for us of imperfect ordering, on our way to becoming more perfect—which means coming to order our loves correctly. Thus this only can occur through suffering. Start here: what ought to be loved above all, my dear Adam, and Eve? If one considers his sermons through the lens of love, which is Paneloux's main point, a reader does not come to agree with Sharpe's evaluation that "Paneloux

---

31   All the quotes in this paragraph are from Thomas L. Hanna, "Albert Camus and the Christian Faith," in Brée, 52; there is no page or volume reference for his note to *Actuelles*.

32   A different way to make this point about what a Christian *knows*, is to say the word in a very unordinary way: "once we know *from the divine word* the crucial facts of man's destiny—the history of the Fall and of redemption—we can understand all the things that would otherwise seem depressingly unintelligible and revoltingly absurd." Leszek Kolakowski, *God Owes us Nothing* (Chicago: University of Chicago Press, 1998): 159, emphasis mine. Paneloux himself uses the word in its ordinary sense; this does not mean he is outside the faith of his first sermon.

33   *Expositions on Psalms*, p.141 (Ps 44) and p. 58 (Ps 22).

hypostasizes God's omnipotence at the cost of rendering his providential omnibenevolence wholly beyond human understanding";[34] rather, one begins to understand the superhuman, indeed supernatural, love we are invited to participate in. We have been vouchsafed an ordeal, not a "consolation";[35] or rather: having been vouchsafed this ordeal surpasses consolation. This high and glorious calling is possible for a human being; there is a model, and many less perfect have followed him. Madame Rieux figures both the divine and the human version of this in the novel. Tarrou remarks frequently on her "lightness," "on her kindness...he discerned its gentle glow in all she said and did; on the gift she had of knowing everything without (apparently) taking thought; and lastly that...she quailed before no light, even the garish light of the plague" (*P* 248). To consider this vocation as self-contradictory or a version of masochism is to deny even pagan virtue. It is looking through the wrong lens.

A less terrifying example can be given: suppose that (1) the highest love of the mind is to know all truth, but (2) the mind itself does not have it and (3) cannot own it. These strike me as likely premises. The first virtue one must have on the way to fulfillment of this love, then, will be humility: the humility to accept what is taught or discovered. Avoiding humiliation, should such humiliation be necessary in order to reach the truth, would be to give up the mind's highest love—for truth: a thing which is not the mind itself and cannot be owned by it—and replace it with what? Whatever it is that one wills more highly. Avoiding humiliation has become that mind's highest love.[36] Pride was once considered the root of all sins. Augustine thinks that sin—even that seeming smallest sin of stealing a few pears and feeding them to pigs—finds its deepest root in the desire to be God, to be able to define what the good is, to be oneself the highest good. Suppose we are not; then our love must be different from Rambert's, more like Joseph Grand's—"who joins the sanitary teams out of an unassuming sense that it is the only decent thing to be done."[37] Perhaps these two examples are not

---

34 *Camus, Philosophe,* 123.
35 Ibid.
36 This seems to be the driving motive of Clamence, who has begun to hear laughter behind him.
37 *Camus, Philosophe,* 97.

merely two, but find their deeper unity in this: without the courage of humility, even the acceptance of humiliation, one cannot really love. There is a model for this.

Jean Onimus catches some of the nuances of the Augustinian position to which Paneloux is giving voice, presented for the modern man who lives "the tragedy of the intellect."[38] "Where no logical human response is possible there must be an *excess* of faith and confidence for one to bow one's head and love what God permits to happen. This is the virtue of acceptance; not any banal resignation but humiliation consented to out of love…neither resignation nor fatalism but crucifying acceptance joined with a will to struggle against Evil."[39] True, Christ demands more than taking up one's destiny, or mere resignation to it; he asks Simon Peter one question three times: Do you love me? For Augustine—as for Peter—whose being and consciousness arise out of love, and is oriented to love, this answer is no easier than it is for Paneloux, but let us note that Augustine, unlike Rieux, does not begin with a demand for a lucidity of intellect (cf. *P* 38) which is a founding consumption "afflict[ing] the vital forces of the soul and wither[ing] everything right up to the heart"[40]—we might call it the modern form of tuberculosis. To such modern consumption, or intellectual TB—coughing out its own substance, Paneloux's response will *look* like "an *excess* of faith," but it *is not* that—in this word Onimus is mistaken, it is merely faith, as Paneloux himself seems to suggest to the doctor.[41] Thomas Merton agreed in saying that Camus' modern man is one "consumed by a plague of cerebration" (Merton, 219). But we are not, according to Augustine, first of all Cartesian minds seeking clear certainties, rather, "our hearts are restless." And the love that is called forth from us is to be as unconditional as that which calls it forth; that is the challenge of life, the vouchsafed ordeal, if you will. This is both divine justice and divine love; they do not exist apart; that is as little possible for God as it is for faith and love to exist

38   Onimus, *Albert Camus and Christianity*, p. 21; his description of the tragedy of the intellect is our modern consumption, or TB.

39   Onimus, p. 47.

40   Onimus, p. 21; cf., p. 55: "everything devolves on the intellectual level, in a rarefied atmosphere of coldness and lucidity."

41   After the doctor's rejection of the scheme of things, Paneloux responds "I've just realized what is meant by 'grace'" (*P* 197).

apart in human beings. He addresses us: Is Christ's question unjust? Let us admit, with Peter, the terror of the question. For Peter cannot answer directly. Part of this point is lost in translation. In the Greek, Christ's first two askings use the verb *agapan*, Peter responds with *philein*—Aristotle's word for friendship. The third time Christ is merciful; he finds Peter at his own level and asks using *philein* (Jn 21:15–17). That was an act of the higher love, a love which does not expect return in kind, but empties itself for the beloved. That is God, giving his full assent to His own humiliation.

What follows from all this? God's freely given gifts of life and the opportunity to love as freely unto death has a reverse side: If the world is not a place where we see this love, it is because we do not live up to it. Even God, who became incarnate, could not make us live this love; to force the issue would be precisely to destroy this highest good available to human life, and to destroy the human. Who would want that world? "All or nothing," Paneloux says, is *our* choice in the world of plague. It seems to me he is right, and our world is that world of plague. Perhaps the pagans did not choose Christianity out of weakness and a desire for consolation, but because its challenge and its promise were the same: life with God. In this, what they had always considered the primary virtue found its true weight and worth, its home and the kingdom worth defending by all, everywhere. "Glorious things are said of you, O city of God…"

Let us pause for a moment here to consider something Camus said of rebellion: In his "no" every rebel "experiences a feeling of revulsion at the "infringement" of his rights and a complete spontaneous loyalty to certain aspects of himself.… . The part of himself that he wanted to be respected he places above everything else and proclaims it preferable to everything, even to life itself.… [He] suddenly adopts…an attitude of All or Nothing" (R 13–15). Rebellion against the plague, against this "natural" infection, this nothing which absents us from what is best in us—perhaps that is the first step towards love. In fact, the deepest love already lies under this rebellion. For how do we recognize that infringement? What powers that "spontaneous loyalty" in the face of death? What is that "best in us" inspiring our revolt? Both Augustine and Paul complain of their weakness and incapacity to carry out *this* rebellion. "I was overcome by your truth, I had no answer whatsoever to make, but only those slow drowsy words, 'Right away. Yes, right away.'…But 'Right away—right away' was never now, and

'Let me be for a little while' stretched out for a long time" (*Conf* 8.5.12). "For not what I wish do I do, but what I hate, this I do" (Rom 7:15). These two recognize that there is some part of ourselves which is worth everything else; they revolt against what keeps them from it. And that, too, is part of us. Aristotle, too, encouraged the recognition of such a thing, and a revolt against that nature which might enslave us: "For we should not listen to those who advise us that being men we should think of human things, and being mortal, of the mortal, but we must so far as possible strive to live in accord with what is best and most divine in us; for though it is the smallest, yet it exceeds everything else in its power and worth" (*NE* 1177b 31–35).

There is, of course, another possible answer to the suffering in our world, and another way of thinking about it—that which is enacted by Dr. Rieux himself immediately after the child's death: revolt, or a different revolt. "That child, anyway, was innocent, and you know it as well as I" he shouts at the priest. Then, by way of apology, he says that sometimes "the only feeling I have is one of mad revolt" (*P* 196). It is mad, because in the end, there is nothing one can do about the world "where innocent children are put to torture." In fact, the doctors' own efforts only succeed in making the child suffer longer, as Castel admits, and Rieux seems angered to hear suggested by Paneloux. Rieux's rebellion may be mad and blind, but it is not therefore entirely incorrect. Rather, his madness reveals something deeper than what appears to him, for we are not simply powerless before what looks to be the mere absurdity of evil and suffering: we *see* evil as evil, and death as a prime evil—the absence of a good which should be present. Rieux is right about this. Camus considers this a case of metaphysical rebellion, which is "the *justified claim* of a desire for unity against the suffering of life and of death."[42] But *by what light* does one see this as justified? In a world of mere things concatenating, the idea of justice is simply an illusion, as is any love pretending to be something other than desire. The rebel demands more, and is right in that demand, but by what light do we know this and agree?

Sharpe explains Camus' idea of justification as man pulling God to his own level (*Camus, Philosophe*, 110-113); but could creation be just this: that God invites our love to match his, to participate in his? This is what

---

42   *R* 24, but I have quoted the translation in M. Sharpe's *Camus, Philosophe* 110.

Paneloux, following Augustine, is presenting to us. Madame Rieux was calmer than her son: "I am so glad to be with you again, Bernard.... . The rats can't change *that*, anyhow" (*P* 13). Madame Rieux's claim is true, and it stands without any possible justification, in the face of every evil: joy in the presence of the beloved. Yes, plague is a time which makes us "bend our thoughts to first and last things" (*P* 89), not that this particular evil has changed anything—except our attention, perhaps. The presence of evil cannot change the preceding and ever present fact of the presence of God, it does not win out against *agapê*, it does not win out even against friendship—except by killing the friend—but has evil then won? Or has it thereby shown its powerlessness? Of course, not all loves are *agapê*, and few, says Aristotle, are true friendship. Is God present in *The Plague*? in this world in which we are working even now—one way and another? That is for us to answer, as St. John wrote, and Madame Rieux and Joseph Grand seem to illustrate: "By this we can be sure that we know him, if we keep his commandments.... . He who keeps his word, in him the love of God is truly perfected" (1 Jn 2: 3–5).

The scene of their argument after the death of the child ends with Rieux apologizing:

> "Again, please forgive me. I can promise there won't be another outburst of that kind."
> Paneloux held out his hand, saying regretfully:
> "And yet—I haven't convinced you!"
> "What does it matter? What I hate is death and disease, as you well know. And whether you wish it or not, we're allies, facing them and fighting them together." Rieux was still holding Paneloux's hand. "So you see"—but he refrained from meeting the priest's eyes—God himself can't part us now" (*P* 197).

The doctor, besides holding Paneloux's hand, seems also still holding on to his revolt against creation, against the "scheme of things in which children are put to torture." He says that they are allies, and he is right to an extent: both are working for the good of their fellow citizens. But he cannot meet the priest's eyes for he knows that true as this is, it is not the whole truth: God not only can separate them, He already has. The doctor is only a citizen of Oran, and, as he confesses, is only working for health; the priest has dual citizenship—in Oran and the city of God, and it is the second citizenship which is primary and true—he works for salvation; in the first city he is more like a resident alien. He will fight for its good, though he knows of and lives something better, in which all the others, too, can participate if they will. "As this life is common to both cities, so there is harmony between them in regard to what belongs to [the earthly city]" (*DCD* 19.17). The doctor, like Camus, must know enough about Christianity (if not Augustine) to know this about the priest, so he cannot meet the priest's eyes. The grounds upon which the doctor understands his solidarity with the priest and the people of Oran is a true, but limited, view of human solidarity. From this view, friendship based in working together virtuously for the goods of the world—as that friendship perhaps existing between Tarrou and Rieux—is the most complete version of human solidarity. But the priest lives in a world where solidarity is not based on virtue or shared suffering, or merely common feeling as Rambert suggested, though the father willingly embraces all of these insofar as they do not hinder his first citizenship. And they do not necessarily do so: father Paneloux considers human solidarity to be based on the self-emptying *agapê* which is the gift of God. When he dies, Rieux marks the card "doubtful case" (*P* 211). The doctor cannot say whether Paneloux *was taken* by the plague, or *gave himself* totally in that love which unites the members of the city of God. Judgment about such matters is something more than a chronicle can contain, something further than metaphysical revolt imagines, or any empiricism—medical or ethical—can trace. It does not, then, seem accurate to suggest that Paneloux would deny human beings "an inalienable right to resist all forms of evil," or to oppose "the imposition of innocent, useless suffering," nor does he "rationalize away the immovable scandal represented by such suffering;" none of those would be "keeping faith with that great figure of all suffering."[43]

Rieux's metaphysical revolt itself does touch upon something further that is also limned in the darkness of *The Plague*. Some critics think Camus made a mistake, and a seriously confusing one, by presenting

---

43   The first three quotes are from M. Sharpe, *Camus, Philosophe*, 112; the last is from Paneloux's second sermon (*P* 202). It is what the man says, and does.

moral evil under the guise of a natural evil.[44] In so doing, they say, he makes moral evil as senseless and absurd and seemingly causeless as physical evil. But in fact, their unity is merely the truth if we ask Augustine, for how does so-called natural evil come into the world except by sin? Or how do we come to see something natural as evil? As we have seen:

> Certain things are thought to be evil because they do not agree with certain others. Yet these same beings agree with others still, and thus they are good..... All these beings, which do not harmonize with one another, nevertheless are in keeping with that lower part of things, which we call the earth (*Conf* 7.13.19).

Even the infant is born objectively disordered (*Conf.* 1.7.11). The novel gives voice to this also; as Tarrou says, "I had plague already" (*P* 222), even "through all those long years in which, paradoxically enough, I'd believed with all my soul that I was fighting it" (*P* 227); "we all have plague" (*P* 228), "no one on earth is free from it" (*P* 229). We were not even free of it when "young.... [and] liv[ing] with the idea of [our] innocence; that is to say, with no idea at all" (*P* 222).[45]

Tarrou seems to agree with Augustine that we are in this state from birth, for "the order of the world is shaped by death" (*P* 117), and "the social order [built]...on the death sentence" (*P* 226), and we come into it

---

44 Among them, Gaëtan Picon, in "Limitations of *The Plague*," and John Cruickshank in "Levels of meaning in *The Plague*" both available in *Readings on The Plague*, edited by Jesse G. Cunningham (San Diego: Greenhaven Press, 2001) as well as Roland Barthes in his 1955 review, "*The Plague*: the annals of an epidemic or a novel of isolation?" (available now in *Œuvres complètes*, ed. Eric Marty (Paris: Seuil, 2002) Vol 1: 540–545). Adele King also has several problems with the plague's symbolic incongruities, *Camus*, 74–78. Cruickshank does argue that the incongruities "strengthen [the symbol's] metaphysical application" (*op. cit.* 74). Sharpe orients these criticisms toward a deeper discussion of evil in modern thought (*Camus, Philosophe*, 62–65, 105–110).

45 Tarrou, then, is cured of one aspect of the absurd man's freedom. For such a man "feels innocent. To tell the truth, that is all he feels—his irreparable innocence. This is what allows him everything" (*MS* 9).

unknowing.[46] This may sound like mere repetition, but I wonder. That Creation is a work of love does not disallow that the natural world is shaped by death; from Genesis onward it is clear that if you fail to obey the rules you shall surely die: Go out by the window rather than the door, go out into the jungle at night where tigers are prowling, build your house on the sand of a barrier island, allow a certain segment of your city's people to live among the garbage with the rats. But even in its perfection it was so: "you may eat of all trees except…on the day you eat of it…" (Gn 2:16–17). Any order of nature, as every nature, has edges, or there is no nature.[47] Social orders differ, not being universal, but they are no less determinate about what will cause death, or at least social ostracism (Cottard may end up suffering both): murder (what counts as that is differentially determined across societies), driving on the left side of the road, eating bacon, or eating hamburger—or maybe even eating meat at all. Every order—natural and social—is like a knife: it has edges. "We can't stir a finger in this world with the risk of bringing death to somebody" (*P* 228). On the other hand: no edges, no order, no nature. We should expect that defunding the police will only exacerbate the murder rate; even threats and protests to do so seem to take the edge off in our larger cities.

Paradoxically enough in such a world, Tarrou wants not "to be pestiferous, that's all" (*P* 226), he wants to be "a saint without God" (*P* 230). Given the natural and social orders of the world, the first looks impossible. It is impossible if "not pestiferous" means not participating in death-dealing;

46   I am giving a bit more detail than Cristaudo, who also rates Tarrou's analysis here as "a very orthodox and well-put account of original sin" ("Johannine Christianity," p.151), which is quite accurate, as is his conclusion, a bit later, that Camus' attacks are "attacks upon phantasmic Christianity, which far from breaking with some core Christian concepts actually reproduce them" (p. 152).

47   David Hume, one of the founding fathers of modern empiricism, wishes to imagine a better world than the one we are lumbered with—which has rather sharp edges; but at least he notices the difficulty: if God, rather than by general laws, conducted all matters via "particular volitions" of his most beneficent will, "no man could employ his reason in the conduct of his life." This minor issue seems not to disturb him much (*Dialogues concerning Natural Religion*, Part 11). Unless, of course, his character is joking here. See my "Empiricism or Dialectical Destruction Thereof? Reading Hume's *Dialogues Concerning Natural Religion* on Evil," in *International Philosophical Quarterly* 61, 2: 139–160.

every order does that. Paradoxically enough, after his long discussion on the rooftop with Dr. Rieux he suggests they go for a swim. They have a pass which allows them to dive into a world others may not enter: "A saint-to-be can indulge in [that], don't you agree?" (*P* 231). Their shared fraternal swim takes them out of the world of plague, where others cannot go—or does it? Part of this picture seems to imply that neither Rieux nor Tarrou achieve what is the highest in an Aristotelian judgement. Their long discussion in their "hour off for friendship" is a discussion of what they consider the po-litical and social goods, and how they came to those positions. But the good of communal contemplation of the highest good they miss. Each discovers how his friend has come to the work he has, but the idea that there could be a something higher—a good for its own sake which is not tethered to use in the world—evades them. Neither Grand nor Paneloux miss that good.

Unless it is just this swim which is their shared "for its own sake." "Be-fore them the darkness stretched out into infinity…. Rieux lay on his back and stayed motionless, the dome of the sky lit by the stars and the moon" (*P* 232). On the horizontal plane of the chronicle there is darkness without end; when he lies down momentarily in the sea things are described differ-ently. It is a resonant phrase, "dome of the sky"—it is not from a chronicle. And the lights are ordered; one can tell time by their movements. The trick of life would seem to be not to escape the world of plague (even together with a friend for an hour)—in which the darkness stretches out to infinity, but rather to live in the world of plague, while not being of it; rather, know-ing of something greater while under the dome of the sky. Grand achieves a transcendence of the horizontal in his poetic creation, it does not seem that Rieux or Tarrou accomplish that. Tarrou does not imagine something greater, but he does imagine being out of this world of death. How? He dives into the sea. At this point a reader is either literate, or confessing him-self to be a mere materialist—a thing that makes intimations impossible. It is clear that what we need, and what Camus has pictured for us, is Bap-tism;[48] a baptism by which we are reborn, by which we re-enter creation—

---

48 Sharpe says that the friendship of Tarrou and Rieux is "baptized in their final swim together" (*Camus, Philosophe*, 97), which is true—though it quite openly seems to be reaching for more significance than an absurd world, or view of the world, allows.

which is not merely a matter of facts following each other in the order chronicled. But in this novel's chronicle it is pointedly not the sacrament which they take, for the water is merely water, their escape merely a momentary (and illicit—for everyone else) reprieve: all things are merely things for the modern man, and the two come forth only to the world of Oran— one still "without intimations," in which, unfortunately, a fraternal swim is merely that: a momentary escape into a world only imagined to be free of plague. Tarrou later founders "in the dark waters of the pestilence" (*P* 260). The order of the world is shaped by death. Who may free us?

Paradoxically enough, Tarrou sounds perfectly Augustinian, even to his definition of the good man, who is "the man who infects hardly anyone, the man who has the fewest lapses of attention" (*P* 229). Tarrou, Rieux and Augustine (to say nothing of Plato) all find the condition into which we are born something we must work against, difficult and omni-present as that condition is. But the rest of Tarrou's self-explanation is decidedly anti-Augustinian, for it is Pelagian:[49] "What's natural is the microbe. All the rest—health, integrity, purity (if you like)—is a product of the human will" (*P* 229). Tarrou, in many ways, seeks to be an agent of grace—without God. He seems more human to Cottard, whom he regularly invites to a second chance, and he shares something human with Cottard even in doing so, for this is our first rebellion: the good is my creation, and wholly within my power, without the need of divine grace. Rieux's mad rebellion is against the symptoms that follow naturally from this first rebellion. Augustine and his friends accomplished the first upon some pears. Tarrou continues, "and it needs tremendous will-power, a never ending tension of the mind, to avoid such lapses. Yes…it's a wearying business being plague stricken" (*P* 229). Perhaps by "lapses" Tarrou meant "the fewest lapses of attention to his disease," but Augustine is deeper, for if everyone has it, by what light do you know it to be a disease? It is certainly *not* abnormal. "What's natural is the microbe." And so to what, or to whom ought we always be paying attention? It cannot be to the microbe itself—to evil, that is. For, even in

49 Echoes of Pelagianism can be heard in Sharpe's descriptions of Camus' own tendencies of thought and self-formation in "Camus and the Virtues," 690– 694; or to use less heretical terms—his Socratic and Stoic efforts at detachment—which also require one to be unwearyingly attentive.

order to understand the plague as evil—which Cottard, for one, does not seem to completely agree with—we must pay attention to something else. It is not our fellow human beings either—for Cottard's situation has become more widespread, and this feels good, having company—life under the plague suits him, and numerous others. Cottard does not, perhaps, help spread the plague, but its coming and continuance in others sets him at ease. Plague dulls the edges of the world *he* is in at least in this way: everyone is now on the edge of death. And how can we, by ourselves, not lapse in attention? I suppose we must drown in it, as Tarrou does—in our own lapses, as well as those of others. Even in a world that is created as grace, a grace which is everywhere available, though now always mixed. It is by our lapses of attention to God that evil comes into the world; and in so lapsing we disorder the world's original good order. That is what lapsing really is: a disordered choice—a preference for the good as *we* see it.

What does this disorder affect? All the world, all of creation, every order. What is natural evil? It is an effect of our "lapses." Do these lapses affect only us? Does the drunk or texting driver only kill or maim himself? Does the CEO of the chemical plant build his house downstream of the effluent openings, or the prevailing winds? The original order of created nature is good, as Augustine takes pains to show in the closing books of *Confessions*, but our injustice, disorder, inattention infects it: pears go to wild pigs, this infection carries on as nature carries on; it becomes one with nature, though this plague was not willed by God. It is become one with nature by our work, as it is one with grace, by God's. God was apparently serious about justice inhabiting matter through us. The order of justice and the order of nature are inextricably linked.[50] They were made that way: "And God looked at all he had made and saw that it was very good" (Gn 1:31). And so it shall be again, when all things are reconciled to God in Christ, for when our love is correct, so are all other passions (*DCD* 14.9). Camus is right, then, as Sharpe argues, to consider that "human beings have an inalienable right to resist all forms of evil or the imposition of

---

50 The ancient philosophical expression for this natural link is Aristotle's—"activities of virtue are naturally pleasant" (*NE* 1099a13, 21). Modern moral philosophy, e.g. Kant, is, at best, agnostic about this connection of natural happiness and morality. Apparently, the world has grown darker.

innocent, useless suffering" (*Camus, Philosophe,* 112). But we must begin *before* Dr. Rieux's rebellion against that suffering, we must begin in that lack of attention to the divine lover which was our first rebellion: there is where we must resist. We must resist that inattentive (or openly rebellious) reordering of the world which Augustine takes pains to explain in book two of *Confessions* as *imitatio dei.*

When Paneloux becomes ill we read that "he seemed to be struggling to force up from his lungs a clot of some semi-solid substance that was choking him" (*P* 209). All his efforts are unavailing, but in all that follows he "never let go of the crucifix" (*P* 210). His attention never wavers. At last he "brought up the clot of matter that was choking him; it was red" (*P* 211); and being rid of it, he dies. Even having paid minute attention to his case, the doctor cannot tell if Paneloux had the plague. Is this "doubtful case" (*P* 211) one of doubtful material nature, or doubtful moral nature? Hard to say. John Krapp holds that despite Paneloux's good work, his "adherence to absolute Truth obviously places his moral voice at some odds with Rieux's."[51] While he *is* at odds with Rieux, his adherence *is not* to some absolute abstract truth as Krapp describes, rather "he would keep faith with…that tortured body on the Cross" (*P* 202), who is also figured in the child, in its "grotesque parody of crucifixion" (*P* 193), and will be seen again later in Tarrou, whose body "lacerated under the spear thrusts of the plague" (*P* 260) proved to the doctor again that his own position could only be that of witness. John Robert Maze suggested that Paneloux "submitted to dying because he was convinced he had committed a mortal sin, and so was dying as a form of penance."[52] This could hardly be considered an argument against Augustine's (or any other orthodox Christian) position, though Maze considers that the sin was that he "had prayed to God to save the child—that is, for God to cancel his willed act."[53] But Paneloux began his second sermon by saying that he had not changed his opinion from the first sermon, in which he had clearly said "this calamity was not willed by God" (*P* 87)—it was, rather, the result of our inattention—our lapses in love, which, if correct, would order all things correctly. And those matters

51 Krapp, *TEAC,* 670.
52 Maze, *Camus,* 70.
53 Ibid., 67.

which still fall incorrectly, due to the lapses of others? How would love respond to these? I suppose it would ask for more weight to be laid on itself. Paneloux says in the second sermon that he may be accused of fatalism, but denies the term is entirely accurate and considers the better term to be "active fatalism" (*P* 204). He never lets go of the figure of the suffering servant: Has the priest been made free of plague by uniting himself to the crucified one?

Merton suggests something like this, and then something surprising:

> We divine that Paneloux, in heroic Christian fashion, has doubtless asked God to lay upon him the punishment of all, the unrelieved suffering of the worst kind of death by pestilence, and to do this in such a way that Paneloux will receive no praise or credit from men... . And, paradoxically, in blindly submitting to God he also manages at the same time to impose his own will on God (Merton 211).

Unless he is a very strange kind of heretic or a madman, Paneloux cannot ask to have the punishment of all be laid upon him, for that job has already been taken; he can consciously unite himself to that suffering one in love. Perhaps he does. Hard to say; impossible to see. No chronicle will tell us. Augustine's explication of Psalm 22, however, intimates his success.[54] Why call this blind submission? He knows to whom he clings; he knows why. That last sentence of Merton's is nonsense then, for there is no place for the will-to-power in uniting oneself in *agape*—or at least friendship—to that being who is *agape*. So did the priest die of plague, or of self-giving *agapê* —having elected "the place incumbent on him—the forefront of the fight" (*P* 198)? Would the doctor or Tarrou be able to tell? They do not yet recognize the light necessary for such investigation. Would they think it sensible even to ask the question? They are modern men.[55]

54 See notes 30 and 33 above.
55 It is almost humorous, given Rieux's self-confessed inartistic chronicling of what things happen when, that Merton says "Paneloux is plainly no saint" (Merton 212); in chronicles, no saints appear. But let us return, at the close, to the person of our *author*: Perhaps he repents of his modernity. He notes a

Paradoxically, the next day is All Soul's Day; so by some accident of authorship Fr. Pan et Lux, or is it *pan-eleeô*—I have mercy on all—died on the Feast of All Saints, having coughed up the bloody mess that chokes us all.[56]

What caused the death of the child then?

Who caused the death of the man on the cross?

"Who will deliver me from this body of death?" (*Conf* 8.5.12)

> Too late have I loved you, O Beauty so ancient and so new, too late have I loved you! Behold, you were within me, while I was outside: it was there that I sought you, and, a deformed creature, rushed headlong upon those things of beauty which you have made. You were with me, but I was not with you. They kept me far from you, those fair things which, if they were not in you would not exist at all. You have called to me, and have cried out, and have shattered my deafness. You have blazed forth with light, and have shone upon me, and you have put my blindness

discussion he had with several of the major French intellectuals of the day: "Don't you think that we are all responsible for the absence of values? And that if all of us who are the descendants of Nietzscheanism, of nihilism, or of historical realism were to proclaim publicly that we were wrong and that there are moral values and that from now on we would do everything necessary to found and illustrate them, don't you think it would be the beginning of a hope?" Albert Camus, *Selected Essays and Notebook*, edited and translated by Philip Thody (Harmondsworth: Penguin, 1962–1979), pp. 282–283. More context can be found in Todd 233–234. The difficulty Camus is having was pointed out by Augustine in his *Soliloquies* 1.8: "the lessons of instruction can only be seen as it were by their own sun"—but in the modern world only one sun is allowed, and it is dark.

56 M. Sharpe (*Camus, Philosophe*, 105–111), following Susan Neiman's *Evil in Modern Thought*, would suggest we consider this feast in an alternative light: All Saints' Day is the anniversary of the 1755 Lisbon earthquake, which brought questions of theodicy loudly into the cultural mainstream. Roger Quilliot comments on the fact that in the manuscript version Paneloux seems to lose his faith, *The Sea*, p. 145, but in the finished work of art it is not so. Divine inspiration? Or authorial choice? A doubtful case. I am merely repeating known facts about what happened.

to flight! You have sent forth fragrance, and I have drawn in my breath, and I pant after you. I have tasted you, and I hunger and thirst after you. You have touched me, and I have burned for your peace (*Conf* 10.27.38).

I do not think going for a swim will be much help.

CHAPTER FOUR
PALIMPSESTS:
OBLITERATING EQUATIONS
IN THE CLASSROOM OF SUFFERING

> There was just enough light to make out the half-obliterated
> figures of an equation chalked on a blackboard.
> *The Plague*, 192

The dramatically central scene of the five-part *Plague* is decentered into Part
IV. In it, all of the named characters excepting Cottard are drawn into a
knot around the dying son of Oran's chief magistrate, M. Othon. The auxiliary hospital in which it occurs "had formerly been a classroom" (*P* 191),
and at the far end of the room there is a chalkboard, on which some pieces
of an equation can still be made out. An equation—whether in mathematics, chemistry or physics—is an abstract summary of a set of relations used
to outline how real particulars are connected. They are the basis for what
Kant called the hypothetical imperatives of science. With them we are able
to solve for whatever x we are attempting to achieve: launch an ICBM at
Beijing, or a stone against the walls of Syracuse; invent a vaccine, a T-cell
adjuvant for a set of diseases, or a hallucinatory drug; induce a chain reaction, or inhibit one. There are equations for reduction and for expansion,
for formation or synthesis, and for ordered analytic assay. That the plague
has changed the whole world of the Oranais into a sick ward and its class-
rooms into hospitals does not change the fact that the classroom is still a
classroom, and there are still things to be learned; rather, it generalizes the
classroom to the whole life of the town. There are still valid equations working in and beneath the disease and the dying; particulars instantiate them
in their variable ways. But the plague might make some wonder why all
these equations matter, for when facing death there may be many such that

suddenly seem much less important to know about. It also seems that none of them are delivering the answer desired. In any case, the school is closed.

There are equations in the social world too; they are more culturally relative than those of the physical sciences. In *The Plague* such equations are symbolized by Tarrou's father and his peculiar hobby. Tarrou's father is, like M. Othon, a state prosecutor; he sets forth and carries out the conclusions of the law upon the individual members of society brought before him. Like a scientist, he does not make the laws, he merely applies them to the subject before him to the very end of their "process"—some are lengthier processes than others. Those laws organize the social world as the equations of science organize the matter of it.[1] Tarrou's father's hobby—memorizing the railway directory—is, writ small, the picture of what would be the knowledge had by the god of social science. "He could tell you the exact times of departure and arrival of the Paris-Berlin expresses; how to get from Lyon to Warsaw, which trains to take and at what hours…. Could you tell me offhand how to get from Briançon to Chamonix? Even a station-master would scratch his head" (*P* 223). He knows how the social world is organized and how one can move in it. We should remember that at this time there were significant borders, with occasional changes of track sizes, and much more complexity about which stations in a large capital city could be the point of departure for which kinds of train. His father knows how to handle all these cross-border issues as well as more local trips like the family vacation to Brittany. He knows how social orders change, and where, and when; he is one part of the machinery responsible for their enforcement.

One of those stations—Oran—is now erased; equations for journeys that began, ended, or changed there are no longer solvable. Rambert, whose heart is set on a journey no longer available, spends some time in the empty railway station, reading of equations that no longer apply in his world (*P* 101). They have been erased: You can't get there from here. Under every set of "travel equations" a society might have, if you were to hijack a train to attempt to go where you wanted, you would undoubtedly cause a number of deaths—on your train as well as the one you hit. Like driving on the

---

1   The narrator describes the series of inoculations performed on Othon's son as "a lengthy process" (*P* 191); so too was the legal process leading to a certain crucifixion, half erased in this scene.

wrong side of the road (whatever side that is in the social world you enter), acting against any part of the system of these social and legal imperatives will bring you, if you survive, before the state prosecutor; a variety of punishments extend to the highest—either way, the social order is shaped by death. Kant considered hypothetical imperatives to be those which one took up on the hypothesis that it would be good to achieve a certain end: under the condition that you want x, do z, then y. This is always true of the ends we set using the hypothetical imperatives of science, whether health or poisoning; but of all these ends we must admit that we do not need to affirm that end, or that end now—they are only hypothetical, not apodictic like those of morality. Another way of understanding hypothetical imperatives is that they could be (or could have been) otherwise. The train routes could have been set up differently, the driving rules and religious dietary injunctions likewise. While it is now a matter of some debate at the higher levels of science whether our world could exist with other basic laws of nature than we have, in Camus' time it would have been thought unlikely that the laws of physics and chemistry could have been otherwise, though even if they could have been, they cannot now change. In this, nature's laws are unlike social laws—like which cases may lead to the death penalty—for the social laws may be changed or even totally erased; perhaps half-erased means mostly uninforced. At any rate, Tarrou's father, like M. Othon, is the cutting edge of the system of hypothetical imperatives which define the society: he knows all the ways to get to the places which have been defined as stations; he knows all the licit ways to achieve ends society allows. He enforces everyone to stay on track in all their choices of ends and means; he is the cutting edge of the "or else" when they do not.

The plague's partial erasure of the equations on the blackboard signifies at least two things then. First, some ends are erased—they are no longer possible. This may happen in a couple of ways—toilet paper, or meat, or "peppermint lozenges" (P 105) may disappear from the markets for instance, or, all airports and train stations may be closed down, or all bars and cafes. Certainly, under quarantine, what is erased is the socially allowed equation joining "where you are now" with some desired end outside the city. We have already discussed Kant's idea that a person cannot even think his maxim: "When in time of quarantine for plague, I leave the city because 'I don't belong here'" (P 79), since, under universalization which makes it like a law of nature, the word "quarantine" becomes meaningless. Therefore, such a maxim cannot be moral. The equation leading to the solution at which Rambert aims looks completely erased empirically also. Rambert discovers every road now leads to one or another part of the city wall; he finds these erased exits re-iterated in making his rounds of "officialdom" (*P* 97–100). All traffic moves in circles. Cottard and his acquaintances, however, have ways around these empirical problems; in other words, they have arranged a set of hypothetical imperatives, an extremely difficult and drawn out equation, which can get your desired end—but "it's going to cost you something" (*P* 132), "a cool ten thousand" (*P* 135), as well as, perhaps, your moral self-respect. Cottard's is a different society than Oran generally, it has invented different hypothetical imperatives for the solution to empirical problems than the usual society allows. This small subset of equations comes to be under the erasure of ends or means to things some people want despite the "legal" society's imperatives, misfortunes, and definition of allowed ends. That this sort of displacement happens all the time might make one think that it is a law of human social nature, as Kant said, to want to arrange things so one is subject to no law whatsoever other than one's own immediate desire. That this unsocial sociability is deep in our nature is a thesis shared by thinkers as diverse as Freud and Augustine. In *Civilization and its Discontents,* Dr. Freud says that my neighbor "has more claim to my hostility and even my hatred" than to my love (*CD* 67), as each stands in the other's way of "the most enticing method of conducting one's life: … An unrestricted satisfaction of every need" (*CD* 26). Augustine's analysis of the pear tree incident makes even friendship a questionable good, for without those others with whom he did the crime, he would not have done it. His desire for the pears was not for the pears *per se*—he had better ones at home, but to have the power of God to define good and evil, which—in order to be experienced as real in the world—needs the recognition of others who agree: "Let's go; let's do it" (*Conf* 2.9.17). Our narrator, on the other hand, thinks such activities as Rambert's "monotonous struggle to recover [his] lost happiness… [bears] witness, even in its futility and incoherences, to a salutary pride" (*P* 127f). That certain incoherences come along with pride is an interesting point for the doctor to make. The equations pride acts on are not universalizable, they are one's own. Many become incoherent if one attempts to universalize them.

Very well, the equations that used to be taught in the classroom are half-obliterated; they are literally scientific or mathematical equations, not train schedules or blackmarket flow charts; they are at the end of the classroom, far from the subject of today's lesson, for the classroom is now the classroom of suffering, and the subject of our attention in this lesson is Othon's son. Our attention has been re-oriented from the usual classroom abstractions to the concrete individual. The central scene of *Republic*—the cave—is openly described by Plato as a picture of "our nature regarding education and the lack of it" (514a), a regard Camus intimates by placing his scene where he does. Both the cave and the classroom-hospital are scenes of education: what are we to learn? "They have been there since childhood," and "they are like us," Socrates says, and as that scene is an inset outline of how Plato's whole book works[2]—as well as life, so too with this equally highly detailed inset of Camus' novel. For we have been in a world of suffering, including innocent suffering, since childhood and since the opening of Camus' book, and these characters are like us; now we will be watching up close. Both scenes are "plays within the play" which write small what each whole book is doing. Such insets are the literary version of equations; the genetic code, as it were, for the growth and flowering of the entire work.

If we begin by superimposing Camus' inset over Plato's scene of education we see that our attention has been drawn away from the wall at the far end—with its half visible equation on the chalkboard, and we are now gathered around the thing itself; we are no longer gazing at abstractions, or shadows, or yet statues, or even puppets in the flickering light of desire as in the cave. Rather, the very thing is placed before us. Neither we readers, nor the characters had "yet watched a child's agony minute by minute, as they had now been doing since daybreak...hitherto they had felt its abomination in, so to speak, an abstract way" (*P* 192f). We readers have been watching the suffering of Oran as if from the distance of an equation, just as the townsfolk listen to the radio announcements of the numbers of new deaths, and the comparisons of ratios from one week, or month, or day, to another. They think such abstractions tell them something, though they do not have any idea what the death rates were in more ordinary weeks and

2   See, for example, Gene Fendt, *Comic Cure for Delusional Democracy*, chapter four.

months, and in any case, they are just impersonal numbers, not personal realities. But in this classroom, on this day, that sort of cool intelligible abstraction is not what we are practicing or attending to.

We see that Camus has reversed the Platonic picture of knowledge. In Plato's extended analogy, including the divided line of intelligibility which immediately precedes it, the way out of merely operating on the cave's flickerings of imagination, or belief in the solid seeming opinions carried by the influencers of the day the next level up, is precisely through the abstract definitions, hypotheses, equations, and proofs of sciences like arithmetic and geometry which prepare one for dialectical hypotheses and proofs in philosophy. Such operations of reason and understanding in the realm of ideas are what knowledge really is according to Plato. In Camus' novel, on the other hand, knowledge is not of ideas, and the real is not an abstraction; rather, knowledge is of individual actualities: today, the torture and death of Othon's son. It is "a grotesque parody of crucifixion" to be sure (*P* 193), but that remark takes us one step away from the actuality Camus puts before us. Or so existentialist interpreters of Camus would have us read. But we have seen that Camus suggests that this is merely the way a novel must work to remain a work of art and not have its life crushed out, as Sartre's *Nausea*, under the weight of its philosophical burdens. It must present particulars as real particulars, not as ideas. But in these particulars, like Othon's dying son, ideas still live.

So, the presumption (or presentation) of an anti-Platonic epistemology, seems, first of all, merely a necessity of artistic creation: no ideas but in things, as Wallace Stevens said. Therefore, this anti-platonic epistemology can, at best, only be part of how Camus' central inset works and what it works to do. For a sign is a sign, and a sign = a sign. This scene is itself a sign, not just the thing. Certainly, it is not a real thing, being a fiction; being made entirely of signs. And so, many more than the particular named characters of this book are gathered here—on purpose we must suppose—by the author. They are half-obliterated, but still recognizable. What happens here is an illustration of an equation in which we are all involved, as many others have been and will be. Camus begins: "That night, after dinner…a lengthy process… . At daybreak on the following day they gathered round…to observe the effects of this…on which so much hung" (*P* 191). Of the son of the magistrate Castel asks—"Any news of his father?" "'No,' said Rieux" (*P* 192). Try not to think that this process begins on a certain Thursday night, being carried over into Friday. "My God, My God, why have you abandoned me?" Especially when it comes to this: "the child lay flat…in a grotesque parody of crucifixion" (*P* 193).

Consider, as well, the disposition of the characters near daybreak: "Tarrou's bulky form was slightly drooping at the head of the bed, while at its foot, with Rieux standing beside him, Castel was seated, reading, with every appearance of calm, an old leather-bound book" (*P* 193). The others come in "as the light is increased" (*P* 192)—perhaps hardening on the upper part of the wall as in Jacques-Louis David's painting of *The Death of Socrates*; though there the other characters are leaving. Add, then, thousands of millions, channeled through "the small mouth, fouled with the sores of the plague and pouring out the angry death-cry that has sounded through the ages of mankind" (*P* 195). Rieux, who gave the child the test serum, is standing in the place of Socrates's poison-presenting gaoler in Camus' modern picture. Neither the gaoler nor he can stand what he is seeing. Thus, Camus' central, let us call it anti-Platonic, scene of the knowledge of individual suffering still presents us with an equation—or a set of equations, only partly obliterated. The child is still the particular child; he is also a sign of two other particulars—Christ and Socrates—and then of every human suffering. So, it is not just the child who is being presented here. Those two other particulars are at least half-visible. And the child's cry is something else—something which is apparently an age-old constant in the equations of human life. So, the child is *res et signum*. A sacrament then: in his being there are many participations; we see them; we hear them; many *are* them.

The actual structural center of Camus' book (Part III) is the shortest; it is one of darkness and presents he generalized working of the plague and preparations for universal death. Its main character is the plague—an abstraction?—which "had swallowed up everything and everyone" (*P* 151). We are deep in the cave, and the narrator picks this moment to show how all the prisoners are being operated upon: The narrator considers that "this moment, registering the climax of the summer heat and the disease, the best for describing, on general lines" (*P* 151) the development and final solutions of the plague's operations on the city and citizens. We are reminded again that "so as not to play false to the facts, and, still more, so as not to play false to himself, the narrator has aimed at objectivity. He has made hardly any changes for the sake of artistic effect" (*P* 163). As we are reminded of his original promise, so his description of town and townspeople is a starker outline of his first descriptions. If the original Oran was "a town without intimations" (*P* 4), this central section now focusses on what everyone must focus on, absent not only intimations, but also the pastimes and the commercial busyness which formerly abstracted them from the (absurd?) truth of their lives. "Treeless, glamourless, soulless, the town of Oran" encouraged a habitual rotation of activities which allowed one "to go complacently to sleep there" (*P* 4). Such a "completely modern" (*P* 4) arrangement, built as to "turn its back on the bay, with the result that it is impossible to see the sea" (*P* 5–6) is now seen as precisely like the plague, which, in the book's center has swallowed up everything and everyone. "No longer were there individual destinies; only a collective destiny, made of plague and the emotions shared by all" (*P* 151). At both times, "the town was peopled with sleepwalkers" (*P* 166). "Or, to put it differently, they looked like everybody else, nondescript" (*P* 166); each had become a faceless Everyman doing what every other is doing. Latterly, the ordinarily well-behaved citizens, who had been working "solely with the object of getting rich" (*P* 4) are seen in the plague's night light to be "changed to hunched misshapen gnomes by the flickering glow from the dying flames and the ornaments or furniture they carried on their shoulders" (*P* 155). And "only the mute effigies of great men, carapaced in bronze…conjured up a sorry semblance of what the man had been" (*P* 155).

Again, we get a half-erased picture from *Republic's* center. Half-way out of the cave, should we turn from the wall of shadows, we would see men carrying images or statues—of things, like furniture, or men or, perhaps, opinions that are important to them. We would see them and their carryings by the flickering fire of desire, which is what lights up everything in the ordinary unexamined cave-life. Camus shows us that these men have become one with what they carry, just as Cephalus had become one with his idea of justice as paying debts and telling the truth, and when, early on, that idea was reduced to nothing—or, in fact, its opposite: injustice—he disappeared from the discussion. Camus tells us that the now fading fires by which we see these misshapen men were once the homes of the plague stricken—the fires are set by the surviving family members themselves. What happens with all those riches the Oranais were chasing and hurrying to carry into their homes at the start? They burn up; some others carry some of it off, but is this carrying off a human life—or that of misshapen gnomes? If it is not a human life now, then was the previous carrying-in a human life? There is no difference. They were deformed gnomes before; now we are merely seeing that life more starkly for what it is. Does this desire for things naturally burn itself down? Or has it perhaps always been a burning out of every significance human life might have? Or do we now see in the plague's light that such activity is not ever a truly human life, but rather that of some peculiar gnome-like creature—half human, half pewter tea urn, or half human, half couch? Man + horse = centaur; man + modern furniture = gnome. Have human beings ever been anything else—as those noble figures carapaced in bronze on the dark streets suggest might have once been true? Was there something else one could have been?

In the thoroughly modern city of Oran, as in the city of Oran under plague, "sentiments can't be taken into account, and all [is] sacrificed to efficiency.... . Indeed, had not the epidemic...spread its ravages, all would have been for the best" (*P* 157–158). Human life is now abstracted into an efficiency equation: *there, that operates smoothly.* That is the equation of modernity; the plague has done this in Oran. Camus' doctor is here suggesting just this—if we were reduced to operating according to the most efficient equations everything would be for the best. It is unfortunate that it takes a plague or total war to get us to do this. His earlier argument with the other members of the medical society we now see functioned in line with this root equation. Then he had said that we must make the declaration of plague—whether accurate or not—or "half the population may be wiped out" (*P* 46). "It's not a question of the term I use; it's a question of time" (*P* 47). Neither truth nor the moral law are the question—or even necessary; efficiency is. Plague and war do make us look for such efficiencies; perhaps if we could get the government to arrange this efficiency without such motivation being forced upon them?—Is that not the organizational *arché* of the modern city? Efficiency. Human resources management. Of course, much that we take for granted would have to be sacrificed, as in war, to achieve such efficiencies, but after a while one would get used to it. One might come to the point of the camp manager, who beams at Tarrou's "very efficient" remark, responding, "'Yes, isn't it? We're great believers in efficiency in this camp'" (*P* 219). Dying would still be difficult—for the individual, though that is perhaps not the right word; "'discomfort' would come nearer" (*P* 5). But perhaps we can even make dying efficient—and so less uncomfortable? Then we would have a perfect world. Let us lay tracks to the crematorium (*P* 161).

Tarrou's father was the embodiment of the practices of social efficiency, not only in his work, but also in his leisure—studying, in his free hours before bed, the European railway directory. Following this avocation he got to know all the timetables and exchange stations, and he could solve any imaginary railroad problem the young Jean could set for him. Every science has its equations, knowledge of the ways in which all its variables are connected is perfection of the science, with such perfection at one's fingers ends one can dictate the most efficient solution to every problem science can solve. Those who attempt things not on the timetable fail to achieve their end, just as those who attempt things not within the laws of city fall to the prosecutor—his father's vocation. "The order of the world is shaped by death" (*P* 117, 226).

While the narrator ends this central section claiming that "our love persisted, but in practice it served nothing; it was an inert mass within us, sterile as a crime or a life sentence" (*P* 167) and then, "blind endurance... had ousted love from all our hearts" (*P* 168), his opening description of the way the townspeople loved had hardly been more promising, less sterile, or less a life sentence: "Men and women consume one another rapidly in what is called 'the act of love,' or else settle down to a mild habit of conjugality" (*P* 4). Oran's endurance is blind, Camus' essays suggest, because modern man, while eschewing intimations, will not recognize the absurd. Not recognizing the absurd, it is also impossible to even begin to love. That is true of Oran, plague-stricken or not; that is to say, it is true of the modern city. In *The Fall*, our Judge-penitent puts it this way: modern man fornicates and reads the newspapers.[3] There are neither intimations nor recognition, and certainly not love. Rather, practiced avoidance of self-examination in accord with the encultured habits: these days he would have to reduce us to pornography and social media (the pornography of social media?), the

3   Albert Camus, *The Fall* (6–7).

previous person to person pastimes of Camus' day having been virtualized. Such willing blindness may become much more difficult to carry off in the time of physical plague, though perhaps not quite so much so in a more virtual world. Or is it? Visibly imminent universal death deepens the darkness of modernity perhaps, but the town is still as spiritually empty as before. The narrator says of the parted lovers (such as Rieux and Rambert) that "they were wasting away emotionally" (*P* 163) and "had lost the power of imagining the intimacy that once was theirs or understanding what it can be to live with someone whose life is wrapped up in yours" (*P* 164)— but had anyone really had that before? In the town of rapid consumption or mild conjugality nothing really has changed; that death is ever present and universal is part of the equation of being human; in plague and war that fact merely becomes more visible, and this may allow the human heart to wish for something more than the daily round it had sentenced itself to, or blindly accepted. "The plague bacillus never dies or disappears for good" (*P* 278). So then, the difference between the opening description of Oran and this starker, later picture in the middle of the book is that now all know where the last stop on the tram line is, and "the faint, sickly odor coming from the east remind[ed] them that they were living under a new order" (*P* 162)—not only no intimations, but no business, no pastimes of gambling or sea-bathing, and no place to go except in circles until taking the tram to its newest terminus: the crematoria. Still, even with their neighbors' houses burning, the gnomes are busy carrying things off. And the newspapers continue to be read, producing all kinds of content from competing experts, including Nostradamus and St. Odilia, whose popularity was waxing. So, not a new order; same order, different variables.

We invent ways to avoid facing such questions as "what should I live for?" by engaging in things that are not able to be the answer. Thus we find recent reports like this:

> The prominent astrologer Susan Miller placed responsibility for the coronavirus on a distant dwarf planet in March after her earlier, pre-pandemic prediction of a "great" 2020 seemed to miss the mark. There were some taunts. But the fact that astrologers did not see the virus coming hasn't made their practice any less popular. In fact, horoscope sites have reported rising

traffic as people look to the stars to give shape to a formless quarantine life.[4]

Thus we turn ourselves into effects, into elements of a chronicle. "These exiles of the plague" (*P* 166) are "home;" they are in the city of their own making, but they will not believe it, they believe it has come upon them "from a blue sky" (*P* 34) and would go away on its own. They consider their individuality taken from them by this external enemy: the plague. But it is not so; the doctor's description of them in this state of plague echoes his first description of the city: "It will be said, no doubt, that these habits are not peculiar to our town; really all our contemporaries are much the same. Certainly nothing is commoner nowadays than to see people working from morn till night and then proceeding to fritter away at card tables, in cafés and in small talk what time is left for living" (*P* 4). The doctor now only lacks the comparison to other contemporaries in other towns; he can no longer see over the wall of the plague in order to discover whether his town is like any others. We must be those eyes. Is Oran now different from our town? "They looked like everybody else, nondescript. They shared in the torpor of the town and in its puerile agitations" (*P* 166). "They had ceased to choose for themselves" (*P* 167). But really to choose for themselves they must first recognize their situation: the world as it is and human desire as it is are at odds; this fact is in their faces now, but they behave exactly as they did before it came to that point—which only means it wasn't so force-fully in their faces. This fact of contradiction between desire and the world, which the younger Camus called "the absurd" seems always to have been true, and the response of the Oranais is always available: don't look; if you do look, look for external causes—the stars, a fated prophecy, a conspiracy. Some in Camus' day said that the plague that takes away freedom and in-dividuality is the Jew; some Romans, in Augustine's time, blamed the de-struction of their city and happiness on the Christians; the names change, the equation which produces the absurd is always true; we invent solutions, some more final than others, but the equation remains, and false answers abound. Sometimes the contradiction is easier to hide from ourselves; at

---

4   See https://www.nytimes.com/2020/05/09/style/coronavirus-astrology-pre-dictions.html.

all times it takes a kind of courage to examine it rather than blame an external source. "Our townsfolk...forgot to be modest, that [is] all, and thought that everything was still possible for them, which presupposed that pestilences were impossible" (*P* 35). But neither plagues nor wars are impossible; far from it: pestilence is merely one element in the equation of human life; it is never really reduced to zero, there are merely situations in which it is easier not to notice. Neither collective action nor individual heroism can erase this fact. So, Camus is correct to consider that the root of all courage is to recognize the absurd—it is the first step of lucidity. But that requires a certain humility, though neither the modern city nor the modern human being is built upon humility. As for the doctor's dream that "[i]t was only a matter of lucidly recognizing what had to be recognized; of dispelling extraneous shadows and doing what needed to be done. Then the plague would come to an end, because it was unthinkable, or, rather, because one thought of it on misleading lines" (*P* 38), that is merely a confession of a lack of humility. That is indeed the modern doctor's dream; but it is no less a dream for being modern and a doctor's. It is a symptom of the madness which forgets to be modest. Or, echoing a more ancient case, we might call it the confession of Pelagius. Only the modern world goes farther: Pelagius taught it was possible for human beings to achieve moral perfection without grace—on our own power; the doctor here is dreaming the dream of the perfect scientist as well: if we discover the correct equations we can change nature, erase plague, deliver ourselves from all evil. That would be our kingdom.

As is the case with Plato's great book, so too, with Camus': when we come to the detailed middle inset we see that what is described there has been operating throughout the whole, and is a picture of our life: "they are like us." There are, once we are made aware of this sort of operation, numerous half-erased equations in many scenes of *The Plague*; or perhaps we should call them palimpsests. Before examining them in more detail, however, we should call up something more of the unreliability of the narrator, in order to exhibit the necessity of carrying a few grains of salt so that we may be sure of the flavor of his "objectivity."

The best picture of the doctor/narrator's untrustworthiness occurs in this (off-centered) central chaplet. It is the scene we examined in the previous chapter, immediately after the child's death. Rieux rushes past

Paneloux and out to the school playground. As Paneloux tries to check him, he swings around fiercely: "Ah! That child, anyhow, was innocent, and you know it is well as I do!" He then confesses to a feeling of "mad revolt," and a refusal "to love a scheme of things in which children are put to torture." He calms down somewhat and admits

> "We're working side by side for something that unites us—
> beyond blasphemy and prayers. And it's the only thing that mat-
> ters."
> Paneloux sat down beside Rieux. It was obvious that he was
> deeply moved.
> "Yes, yes," he said, "you, too, are working for man's salva-
> tion."
> "Salvation's much too big a word for me. I don't aim so
> high. I'm concerned with man's health; and for me his health
> comes first."
> … Paneloux held out his hand, saying regretfully:
> "And yet—I haven't convinced you!"
> "What does it matter? What I hate is death and disease, as
> you well know. And whether you wish it or not, we're allies, fac-
> ing them and fighting them together." Rieux was still holding
> Paneloux's hand. "So you see"—but he refrained from meeting
> the priest's eyes—"God himself can't part us now" (196–7).

The doctor's picture of what is going on is quite clear: both he and the priest are working together for man's health, which Rieux considers an end beyond blasphemy and prayers, and yet not as high as Paneloux's aimed for end—salvation. This is already a curious combination of descriptions, for it would seem that any good beyond blasphemy and prayer would have to be not an early first-achieved or necessary good on the way to others, such as health is classically conceived—a means for the achievement and enjoyment of other goods which are more final, but something very high indeed. "First" would have to mean—for Rieux—of the first rank, superior to all others, indeed the highest—if it is "beyond blasphemy and prayers." Perhaps our modern doctor thinks that health is precisely that kind of good; even in Aristotle's time there were people who would say such things (*NE*

1025 a20–30, 1099a26–27), though Aristotle's argument proves that health cannot possibly be the highest good, or in the highest rank, but only, at best, a part or aspect of the highest: a thing good in itself, but also good as a means, so of the second rank. Perhaps there are other modern folk who would agree with the doctor's implication against Aristotle: all else is to be sacrificed on the altar of health. The highest god is Asclepius. Perhaps this is what the doctor thinks when he says, "health comes first," for if it were merely first in an ordered series of those goods which either lead to or together make up the highest good of happiness, it would clearly be a kind of (at best) intermediate good (both means and end), rather than the highest—which is never used as a means to something else. But one wonders if even the highest good—whatever it turns out to be—could be rightly described as "beyond blasphemy and prayers"; such a good would presumably be the prime object of both blasphemy and prayer. The doctor, here, seems to have taken rhetorical flight into a region of incoherences where reason's wings can find no purchase.

And the conclusion of this scene seconds this interpretation. Despite the fact that the priest clearly states his end—salvation—as the doctor has stated his own—health—Rieux concludes with one truth and one perfect falsity, which makes even his truth but half true, at best. He and the priest *are* allies—and have been, working together against death and disease; but that is all the doctor thinks of, while for Paneloux that fight is just for a "first" good—a good to be achieved so that other higher goods may be sought and found, and a good which may not even be necessary for finding that highest good. And highest of all is salvation; one may lose one's health and gain one's salvation; so health may not even be a means to it, or part of it. The doctor is shaking the hand of his "ally," the priest, but he does not look him in the eyes: he is not telling the truth, and he knows he isn't. For, as we noted earlier, even as the doctor says He can't, God has already separated them. For Fr. Paneloux the corporal works of mercy are already an achievement of the good for both the patient and the worker; their further success—for example, in the achievement of health—is not determinative of their goodness: the work is a good for its own sake. What Kant said of the act of a good will is true of Paneloux's work: "The good will is not good because of what it effects or accomplishes…and even if the greatest effort should not avail it to achieve anything of its end…it would sparkle like a jewel all by itself" (*FMM* 394). As Aristotle said too, virtue and happiness are in the activities, not the results of activity. The value of that health for which Rieux and Paneloux are allies is completely different for these two men; they live, as it were in different worlds, even when they share the same classroom, playground, and work. They are like us. It is not only God who has already, and definitively, separated them. Something in the doctor knows this, so he does not look at the priest. Which of them is telling the truth?

Rieux's non-look certainly intimates something, even something that he knows. He is in the process of erasing something, or perhaps I should put it in the more comfortable passive: something is half erased, yet still not entirely beyond his awareness. We will also see that just before Paneloux's second sermon, immediately following this scene, the narrator notes that most people "had replaced normal religious practice by more or less extravagant superstitions" (*P* 199), a remark which seems to confess that religion is something other than an empty superstition, that there might be a correct and an incorrect way of relating to the divine. It is a strange thing for an empirical chronicler to suggest. Having noticed such difficulties with truth as these, we may now continue with our narrator's descriptions; these descriptions we should expect will be palimpsests—there will be things we may partially see which the doctor does not, even while describing everything objectively.

Before Paneloux's first sermon we are told that "the ecclesiastical authorities in our town resolved to do battle against the plague with the weapons appropriate to them, and organized a week of Prayer" (*P* 84f). If the central scene gives us any insight here, we may understand the narrator-doctor as presuming that the Church is fighting precisely the same enemy as the doctor. But this is clearly not the evil Fr. Paneloux recognizes in his sermon or is most concerned to defeat, and it is not news to him that there has been a plague of a less obviously physical sort around for some time. He is well known in the town for having given "a series of lectures on present-day individualism" to the wider non-specialist public; and there are undoubtedly other sources of "modern laxity" (*P* 84) which a scholar of St. Augustine, such as himself, could point out. One would not need to be much of a scholar of Augustine, nor have read much more than his *Confessions*, to know he would consider the "curious frame of mind, as remote from indifference as from fervor" of our fellow citizens (*P* 84f), as inappropriate for consideration of religion and the prime truths of life. And it is precisely this indifference and "objectivity," this attitude that "Anyhow, it can't do any harm" (*P* 86), that Paneloux's first sermon attacks. The description of the day of the sermon presents a palimpsest of what this modern town's spiritual status is—barely ante-diluvian: For the few days before it we hear of "the swelling tide of…whose backwash filled the neighboring streets…and on the Sunday of the sermon a huge congregation filled the nave,[5] overflowing on to the steps and precincts. The sky had clouded up… and now it was raining heavily." In the middle of the sermon the downpour increases in violence, and the whole congregation slips "forward from their seats on to their knees" (*P* 86–87). The plague is like the flood, a deserved calamity, but "not willed by God" (*P* 87), rather one that is "ineluctable as the order of the scheme of things"—a scheme which Augustine summarizes as "every disordered mind should be its own punishment" (*Conf* 1.12.19): If one does not fervently seek the highest good (which good justly deserves to be fervently sought), one must be seeking (more or less fervently) lesser goods—each his own (as modern individualism would have it). It is both just and an immediate punishment that the highest goods are not seen as highest (if seen at all) by such a one, and so he does not achieve them— unless the highest can be achieved by accident. Moreover, lack of knowledge or acknowledgement of the highest good vitiates, at the root of principle, the ranking of all other goods. So, such a town is already in moral chaos; physical chaos generally takes longer to develop—or be seen. The moral result is immediate, if invisible. Similarly, we did not need to see the priest and doctor go their separate ways after shaking hands; they were already divided, even when hand in hand. The evil which the townspeople are in the midst of, then, is an both an effect and a call: "the hour has struck to bend your thoughts to first and last things" (*P* 89); but that hour is every hour, for in every hour whatever good we are seeking should be oriented appropriately to those first and last things; without such an orientation, all

5   For readers who, like Grand, have forgotten their Latin, the main body of the church is so called from the Latin word *navis*—ship, because its roof's shape mimics an ancient boat, turned upside down; the church is the ship within which sinners are saved from destruction.

the goods of the world revolt against us, they are not healthful, but are a cause of increasing sickness. Camus would have read this famous prayer while preparing his licentiate:

> Too late have I loved you, O Beauty so ancient and so new, too late have I loved you! Behold you were within me, while I was outside: it was there that I sought you, and, a deformed creature, rushed headlong upon those things of beauty which you have made.... They kept me far from you, those fair things which, if they were not in you, would not exist at all (*Conf* 10.27.38).

"A wet wind was sweeping up the nave, making the candle flames bend and flicker" (*P* 90). Is the spirit of Pentecost sweeping into the church during the priest's sermon, as if called in by his passionate words? Or is this wet wind an anti-spirit, a black pentecost? Is Pan/e/loux bread and light or an ironic juxtaposition of syllables? When is the hour to bend our thoughts to first and last things? And what if we never do? "Anyway, it can't do any harm" to consider such questions. Or could it overthrow the whole of modern individualism and its so-called life?

> It is hard to say if this sermon had any effect on our townsfolk. ...M. Othon, the magistrate, assured Dr. Rieux that he had found the preacher's arguments "absolutely irrefutable."
> ...It is noteworthy—this may or may not have been due to mere coincidence—that this Sunday of the sermon marked the beginning of something like a widespread panic in the town, and it took so deep a hold as to lead one to suspect that only now had the true nature of their situation dawned on our townspeople (*P* 92).

Our narrator's juxtaposition of Paneloux's sermon and this immediate reaction in the town might imply a certain condemnation on his part—if he were composing artistically. Perhaps the implication is that widespread panic comes about through the priest's creating delusional religious shadows—that is, not aiding in achieving lucidity, but actively working against it. On the other hand, it is a fearful thing to be caught in the hand of the living God (so someone once said). But is that, objectively speaking, ever our real situation—or perhaps always? And suddenly to be made aware of this, even when not merely whiling away a few hours at a "social" or a club "where large sums change hands on the fall of a card" (*P* 4) could induce that panic. "Will you not look away, nor let me alone to swallow my spit?" (*Job* 7:19). The chronicle does not tell us why "something like widespread panic" followed the sermon, merely that it did. These would seem to be at least two of the possible explanations—the town has realized the true nature of their situation: empirically, plague; spiritually, sinners in the hands of an angry God. The chronicle merely sets forth what happened, it cannot attempt a "why" without stepping beyond the visible empirical facts: Sermon, then panic.

Paneloux's second sermon also presents some scenic palimpsests. Our narrator seems to have become somewhat more lucid than we found him after the death of the child. He points out all of the modern city's choices regarding religion—but what am I saying, there is nothing particularly modern about these choices; they are always the same, a sort of constant in human societies: "most people, assuming they had not altogether abandoned religious observances, or did not combine them with a thoroughly immoral way of living, had replaced normal religious practice by more or less extravagant superstitions" (*P* 199). Rieux clearly understands there is difference between religious practice as an end in itself—a final good, if not *the* final good of life—and the superstitious theurgy which treats God as a means to other goods. Perhaps most people never consider this difference, or are brought up in a gospel of prosperity (not so believable among those who grew up in the middle of a World War) and so have hedges against a more Augustinian understanding of religion; at any rate, "superstition had usurped the place of religion in the life of our town" (200). In this sermon, too, there are echoes of Pentecost: "the wind was pouring in great gusts through the swing doors and filling the aisles with sudden drafts" (*P* 200). No holy spirit is inspiring these people, however. When Paneloux says that

> all trials, however cruel work together for the good to the Christian. And, indeed, what a Christian should always seek in his hour of trial was to discern that good…the people near Rieux

seemed to settle in against the arm-rests of their pews and make themselves as comfortable as they could. One of the big padded doors was softly thudding in the wind, and someone got up to secure it. As a result, Rieux's attention wandered (*P* 201).

The only movement in the cathedral of Oran is to become as comfortable as possible on those hard wooden seats—each to his own arm-rest, and among other things that comfort requires locking the doors against the ... wind. As a result, the doctor's attention wanders. Augustine's *Confessions* shows his own attention wandering quite wildly and for quite some time while he has the wrong idea (if any) of God, so long as he does not allow the spirit of God's love to "set fire to our heavy torpor and burn it away, so that we would not turn toward lower things" (*Conf.* 9.2.3)…that is, so long as he attempts to "stand on [him]self, and thus not stand at all" (*Conf.* 8.11.27).

By the time Paneloux gets to the "all or nothing" challenge of his sermon, "the whistling of the wind outside…had risen to storm pitch" (*P* 203) and he goes on to mention several other cases of plague in history, after which he concludes that "the real problem had been shirked; they had closed their ears to God's voice" (*P* 204), just as someone had closed the doors. Or perhaps, too many other voices distract us, by all their many words we enter "more deeply into the stormy society of human life" (*Conf* 1.8.13); they blow their "smoke and wind" (*Conf* 1.17.27), and we blow our own (*Conf* 2.9.17) and follow it into the "land of want" (2.10.18). Is that what the wind represents; is that what is locked out—so that we may concentrate? But Rieux's attention wanders. Long after we might come to see the emptiness of such smoke and wind, they "pluck at our fleshly garment, and they whisper softly: 'Do you cast us off?'" (*Conf* 8.11.26, cf. 10.30.41–10.39.64). Augustine prays that all these things, and indeed "all things" might "become silent, for they have raised up his ear to him who made them, and God alone speaks…so that we hear his Word" (*Conf* 9.10.25). The doctor confesses distraction—curiously he even recognizes it as wandering attention. And so he misses the point, doesn't quite get it clear. How is such recognition of inattention possible? Perhaps he is merely talking "objectively" about his attention span. But what is attention, Augustine asks in Book X, and what is its span? Is there something which it may grasp, and which grasps it, which is outside the stormy world of its—

and everyone else's—wants and words, smoke and wind? Or should we shut that idea out? Someone got up to shut the door; the spirit of God—if that is what the wind is—is left outside, we are left locked in upon our human comforts, and lose the point of the words. Language itself becomes mere wind; and the plague becomes pneumonic.

When the Mass ends, "a violent gust swept up the nave through the half-open doors and buffeted the faces of the departing congregation. It brought with it a smell of rain.... [An] old priest and a young deacon who were walking immediately in front of Rieux had much difficulty in keeping their headdress from blowing away" (*P* 206). Perhaps even the churchmen have become too comfortable with their place in an earthly order—they cover their heads and try to keep them covered, a symbolism which would be inappropriate for them, as Augustine explains in a once well-thought of discussion in *De Trinitate* XII. There, as he elucidates the significance of the apostolic order that women ought to keep their heads covered in church, while men should not, he proposes that since the human being was created male and female, the two together symbolize what is a whole human being (*DT* 12.7). One part, symbolized by the woman in Paul's letter, signifies that power of the soul Augustine calls knowledge, which sees the eternal reasons which operate in things and is that power by which the human being operates in the world (*DT* 12.2); this would be Aristotle's *scientia*—science (and effectively our understanding of science as well: knowledge of the equations concerning how things work in the world). This part is rightly under (so, covered by) wisdom, Aristotle's *sophia*—the higher power, which is uncovered to the divine light when it operates correctly: this is that power which sees our end in God and so can order all other knowledge and action aright: which equations should be answered here and now. The first is the necessary helpmeet in the world for the second (*DT* 12.3); a finite embodied spirit requires both, but they must be properly oriented to each other and to the divine. That the narrator notices the difference in distinction between an old priest and a young deacon among the departing laity may be significant. The wind, which is blowing both their particular headdress off, then, is rightly seen as the Spirit, whose gift is wisdom, demanding its due: beyond the popular orientation to degrees of honor with which we cover ourselves, and beyond comfort and working upon the physical world to keep it running smoothly. There is something else the human being must be attentive to—at all times, not only in church. This wisdom the world wants no part of; each "protects his face from the wind" (206).

Tarrou seems to see correctly through these figures. Not that he agrees with Paneloux, but he sees him truly; at least he sees more truly than Rieux. Paneloux believes that there were two human beings who perfectly instantiated the wisdom human beings were meant to have; they ordered their knowledge and work in the world in accord with a wisdom completely open to the divine, to which they said, at every moment, *fiat voluntas tua*—even to torture and crucifixion. Tarrou puts it this way:

> "Paneloux is right.... When an innocent youth can have his eyes destroyed, a Christian should either lose his faith or consent to having his eyes destroyed. Paneloux declines to lose his faith, and he will go through with it to the end. That's what he meant to say."
>
> It may be that this remark of Tarrou's throws some light on the regrettable events which followed, in the course of which the priest's conduct seemed inexplicable to his friends. The reader will judge for himself (*P* 207).

What we are meant to judge for ourselves in the events that follow—Fr. Paneloux's death—must not only be whether he is operating precisely in accord with his faith, but also whether that faith, with its half-erased explication by Augustine, is the proper way for a human being to be. Let who has eyes to see with see. We have already discussed this death in detail above (chapter three).

These palimpsests of Pentecost beneath the scenes of the priest's sermons are "objective" revelations. The doctor merely describes what happens—are they revelations? Are they signs, or merely things that happen? This open question seems in accord with the way of approaching the world that Camus presented in some statements made at the Dominican Monastery of Latour-Maubourg in 1948: "I shall never start from the supposition that Christian truth is illusory, but merely from the fact that I could not accept it" (*RRD* 69f). Tarrou's response to the second sermon certainly exhibits this sort of understanding without acceptance. But the narrator's unremarked-upon palimpsests show also that the Christian view of the world is not objectively illusory—it is possible for any reader to see that Christian understanding working in the world Camus has set before us through a narrator who is merely reciting the facts. The facts do not extend so far as the Christian understanding; reading them can. Let him who has eyes to see with, see.

And Paneloux himself, including the death which follows his sermon, lives up to what the unbeliever can rightly demand of the Christian, besides those "duties it is essential to ask of any man today" (*RRD* 69). Namely, "that Christians should speak out, loud and clear, and that they should voice their condemnation [of the evils of the day] in such a way that never a doubt, never the slightest doubt, could arise in the heart of the simplest man" (*RRD* 71). The narrator's description of Paneloux, before his first sermon, as not only a highly respected scholar, but as a man who could speak to the non-specialist public in a way which championed "Christian doctrine at its most precise and purest, equally remote from modern laxity and the obscurantism of the past," such that he trounces "his hearers with some vigorous home truths" (*P* 84) is the perfect mimesis of such a Christian. This sort of mimesis of Christian teaching Camus encountered personally, and battled against, personally, immediately after the liberation. He admits to his Dominican audience on this somewhat later occasion "that for the fundamentals and on the precise point of our controversy François Mauriac got the better of me" (*RRD* 70). It is not because of Mauriac's scholarship that Camus admits this; rather, Camus sees Mauriac had the morally superior position.

The debate he refers to here took place in the newspapers of late 1944 and early 1945 concerning figures who had collaborated with the Nazis. Arguing against the well-known, older Catholic author, Camus had written strong condemnations of moderation being a virtue, and was dismissive of Mauriac's calls for mercy rather than the death penalty. Like the younger Tarrou, Camus had argued that without a belief in divine justice, man's only hope was in the human version of justice with all its imperfections.[6]

6   See the fine discussion of this debate, its relation to Camus' early life and work, and its historical likenesses in French history in Chapter Two of Robert D. Zaretsky, *Albert Camus: Elements of Life* (Ithaca: Cornell University Press, 2010), particularly, 65–74.

Tarrou, during his time as a communist it seems, had justified his group's activity in the usual way: "These few deaths were inevitable for the building up of a new world in which murder would cease to be" (*P* 226). Like Tarrou, Camus soon changed his mind, being reminded on his own watch of "the same dazed horror that [he had] experienced as a youngster" (*P* 226) at the execution of a criminal. Thus, these aspects of Tarrou's life story, and his reaction to Paneloux's sermon, are written over a still readable fragment of Camus' own life. Reality is frequently a palimpsest of itself.

Perhaps the most peculiar figure among the novel's characters is Rieux's old asthma patient. He is introduced on the same day—the feast of St. Bernadette—that we meet Dr. Rieux. He sits in bed with "two pots of dried peas" (*P* 9). Little by little we discover "his usual occupation, counting out dried peas from one pan to another" (*P* 56). Tarrou, who meets him on one of the doctor's regular visits, finds him quite interesting; so much so that he goes alone to visit him the next day. He had taken to his bed at 50, and was now 75; according to his own account, he "worked out the time—that is to say, the time for meals—with his two saucepans...[which he filled] pea by pea, at a constant, carefully regulated speed.... Time for him was reckoned by these pans, and he could take his bearings in it at any moment of the day" (*P* 108). He is a figure of Augustine's famous investigation of time in Book XI of *Confessions*; the moving hand of the present takes one moment from the pan of the future to that of the past; in Camus' novel the present is the size of a dried pea, for Augustine, it was an infinitesimal, which "has no space" (*Conf* 11.15.20). Augustine had denied that "the movements of the sun, moon and stars constitute time" asking whether, if they all went dark, "while a potter's wheel was kept moving, would there be no time?" (*Conf* 11.23.29). In the course of the plague, time seems to various characters to stop, drip, drag, and then move altogether too quickly to be believed; there were times when "time had never moved quickly enough...and they were always wanting to speed its flight...[and times when] they would have liked to slow it down and hold each moment in suspense" (*P* 265), but the old asthma patient performs the objective and simple truth Augustine saw: each moment of time is as like every other as one dried pea to another: plague or no plague. The question is, as Augustine reminds us, what do we do with each moment's attention? Can the moments be filled, or are they all merely dried peas? And is not a certain verticality of spirit necessary even to be able to be aware of this passing of time? The asthma patient is outside both bowls. Otherwise, one could not step into the river knowing it to be *the same* river and so even ask if one can step into it twice. There would only be one, one, one… . "Something in my memory…remains fixed…[therefore] it is in you, O my mind, that I measure my times" (*Conf* 10.27.35–36). But how can a changing mind remain fixed? How can it notice passing moments? What is the condition for this possibility? It can only be something that transfixes this changing, and frequently forgetting, human mind: "You are that abiding light which I consulted concerning all these things, as to whether they were, as to what they were, and as to what value they possessed" (*Conf* 10.40.65). Paneloux has been transfixed by this light and orders all things accordingly. Each moment is precious to him who attends correctly. To the asthma patient, as to the chronicler, they are as dried peas.

During the plague, "one had the impression that all cars were moving in circles" (*P* 70). Before the plague, the citizens had all run in the same circles of habit: work, work, work, work, work, weekend of rapid consumption or sea-bathing, "bowling, banquets and 'socials,' at clubs where large sums of money change hands on the fall of a card" (*P* 4); repeat, repeat… . From among all the townspeople Tarrou picks this asthma patient to be "a saint… if saintliness is an aggregate of habits" (*P* 109). His habits measure up to sanctity, unlike those of other citizens, because he "infects hardly anyone… [He] has the fewest lapses of attention" (*P* 229); he makes no one his victim (though we may wonder what his wife thinks about that), he depends least upon the social order continuing to keep its edges, he dares nothing in the natural order. But Tarrou is clear that being a saint is "less ambitious" than the doctor who says that "heroism and sanctity don't really appeal to me… . What interests me is being a man" (*P* 231). Tarrou is in earnest—his sort of saint will be less than a man. To be uninfectious one may not participate at all in the social order, for the social order is shaped by death (*P* 226); the asthma patient is as close to such as is possible (but, again, we must neglect his wife). "Even with the best of intentions, even at many removes…we can't stir a finger in this world without the risk of bringing death to somebody" (*P* 228). One, one, one…

At the end of one day, the doctor and Tarrrou make their regular visit to him. "They heard footsteps overhead," and the asthma patient invites them "why not go up and have a look?...They found nobody on the terrace—only three empty chairs... . 'A pleasant spot,' said Rieux... . 'You would think that plague had never found its way up here.' ...'Yes,' [Tarrou replied]...it's good to be here... . Three times the glow spread up the sky" (*P* 220f). They seem to have entered a purer realm, above the ceiling plague has put upon the town, beyond what has become natural in Oran.

The transfiguration is frequently described as a proleptic resurrection scene; after it, Jesus tells Peter, James and John not to speak of what they have seen until after the son of man has risen from the dead; they are puzzled as to what this means. But when these two modern disciples (Jean and Bernard) climb up they find no one is there; the three empty chairs take the place of the three tents Peter wished to set up for Jesus, Moses and Elijah, though there is still a brightness that goes up three times. It is still "good...to be here" (Mk 9:4), though nothing miraculous happens. Tarrou wishes to take this hour off "for friendship," but "all that could be seen of him was a dark, bulky form outlined against the glimmering sky" (*P* 222). And this particular modern version of the transfiguration makes the point that there will be no other place or time granted in the future. Such verticality and freedom as these two seem to be granted here is merely the effect of a temporary inattention to the very facts that Tarrou confesses in their conversation: "we all have plague, and I have lost my peace" (*P* 228). There is no peace as this world gives it—except in inattention, an inattention which the modern town practices and encourages, under every circumstance. If it is true that "the good man, the man who infects hardly anyone, is the man who has the fewest lapses of attention" (*P* 229), then this hour off for friendship seems a mutual encouragement of vice. They are acting as if they can be free when "no one on earth is free from it...and nothing remains to set us free except death" (*P* 229). Early in his *Confessions* Augustine recognizes the "flawed and shadowy beauty found" in such inattentions to the greater scheme of goods for the sake of one more particularly desired at the moment as a "deformed liberty...bearing a shadowy likeness of your omnipotence" (2.6.12, 2.6.14). He confesses that without others to go along with such thoughts and actions, without the "rubbing together of guilty minds" (2.8.16), he would never have done it. Perhaps there is a very old reason why this modern scene of transfiguration lacks all transfiguration of any human being—we are all but dark, bulky forms. If one needs others to affirm, to go along with, to recognize as true one's own belief in the absence of transfiguration and what it proleptically figures, then these two modern souls, sitting on the dark roof of the world have lots of company. But who are they really—these bulky darknesses? They are certainly, between them, the incarnation of the spirit of our time. Is this empty transfiguration what must come of their climb together? The light went up three times, and the darkness grasped it not. Suppose it is true that one cannot receive what one does not wish for; one does not deserve a good which one does not wholeheartedly desire. Then what will be the case for these modern men?

Tarrou speaks of there being pestilences and victims, but since "each of us has the plague within him" (*P* 229) we are all both. He wishes, as "a carrier of the plague germ...to be an innocent murderer" (*P* 230). I wonder how this can work. Could someone who knows he has an infectious disease be an innocent murderer? Earlier he had said that the idea of one's own innocence is the equivalent of "no idea at all" (*P* 222), so we must wonder how he can be thinking these ideas come together coherently. Is there any way "to get the plague out of [one's system]" or is it that "nothing remains to set us free except death" (*P* 229)? What could it mean to suggest "a third category: that of the true healers" (*P* 230)? If the world is made up of victims and murderers (and we are all both), who could these true healers be? What would such a being look like? The plague is natural, and no one is free of it. Tarrou admits "it's a fact one doesn't come across many of them, and anyhow it must be a hard vocation" (*P* 230). Wouldn't such a healer first have to heal himself, in order not to carry the infection further? In order not to be a murderer. But if this were so, if he did not himself carry the plague, is it not the case that the true healer is pure victim? Does he become this in dying of the plague?

As they are ending their discussion on this what we might call dreams of a third category, near the end of this (non) transfiguration and just before they go for their swim, the narrator notes that "the dispersed shouts they had been hearing off and on drew together on the outskirts of the town, near the stony hill, and presently there was a sound like a gunshot. Then silence fell again" (*P* 230). The dispersed shouts of their limited world gather around a stony hill.... As they are descending the hill of transfiguration Jesus tells Peter, James and John of his coming crucifixion and death, and warns them not to speak of what they have witnessed until after his resurrection from the dead. Is that what is needed? Death to free us, and then, a new life? "The breeze freshened and a gust coming from the sea filled the air for a moment with the smell of brine" (*P* 230).

On January 25, known to Christians as the Feast of the Conversion of St. Paul, "the weekly total showed so striking a decline that…the authorities announced that the epidemic could be regarded as definitely stemmed… [that night] was the occasion of much festivity" (*P* 245). The townspeople spend the night parading and singing in the streets; one might wonder if any of these gentiles have been converted from their previous lives, or are merely released back to something more usual and more perfectly suiting their desires. Some weeks later, after the town is opened, Rieux visits his old asthma patient, who knows one pea is most like another, and he is most realistic: "They're just the same as ever really." And when the doctor affirms the news that some sort of monument will be put up, he responds, "'I could have sworn it! And there'll be speeches.' He chuckled throatily. 'I can almost hear them saying: *our dear departed*… And then they'll go off and have a good snack'" (*P* 277). The horseman of pestilence would appear to have knocked no one off of his usual horse. Rieux calls this "their strength and innocence" (*P* 278). I think we may be permitted to wonder about our narrator's judgment; Tarrou, at least, considered that the thought of one's innocence was the equivalent of no idea at all.

Between the official announcement and the opening of the town there is a third death to which we are brought, and which we are assigned to watch closely: that of Jean Tarrou. When he is taken sick, Rieux's mother begs her son to keep him with them (he had earlier come to live in their house), and, despite the danger, let her stay too. Tarrou knows the ordeal he is facing, and says "I don't want to die, and I shall put up a fight. But if I lose the match, I want to make a good end of it." Rieux responds, "No, to become a saint, you need to live. So fight away!" (*P* 255). If death is, by his own admission, what will finally free Tarrou of the plague, is Rieux's response true? Tarrou seems to think he can lose the match and yet still make a good end. What is the good he may accomplish in dying? There is a palimpsest, if not an answer, which seems readable through Rieux's chronicle. "Tarrou showed symptoms of both varieties of plague at once" (*P* 256), as if all the evils of the world had settled in his body. "Rieux knew that his

grim wrestling with the angel of plague was to last until dawn. In this struggle Tarrou's robust shoulders and chest were not his greatest assets; rather,
the blood...and in this blood, that something more vital than the soul,
which no human skill can bring to light" (*P* 256). Tarrou wished to be a
saint without God; could one be the Christ without being God? Christ's
blood would have something more vital than soul; Tarrou's blood, events
will show, does not have that.

Unlike the death of the child, where we saw Rieux take the child's
"pulse—less because this served any purpose than as an escape from his
utter helplessness," and, for a moment their heartbeats linked, but then
"the child escaped him, and again he knew his impotence...and moved
back to his place" (*P* 194), the doctor now seems to know his place from
the start: that his "task could be only to watch his friend's struggle" (*P* 256),
to be a witness, as they all were to the death of the child. It is only in *l'é-
vangile de Jean*, that there are any witnesses close to the scene of suffering—
the disciple whom he loved and some women, including the mother; this
Gospel's suffering both Othon's son's and now Jean Tarrou's suffering and
death echo. Rieux tries to send his mother away, but "she shook her head,
and her eyes grew brighter; then she examined carefully, at her needle tips,
a stitch of which she was unsure. Rieux got up, gave the sick man a drink,
and sat down again" (*P* 257). Throughout the process Madame Rieux
spends long hours

> sitting close beside the bed, her hands folded on her lap.... Tar-
> rou was gazing at her so intently that, putting a finger to her
> lips, Mme Rieux rose and switched off the bedside lamp....
> Bending above the bed, she smoothed out the bolster and, as
> she straightened up, laid her hand for a moment on his moist,
> tangled hair. Then she heard a muffled voice, which seemed to
> come from very far away, murmur: "Thank you," and that all
> was well now (*P* 259f).

There is a way of understanding that all things are well in St John's gospel's
scene of the pieta, but what can it mean for Tarrou? I think it must be that
Tarrou feels Madame Rieux's love accompanying him even into death; can
human friendship go so far? He had commented "on Mme Rieux's

self-effacement," though the "gentle glow" of her light could be discerned "in all she said and did." She has "the gift ...of knowing everything without (apparently) taking thought." She reminds him of his own mother, "and it's she I've always wanted to get back to" (*P* 248).

Rieux, who tells this story, seems only to get to the door, and then he has

> before him only the masklike face, inert, from which the smile had gone forever. This human form, his friend's, lacerated by the spear thrusts of the plague, consumed by searing, superhuman fires, buffeted by all the raging winds of heaven, was foundering under his eyes in the dark flood of pestilence, and he could do nothing to avert the wreck. He could only stand, unavailing, on the shore, empty-handed and sick at heart (*P* 260).

Rieux's "chronicle" seems now to contain something more than merely the facts in this last struggle; it seems more the description given by an apostle whose beloved Christ has been lost, as Dido lost Aeneas on that same North African shore, as Augustine's mother thought she had lost him (*Conf* 5.8.15). Tarrou's description of his mother makes his tragic chronicle contain even more than that, however. Rieux's self-protective "hidden narrator" chronicling has given way to a superior narrator. To him the silence that follows this long battle is "the silence of defeat...[and] this defeat was final, the last disastrous battle that ends a war and makes peace itself an ill beyond all remedy" (*P* 261). But Tarrou had looked for a peace in death that was something other than an ill, and it had seemed to him, near the end, that all was well now—while Madame Rieux was stroking his brow. It is he who originally testified to the light, which is Madame Rieux, one like his own mother. Afterwards, "Mme Rieux sat near the bed in her usual attitude, her right side lit up by the bedside lamp. In the center of the room, outside the little zone of light, Rieux sat, waiting" (*P* 261).

And so, as they keep their silent vigils, Rieux will once again miss what it seems his mother is, what her love is, what it does, what it has done:

> "Bernard?"
> "Yes?"

"Not too tired?"

"No."

At that moment he knew what his mother was thinking, and that she loved him. But he knew, too, that to love someone means relatively little; or, rather, that love is never strong enough to find the words befitting it... Thus, too, he had lived at Tarrou's side, and Tarrou had died this evening without their friendship's ever having had time to enter fully into the life of either (*P* 262).

But somehow Madame Rieux's love had made all things well for Tarrou—so he seemed to say; it must be a love stronger than the friendship between the two men, a love which enters more fully into a person's life, one which—perhaps?—redeems it. But as to this, doctor Rieux is sitting in the dark; his mother, witness with him to every moment of Tarrou's suffering, is not. She is lit up on that side nearest the bed of suffering.

Curiously, Tarrou's death scene, as that of Othon's son, also has an element of that good death Plato described Socrates as having. After administering the poison, the gaoler examines Socrates' feet and legs, and, keeping his hand upon him, notes for his friends the coldness slowly moving upward; when the coldness reaches his waist, Socrates tells Crito that they must offer a cock to Asclepius, the healer (*Phaedo*117e–118a). Is it because Socrates regards death as healing and setting free, or is it a sign of gratitude, or both, or something else? Plato does not say; Phaedo, who was there himself, merely tells the story. "Rieux was sitting on the side of the bed. Beside him he could feel the sick man's legs, stiff and hard as the limbs of an effigy on a tomb.... 'The fever'll come back, won't it, Rieux?' he gasped. 'Yes. But at noon we shall know where we stand'" (*P* 259).

So, in his considerations following the death, Rieux again seems to be lost, projecting into the world his own refusal to enter the light.

How hard it must be to live only with what one knows and what one remembers, cut off from what one hopes for! It was thus, most probably, that Tarrou had lived, and he realized the blank sterility of a life without illusions. There can be no peace without hope, and Tarrou...Tarrou had lived a life riddled with contradictions and had never known hope's solace. Did that explain his aspiration toward saintliness, his quest of peace by service in the cause of others? Actually, Rieux had no answer to that question, and it mattered little (*P* 262f).

Let us start in the middle of what seems to be Rieux's projection of his own life and (lack of) feeling on to his friend, for that center, under one reading, is mistaken. While one would hope for it before achieving it, the perfect peace would not have hope at all, since it would be the fulfillment of all hopes; that peace would exist without hope. In his book on the peace of the city of God, Augustine described it as "the peace of freedom from all evil"—including the impending loss of death (*DCD* 19.20). The more ordinary peace, a peace with hope, is still restless, there is still something it seeks and hopes for, as Tarrou hoped to be set free, in death, from being a plague carrier. Friendship has such hopes and expectations; Aristotle suggests expectations of continuing virtue, at least of improvement; when these are destroyed, the friendship is abandoned (*NE* 9.3). Among other hopes, Tarrou had hoped to help others to cease their participation in evil, as we see in his constant efforts to bring Cottard into some more regular community with the town. These hopes are not solace, but springs of action. Further, it is not clear, even though he fails with Cottard, that all his efforts are a blank sterility. They have allowed some fruit *in him*: he is able to see and accept Mme Rieux's love, and it matters to him: all was well now. Clearly any aspiration—whether toward saintliness, or peace, in service, or in marriage—by definition includes hope. And if peace is to be hoped for, then it matters quite a bit for what peace one hopes (as Augustine argues in *DCD* 19.10–17), and it matters whether that hope is illusion or not. But, of course, if hope is for things unseen, that one cannot see it—as things unchronicled go unseen—that matters little.

Augustine taught that without hope in the forgiveness of sins and resurrection of the dead, the best life—that of the virtuous man for whom things go well—can only be, really, a life of brave misery. For, "a man who is happy in hope is not yet happy...[and] as for the man tortured without any such hope...however much endurance he shows, he is still not happy, but bravely miserable" (*DT* 13.3.10). This must be true of one who knows he is cut off from what he hopes for, as Rieux describes Tarrou. And even if happy, such a one must know—at every moment of his "happy" life—that this happy life will be taken, despite his will to hold it, despite his desire to continue in it, despite his human excellence and enjoyment of the goods of human nature (*DT* 13.3.11). To forget this is not to be paying attention to the truth of things; it is to suffer delusion about the good one possesses. The less lucky virtuous man—Job comes to mind—will remind him of it. Rieux, at his best, seems to be this modern, bravely miserable, Stoic; but the Stoic loved his friends and family in a way which Rieux's inattention and abstraction disallow him from enjoying with, for instance, his wife. Has Tarrou's life, under the ministering hand of Mme Rieux, been one of either brave misery or inattention? Or has he, finally, admitted himself into the presence of a different, and superior light, one which the darkness—even the darkness of plague and death—cannot overcome? Unlike Paneloux's death, which may not have been brought upon him by the plague at all, but embraced as a participation in the love of Christ, Tarrou's death is brought upon him by both kinds of plague at once. Still, his last recorded words are "Thank you." And at the end he seems illumined within a light in which Dr. Rieux does not share, though that light is his own mother.

Camus' description of how the art of the novel works, and how it fails in cases like Sartre's *Nausea*, requires the kind of what may well be called sacramental reading that has been practiced here: The characters, what they do, what happens to them, their situations must not be teaching us philosophy, they must be real, have the nature of *res*. They are, at the same time, put together precisely as signs as well. Each, at once, *res et signum*; and if Camus' own confessions require that they not be *res et signum gloriae*, what we have is merely his confession—what *he* accepts and will not accept. But we must point out that it is Camus who plans Rieux's narratological strategy and its explosion. But even some of his characters behave differently, and as if the world is quite different than Camus confesses—Paneloux, Grand, Mme Rieux. They are different; while dwelling in the modern plague-stricken town, they are not true citizens of the modern town—places where each thing just is what it materially is, or perhaps where all things have been sucked into the virtual—the world of signs. Paneloux and Grand are wayfarers in the modern—and the narrator at times hints that we are all "wayfarers" (*P* 246, 257). Is that so modern, after all?—namely, that town which exists, those people who exist, "without intimations." It certainly intimates the modern materialist vision of the world. But if we are wayfarers, as more ancient and Medieval people held—whence, and whither? Paneloux, Grand, and Mme Rieux surely are wayfarers in that town, a town which would not understand them, but even though not truly at home in that world, these three care about the citizens of such towns as ours; in fact, they are literally made to exist for us. Camus himself does not call them delusional or foolish, though some critics of the novel have; he only says, *je n'accepte pas*. Anyone is free to do otherwise.

As the old asthma patient says near the novel's end, having heard of Tarrou's death from plague: "But what does that mean—'plague'? Just life, no more than that" (*P* 277). The world of *The Plague* is that: "They are like us," living in the post-lapsarian world of the fall, where, speaking objectively, one may well wonder if the savior has come, and if any savior other than the death Tarrou waited for can release us. Father Paneloux believes otherwise, and works otherwise even while working just as hard, and side by side with the doctor, who does not accept it. Grand believes that the beauty of his horsewoman will be seen by his readers to be worthy of having dedicated his life to setting before them perfectly—that his work has to do with "the growth of a personality" (*P* 40). The perfection with which Grand organizes his duties, all under "one's got to help one's neighbor" at all times, even at the cost of what he, personally, seems most to value, and even at the risk of death, exhibits the fact that a personality grows to perfection under obedience. It is not, we have seen, obedience to the neighbor, for he expects the neighbor to see that he "is busy with his work" (*P* 31), but obedience to a law of which even the people of a modern town know the source. A funny thing—to know the source of something, to see that same thing in action, and not to accept the source, or to disbelieve even that the source exists. Grand is an impossible character for modernity; yet, as we saw, our objective chronicler named him the hero. If *The Plague* is Camus' confession, if the narrator speaks for Camus, what does that choice confess? We must prefer to say that *the novel* speaks for Camus, not this or that character. And that fact gives us something further, which the next chapter will attempt to make clear.

CHAPTER FIVE
LOVE AND POLITICS:
VERSIONS OF SOLIDARITY
IN THE MODERN PLAGUE

The palms and fig trees drooped despondently around a statue
of the Republic, which too was coated with grime and dust.
The Plague, 78

A character is never the author who created him. It is quite
likely, however, that an author may be all his characters simul-
taneously.
The Rebel, 37

After considerable travel through recent and more ancient history—secular
as well as sacred—of several cities, Augustine arrives, in his *City of God*, at
the question of what makes a city, which, it would seem, must be more
than merely a collection of bodies dwelling within a certain walled area. In
the course of his meanderings Augustine brings a cast of thousands into his
stories; Camus is more efficient. But to understand either man's *mythos* we
must grasp what a city is before we can ask about the possibilities for, or
actuality of, any happy city. To lead us into this interrogation Augustine
chooses the Roman philosopher and senator Cicero's definition of a republic, as given through Scipio, in his dialogue *De Republica*: a republic is

> the good of the people... [and] the people, according to his defini-
> tion, is an assemblage associated by a common acknowledgment of
> right and by a community of interests. And what he means by a
> common acknowledgment of right he explains at large, showing
> that a republic cannot be administered without justice. Where,
> therefore, there is no true justice there can be no right (*DCD* 19.21).

The issue then becomes, "what is true justice"? Augustine's is a some-what more demanding vision of human solidarity than it seems Camus takes up in his work up to and including *The Rebel*. There, according to Matthew Sharpe, Camus' "metaphysical skepticism…points toward an un-relativisable primary value: that of solidarity with other human beings whom we *know* to exist, this side of all metaphysical disputes and confab-ulations: 'In the light, the earth remains our first and our last love. Our brothers are breathing under the same sky as we; justice is a living thing.'"[1] But some of these brothers are, have been, or would be, murderers; others would merely use us as it suits them—an injustice according to both Kant and Aristotle, to say nothing of Augustine. So, how does justice live in this world—the world of more and less deadly plagues? A world, for example, of Nazis, spies, collaborators—all breathing the same air as the Free French and the resistance, among them the writers of *Combat*!? A world in which even friends of pleasure or of use, not only those of virtue, are called by the name of friend; a world in which brothers (and sisters) fail in greater and lesser ways to recognize brotherhood and sisterhood—or even, as Kant would call it, personality: the ability to make one's own maxims accord with the categorical imperative. Even "loving the earth" in some people seems to take the form of loving what can be got out of it with the least expense, and it is an analogy to the friendship of benefit. Knowing we breathe under the same sky seems to echo a romantic longing for unity that a simple look at the world, and a realistic look at those around us—or even ourselves, would not be able to consider real solidarity. The Brownshirts and the Stal-inists breathe this air, the Republicans and the Nationalists, the police, the child rapists, the victims; if justice is a living thing, does it pay no attention to those brothers and sisters whose breathing has been stopped? Tarrou sug-gests that the state prosecutor is "Enemy Number One" (*P* 134), but would any society be less murderous by defunding his office? And yet, so long as that office continues, do we not all—even if at many steps removed—par-ticipate in the deaths of others as Tarrou has said?

In short, to breathe together in living justice, it would seem that we all need absolution, and we all must practice the forgiveness of sins: seven

---

1   *Camus, Philosophe*, 25, emphasis in Sharpe; quotation from *The Rebel*, 306, within the quote given by Sharpe.

times seventy. Is such absolution only available if we cheat, philosophically speaking? Sharpe argues that according to Camus we must stay "awake to… and preserve the 'absurd' divorce between the human longing for absolution and its unavailability, unless we philosophically 'cheat'" (*Camus, Philosophe* 25). I agree that he is entirely correct about the thought of Camus in *The Rebel*. I am fairly well convinced that "the absurd" is a metaphysical rather than phenomenological matter for Camus, and more importantly in the *Plague*, for Rieux—whose inconcinnities we have seen much of.[2] I am, however, not convinced that it is possible to hold these three—1) the "absurd divorce" between the need for absolution and its unavailability, 2) the existence of murderers and rapists, as well as lesser criminals as perhaps Cottard is, and 3) "justice as a living thing in which we all breathe the same air"—together coherently.[3] And I do not mean to point out problems with mere passional coherence—such as that between the human desire for happiness and the world's arbitrary crushing of it (the first version of the absurd in Camus[4])—nor do I mean problems with simple logical coherence here, for that is what absurdity, in its usual first sense, is. There is, most importantly, what Kant would point out is a deeply practical incoherence here; a practical incoherence so deep that *practical reason could not begin to act*, for practical reason cannot order itself into a work of absurdity, which any attempt to put these three together is. We may passionately act in the face of absurdity, but such action—with *knowledge of the impossibility* of the act succeeding—is delusional; more delusional than acting on that cloudy ideal of the imagination Kant called happiness, for you might get lucky in that cloud. We could ask Io about that, but one good empirical result proves nothing. Most accurately, we should have to say that practical reason could only *ever* begin to act "by virtue of the absurd" to quote a famous line by a voice in Kierkegaard.[5] It may be that only a love empowered by such faith

---

2   For use of this distinction—metaphysical/phenomenological—with regard to Camus' notion of the absurd, see Thomas Pölzler, "Camus' Feeling of the Absurd," *Journal of Value Inquiry* 52, 4 (2018): 477–490.

3   Perhaps the addition of the second and third elements merely raise absurdity to a higher power. But at a certain point we should recognize there are practical contradictions, and these disable rational action.

4   See above, ch.1, section 3.

5   Søren Kierkegaard, *Concluding Unscientific Postscript*; of course, Camus con-

can even begin to hold the contradiction of this trinity together. On the other hand, if in God's love all things really are possible, then the idea of the absurd is a limitation of human reason, so not a ground for any metaphysical rebellion: *every* moral action is a leap beyond what practical reason can allow or order. Let us see whether a work of art can open a door the artist perhaps does not yet see, or perhaps merely does not want to accept, or has not yet adequately considered.

We will, in what follows, consider how Camus' deeply felt expression of human solidarity in this novel is the beginning of his own breaking through to the third level he thought present and finally coming to the fore in his last works. Let us consider solidarity, then, as an umbrella term for all forms of human love and connectedness, and examine their presence, their shapes or kinds, and the extent of their reach in *The Plague*. In Aristotle's investigation of friendship, he points out the relations based on pleasure or on use, or on mixtures of those ends are also called friendship by analogy to the true one, based on virtue. By contrast, I do not think that Camus is illustrating or presuming that there is only one true form of human solidarity, the others being solidarity only analogously. Several of those thinkers with whom we have seen he is in dialogue may well have thought that: Aristotle, in his way, and Augustine in another, for example. Camus, rather, seems to present real diversities of solidarity; perhaps these are diversities of incoherence, which would not be surprising given the trinity he is trying to hold together. In what follows we will discover agreements and differences among types of solidarity, we may evaluate one or another as superior, but the philosopher's task is first to exhibit the distinctions.

1. Cottard and the Shifting Coefficients of Solidarity

What we might see as the first sort of solidarity in Oran will not achieve the status of Scipio's republic. There may be a "community of interests," but the common acknowledgement of justice is not present. This sort of solidarity finds the origin of political unity in plague-stricken Oran to be precisely the plague as physical threat. Part 2 begins "From now on, it can be said that

siders that Kierkegaard is cheating. On the contrary, he is taking Camus quite seriously.

the plague was the concern of all of us. Hitherto…each individual citizen had gone about his business as usual. … But once the town gates were shut, every one of us realized that all…[were] in the same boat" (*P* 61). In the face of a patently visible enemy, every enemy of my enemy is my friend; at that moment when we all have the same enemy, we are all friends—comrades at least: workers of the world, unite! If the boat is to be saved, we must all row together. This sort of solidarity does not have much to be said for it, for numerous reasons. First of all, there are no real common goods or mutual care among persons. Rather, we should see that a shared hatred or enmity produces an anti-human solidarity, as we might see illustrated in Milton or in Lewis' *Screwtape Letters*, or even in what Aristotle says about friendships of use or benefit: "it is not for being the person he is that he is loved, but insofar as he is useful" (*NE* 1156a 18–19). Underneath that use lies nothing important, nor are we looking for anything further. But this is already too many words: underneath that mutual use—nothing; row!

Really, such solidarity depends upon two things: the absoluteness of the enemy, and a very limited set of interests among the people united against that enemy. Identity politics, or special interest politics, can only keep the group together so long as that interest or identity is both singular and overrides any other identity or interest for each member of the group. What keeps such a group powerful is precisely its single-minded fanaticism. This does not sound at all like the kind of solidarity Camus has in mind, though one cannot doubt that it is a form of contemporary solidarity.

On the other side, the group's solidarity is only as dependable as the enemy. If another enemy comes along that at least some people think is worse, those who think so will be less fully our comrades, if our comrades at all. So, this solidarity depends on the enemy being equally threatening to all in the same way. The Nazis were well versed in making some among the equally conquered French or Belgians or Poles feel more welcome than others; their enmity was differentially ordered against some elements of the conquered much more than against others. If you didn't want to find yourself directly under the boot, your solidarity with others among the conquered—particularly those who were directly under the boot—grew considerably weaker, if it did not turn into enmity itself. Among natural evils, as, let us say hunger is, this form of solidarity also requires that our work against the common enemy does not destroy my personal good, as someone living on the edge of a city with a garden might know is the case if she shares with the city dwellers living in block housing with no gardens at all. Even though hunger is the enemy to both sorts of person, it is unclear how solidarity before this common enemy is not going to destroy the good of the woman on the edge of the town. It seems to her the common enemy becomes more potent precisely because of those other people. This same division is the first effect any literal plague produces: under it, isolation is a safeguard, and one of the better prophylactic measures. Any practice of solidarity itself increases one's risks. These facts about natural evil are what the Nazis imitated in their differential treatment of various sub-groups. The general rule was formulated in Caesar's Gallic War commentaries: divide and conquer. Supposing one knew all the variables in these regards, one could write stress and shear equations, as an engineer does, to summarize the relations among all these people and the result would be a co-efficient of solidarity for each person with each other: Solidarity, or S, $=\dots$

I have insufficient experimental knowledge of the weights and shear values connected with individual interests and fears to adequately define such coefficients of solidarity. Clearly, given that each of us has his and her own choice algorithm, our co-efficient of solidarity, S, will vary with each other person we come across or act at a distance upon. One thing is certainly true about the process of making such equations, however: it treats the human being as just another material thing. What kind of solidarity is it which could base itself on such a premise? Not a human one. Some forms of solidarity, as I said, are anti-human. One could, if she knew enough about kinds of trees and their variable placement (so soil viscosity and nutrients, etc.) across a piece of land, develop such equations to predict which would shear or uproot in different categories of tornado or speeds of straight winds. Some contemporary philosophers (not just Google engineers) explain human activity this way. Barbara Herrnstein Smith sets out a view of the individual human being as an algorithm for particular evaluations. The algorithm is built up by the usual inputs, which, because they can vary through life, make the algorithm vary. Each particular evaluation or action of a person comes as the solution to a multivariable equation of innumerable variables; she gives a list of the *kinds* of variables, but probably could never list all of the variables precisely. Here are just a few of her kinds of variables:

a) various psycho-physiological structures, mechanisms, and tendencies that are *relatively* uniform among human beings;
b) other psycho-physiological structures [etc.] that vary quite widely among individuals;
c) such more or less obvious particulars of personal identity and history as gender, age, the particular physical and social environment into which one was born, ethnic and national culture, formal and informal education, and so forth.[6]

The list of evaluative outcomes which are produced (the passive voice is required) by these individual equations will similarly range from detailed position papers to more and less articulate grunts of approval and disapprobation, "most of which," she says, "are performed intuitively and inarticulately, and many of them so recurrent that the habitual arithmetic becomes part of our personality and comprises the very style of our behavior."[7] She thinks that the great advantage of this view is its reductivism, which it certainly is: the human being is a feedback algorithm like every plant and animal, though with more input variables. Real autonomy would be an illusion reified by the difficulty of getting the algorithm correct. It is a weird sort of Platonism: the real is the algorithm, what the animal, vegetable or human does is its expression at moment (m) of its participation in that mathematical reality. "In accord with such an account, evaluative divergences and the exhibition of so-called bad taste would be seen as the product of the *same* dynamics—the playing out of the same *kinds* of variables, but with different specific values—that produce evaluative convergences and the exhibition of so-called good taste."[8] The adjective here is an absolutely necessary element of the end result. There would be no such thing as *real* bad taste or good taste, much less barbaric or civilized choices; Smith is correct that what *is true* concerning these matters is what is "so-called"; in other words, what elicits the response (good or bad, civilized/

---

6 Barbara Herrnstein Smith, *Contingencies of Value: Alternative perspectives for critical theory* (Cambridge: Harvard University Press, 1988), p.38.
7 *Contingencies*, 43; I wonder what "intuition" means here, though "inarticulate" seems correct.
8 Ibid.

barbaric) from the larger number of presently operating algorithms is definitive. From this mathematicised reduction we can produce another: Each real person having its own algorithm, when combined with another, results in a distinct value for S (at moment m, for persons x and y).

Though now scientifically stated, this way of determining the truth about values was described just as precisely by Plato, whose cave dwellers gave awards to the person who was "quickest to make out the shadows," which can only mean was the quickest to call each shadow what most of the cave would call it, since no one knew the things themselves (516c–d). So let us call this the evaluative convergence of the cave: that is good taste, that is the morally correct, that is justice: what most people say at moment m. Being modern, we can now (perhaps) be more exacting about the coefficients of solidarity of these cave convergences. At least it will look more scientific (I trust we all agree on that), and that will convince the cave that it is so. The word 'algorithm' has great hypnotic powers. According to Smith, this alternative view can be played out with regard to all human preferences, from art to food, from sex to religion, "or even [to] types of logic."[9] In this last case the cave's evaluative convergence becomes an openly epistemological one; truth is what we say it is, at moment m. I would not dare argue against such a view, but merely wish to point out that the fissures in solidarity between such beings are many times more multitudinous than the number of equations for choice and evaluation each unique being himself, herself, itself and theirself instantiates. The solution for that larger equation determining values of S at each moment m (the number of possible combinations all the personal equations can fall into regarding each other) is, precisely, x! (x factorial)—at every moment m, where x is the number of algorithms whose solidarity we wish to measure. Go to Google for the details on the individual algorithms; with those details you would be able to form various groups with differential coefficients of S. The number of distinct communities of solidarity will be uncountably more than there are churches, including storefronts. That is fitting, for this is the mathematics of demons. The dream of such a reduction, though the math would be impossible for even the most glorious of supercomputers, is itself the destruction of all *human* solidarity, since, while it treats all human beings equally, does so by treating them all as things.

9   *Contingencies*, 39 and 43.

Cottard seems to be an example of this sort of solidarity at work. Generally, he feels "much more at ease here since the plague settled in" (*P* 129) as others now share a potent, life-threatening enemy with him. In fact, Tarrou finds him "blossoming out. Expanding in geniality and good humor" (*P* 174). When they are under an equally dire threat, he is not so separated from the usual law-abiding citizen. As the plague ebbs, the fissures in his solidarity with others come to the surface; he is in a state of "consternation" (*P* 247), unsure which way pressures will break. Thus, he exhibits coefficients of solidarity that vary on a daily, if not hourly—or moment *m*— basis, "his abrupt changes of mood" (*P* 249) seeming inexplicable to neighbors and acquaintances, though increased anxiety on the part of others about the reality of the plague's decline generally reassures him and brings him back to "friendliness"—for the moment. Friendship, by contrast, is beyond the capacity of such as Cottard: he can only estimate who would take his side, or at least not give evidence against him, under the shifting tides of all those variables. When the tide comes in all stones are underwater; as it goes out, they dry separately; their separation and differences become noticeable again, and there are uncountably many. As for the tides, I think the last century proved empirically that the more violently irrational sources of social cohesion are considerably more effective than the slow spreading puddle of bourgeois comfort (also an irrational source of cohesion).

As Kant said, "everything in nature works according to laws. Only a rational being can act according to its conception of law.... This capacity is will" (*FMM* 412). Note Kant's realism: we *can* do so; he will also say we should, but such sentences are not empirically provable. Herrnstein Smith's reductive view of human nature and solidarity treats the human being as not forming the law for his or her own action, but as being formed by the inputs of nature, enculturation, and happenstance upon his and her particular physiology, etc. Herrnstein Smith, of course, formed this law—for the reduction of everyone; that includes herself, and her choice of logic. Aristotle, as we saw in the first chapter, called beings who could not set their own ends natural slaves; he thought whole cultures could enculturate to such slavery. Perhaps Dr. Herrnstein Smith is a crypto-Aristotelian? Certainly, anyone who has such a view must regard herself and all others as what Aristotle called slaves of nature—of course, there is still a wide variety of masters amongst us, but the category is clear. It is neither hate speech nor hurtfully divisive if it is true of all: we are all barbarians now. That the science of human behavior and evaluation is unfinished, and perhaps unfinishable (if the variables within each kind of variable Herrnstein Smith enumerates are innumerable) changes nothing about the logic of this evaluation of the being: thing, or to quote Aristotle, living tool. We can get close to what the individual's response will be, that is all we need to sell advertisements for the proper flotsam (racial, genderal, bourgeois, socialist-realist...) to the appropriate barbarian, to get them to jump on the appropriate bandwagon, or to get them to hang a little longer in solidarity with certain others. As "choices" are logged, the equations become more exact.

But Camus opens a wider picture of possibilities for human solidarity than this reductive, empiricist, feedback equation chronicling individual acts and events and then attempting to draw lines of solidarity between different versions of such equations. Perhaps a simple attempt at charting such solidarity among individuals would look like geographical contour maps. Unfortunately, such maps only measure one variable—height; the equation for a single human being would require many more kinds of variables, as we have noted above; soon any contour map for communities of solidarity (and each individual's depth of commitment to each variable) would be unreadable. In what follows we will examine the sorts of love and solidarity exhibited among the characters in a way quite different from this proposed science.

2. Rieux and the Solidarity of Utility

It is Dr. Rieux, the narrator, who notes the statue of the Republic in the square is covered with grime and dust. Curiously, for someone whose "business is only to say: 'This is what happened'" (*P* 6), he describes the fig trees as "drooping despondently," as if these vegetable souls are disappointed in their supposed betters, who notice the statue they are all gathered around, but know as little of its meaning as the vegetables do. The palms and figs do share a common ground, but as we saw in chapter two, neither Rambert nor Rieux—looking for some common ground on which they could meet (*P* 80)—understand either any Kantian or Augustinian picture of 'where', as the kind of being they are, they already share ground: a certain republic, or kingdom—not socio-political or geographical, but moral or spiritual. It's a dusty idea; who attends to such? The journalist is operating on his inclinations, the doctor is reasoning in accord with hypothetical imperatives like greater health or happiness. Regarding the doctor, this is best exemplified in the sending off of his wife, who is shut away in the sealed railway car and sent off to be taken care of according to the best scientific principles. She dies alone, unseen. Rambert and Rieux are breathing on the same earth, but justice is not a living thing—it is a statue, and not well tended.

In the middle of Plato's *Republic* we see that a prisoner, should he be forced up from his seat along the wall and turned around, would discover that the cause of those things he has been so vociferously discussing since childhood are statues carried by other human beings he never knew existed. In the first book several of these "statues" were claimed by their carriers—Cephalus, Polemarchus, Thrasymachus—to be justice, and were shown in short order not to be living justice by Socrates—they were reduced to incoherence by his questions.[10] That neither Rambert nor Rieux can find their common ground while talking beneath the statue under which they have spent their entire lives is a replay of that classical picture of incoherence concerning justice, and so, the concomitant vacancy of the word "republic." Rieux is sure there is some common ground; Rambert is perplexed (*P* 80), though admits he rather thinks so too—in spite of himself and what he had been saying (*P* 81). Rieux concludes that "the journalist was right in refusing to be balked of his happiness. But was he right in reproaching him, Rieux, with living in a world of abstractions?" (*P* 81).

"The doctor glanced up at the statue of the Republic." Sometimes a statue is just a statue, I guess. The journalist has a very definite empirical version of happiness he is aiming at in this moment (*m*), and the doctor *is* balking him. If it is not an abstraction that is in the way (like that of a republic, or a moral law—to which ideas Rieux pointedly does not turn), it must be some empirical hurdle in the doctor himself which is preventing him from working with Rambert to achieve what he rightly refuses to be balked of. This difficulty in finding common ground exhibits the problem

10 On the way things work in the cave, see my *Comic Cure for Delusional Democracy*, chapter four.

with all utilitarian calculations: the co-efficient of solidarity (S) for any individual, x, with the happiness of any other (y) produces shears and stresses against (or for) the happiness of every other (z...) upon whom one's proposed act will have some effect. The doctor has relations not only with Rambert, but with all the other citizens of Oran, as well as the rest of France—which government sent the order to close the city. The judgment of the correct thing to do at moment (m) must draw a line connecting all of them. No republic can be built with such shifting agglutinations of seashells. Or more exactly, such shifting agglutinations are no real moral thing, but merely the shadows of shifting material incentives and feeling. A fig tree is more real—it has a real unity of being, in which all parts participate for the good of all the other parts, which do not have their good as mere parts; for moral beings such real unity must be a principle of reason or something else universally shared, not a happenstance agreement of desires with a plausible technically rational (e.g., mathematical) rule for the accomplishment thereof for all—for that rule does not exist, and your desires are not my desires. Though they speak with each other, even ending in a friendly-looking agreement, there is no real solidarity between Rambert and Rieux at this moment (m), under the statue of the Republic, surrounded by the defeated figs. Real solidarity among human beings requires a moral or spiritual agreement, as Scipio, Augustine, and Kant point out:[11] an idea of justice, an agreement on the ranking of ends, a mutual love for a common interest that all can share, an imperative each one of us affirms, which orders our relations to each other—with or without the threat of a death penalty.

Perhaps, then, there is something deeper than shifting seashells in Rieux's not being able to look the priest in the eye as he confesses to the solidarity of "working together" with him for man's health. That he cannot look the priest in the eye is the symptom of his recognition of something deeper than what he is admitting. There are times when putting health at risk is exactly what he is up to himself (in his everyday work visiting plague

---

11 We should add Aristotelian *homonoia* (chapter two) as well. *Homonoia* as Aristotle means it is not possible for these algorithmic beings—for identical algorithms are merely the same thing, not individuals with an agreement of mind.

victims) and what he encourages (as he does Tarrou, in the formation of the groups of helpers). As with health, so with all other singularly possessable goods: it is not clear why, or on what grounds, a utilitarian would consider the pleasures and pains of every individual to be a necessary part of the moral equations and decision procedures for any republic. It is obviously dangerous to my pleasure (which is the good for me as a utilitarian); it is also an unpleasant principle, as it is certainly quite painful to have to concern myself with the pleasures of others, considering what many of them think pleasant. Further, such a principle is unhelpful: it makes every decision interminably difficult. In fact, utilitarian mathematics is impossible, since it must put in the balance of pleasures and pains not merely those of the people nearest them, but the pleasurable and painful effects redounding to all for the rest of history. This includes, as a small example and subset, the city of Paris while you are off in North Africa. Unless, perhaps, those people and their pleasures and pains don't count? Perhaps something in Rieux knows that the common ground he seems attempting to visualize is an illusion.

Perhaps the problem he is *feeling*, which disallows looking into the priest's eyes, is deeper. Perhaps he has some intimation of the truth about values which Kant states this way: "Reason can never be persuaded that there is any intrinsic value in the existence of a human being who lives merely for *enjoyment* (no matter how industrious he may be in pursuing that aim), even if he served others, all likewise aiming at enjoyment, as a most efficient means to it" (*KU* 208, emphases in Kant). If health is the first good, it must be because it is part of and means to all the other enjoyments of life which go by the name of happiness, and which Rambert sums up as "a woman" (*P* 78) or his "wife"—"it comes to the same thing" (*P* 77). But this sort of human being is precisely what a utilitarian aims to be insofar as he aims to be a morally good utilitarian: an efficient means to the enjoyment of all: we suit each other perfectly. When Rambert decides to stay— turning down his own happiness as the doctor sees it—Rieux also confesses that he is turning his back on what he himself loves "though why I do not know" (*P* 188–89). He does not re-affirm his remark to Paneloux about the primacy of health among those which tie up into happiness (and for its part in the good "beyond blasphemy and prayers" which would fully encompass his aims), but instead pleads ignorance: "man can't cure and know

at the same time" (*P* 189). This confession seems to admit much more difficulty than that which came out on the playground after the child's death,
for here he seems unwilling to take the time to investigate the order of values, forced as he is to continue at breakneck speed in the technically rational
project of curing: so perhaps health isn't the first thing? In any case, we
don't have time to investigate that now, we must accomplish it—and as
quickly as possible.[12] The doctor, then, is one of the early described citizens
of Oran, who, due to "lack of time and thinking," must hurry through their
day rapidly consuming or practicing a mild conjugality before they get back
to work (*P* 4). He apparently does not work only to become as wealthy as
possible, but, given that difference from the usual Oranian, he does not
have any idea why he returns so regularly to his work.

He does not interfere with Rambert's attempts to escape, rather, in fact,
gives him several warnings about the approach of the prosecutor. He also
does not interfere with Paneloux's end "salvation," but he is willing to accept
the help of both men for as long as they are willing to give it in his project.
It is plausible, however—his good feelings for them both notwithstanding,
that a more efficient utilitarian, a more lucid and clear-headed one, would
see both men as dangerous to his project of health in time of plague, and
so engaging in activities which must in any case be stopped. He should report Rambert and his cronies to the authorities, and he should close all the
churches. But let us point out that to do so is to require all citizens to agree
with his statement to Paneloux—that health is the first good, and perhaps
"the only thing that matters" (*P* 197). But health is not a necessary first
good for acting in accord with virtue, and so for happiness as Aristotle explains it, nor is it the primary good among all those other satisfactions
which together make happiness for Kant—and Rambert. Of course, perhaps we can't cure and think at the same time; but we can see this: under
the pressure of a lucid utilitarian calculus by such health professionals as

---

12 This kind of technically rational activity, which must be accomplished before
taking any thought concerning an order of final ends, is precisely the kind of
activity which J.M. Keynes recognized his world had organized itself to accomplish, and in which we found him hoping for a better world: one in which
his grandchildren would have time to consider their ends and to order them
aright. See chapter one, pp. 13–14 and note 19.

Rieux (were he efficient) ought to be, all other values will be relegated to the waiting room where there is world enough and time to think about their proper order. Rieux is reducible to Cottard, but he wears what seems a to be a better quality suit—at least at this point it is not a straitjacket as Cottard will find himself in, though it is, perhaps, a white coat.

At any rate, he doesn't find common ground with Rambert, and he can't look Paneloux in the eye. That's what happened. The utilitarian solidarity Rieux seems to be looking for with Rambert under the statue of the Republic, and in the meeting of the health committee just is that shifting seabed of rocks and shells defined by equations for S. In the presence of the priest, he seems to feel its inadequacy, and in responding to Rambert, as the latter decides to stay, he admits he can give no cogent explanation for why he does as he does. Practical reason's inconcinnity is confessed. He seems a morally superior character to Cottard, but this is only because he considers, or at least tries to consider, the pleasures and pains of others in his own algorithm, whereas Cottard does not; of course, that he feels—and in some way knows—the inadequacy of his way of proceeding is a good beginning: without such an admission one would never look for a more perfect solidarity.

3. Othon/Tarrou's Father: The Limits of Legal Solidarity

In the course of the novel, according to Adele King, Othon "loses some of his uncompromising rigidity, his respect for law and order" (70), but while the first may be true, the second is not. He does add mercy, corporal works thereof, in order "to feel less separated from [his] little boy" (*P* 235). Both he and Tarrou's father are figures of the god of the law: the latter is abandoned by his son after Tarrou sees him win a capital case which leads the criminal to the guillotine; the former is not able (by law) to be with his son as the son is dying and loses him to the plague. He accepts the quarantine's law, which separates him from his son, as one of those matters in which "we must do as we are told" (*P* 190). This acceptance of the law of the community as a law imposed from an outer authority enacts the civic solidarity which every social order requires; one may accept it out of fear of its penalties (as Cottard, in fact, does not), or one may accept it as Othon seems to—because there is no social order without such obedience. The social order's commands ought to have some relation to the commands of reason as Kant lays them out, certainly the maxim "when I am able to act against the social order, I do so, in order to fulfill my desires" could not be made a universal law of nature without rendering the phrase "social order" meaningless. It is a perfect duty then, to obey the social order despite one's own desire. As for other purposes and motives for disobeying a social order, we must leave that great question aside. Othon's way of putting the matter, in any case, does not make this Kantian kind of connection, and sounds suspiciously like those Nazis and their Vichy collaborators who attempted to defend themselves with precisely this line: I was only following orders. A good Kantian would see that if the legal order cannot be made a universal law by each rational being, it is an illegitimate law.

If we see that the legal solidarity Othon here consents to may be just as morally corrupt as Cottard's illegal solidarity with his blackmarket "friends," we are seeing something of what justice as "a living thing," which Camus thought must be an element of all human solidarity, must be. We are recognizing this good precisely by the seeming absence of its working here in Othon. Such living justice must judge of the dead letters of the law, which Othon has spent his life defending. Living justice must be something ever active in the application of, and obedience to or disobedience of the legal. It is not clear that Othon ever reaches the point of entering upon such living justice; perhaps his continual practice of the application of the letter to the individual case has been rather like that of a calculating machine. His inevitable formal dress and coldly disciplinary eye upon his children make us think so. He does, however, add mercy to his acts, though in order to do so he feels he must take a leave of absence from his job as prosecutor (*P* 235). He is unable to bring both sorts of act together, as if the law just is the letter. Camus also could not temper post-war justice with mercy; he realized his mistake, as we have seen (chapter four).

Tarrou's father held a similar position; "underneath his red gown" (*P* 224), however, there appears a different person—he is not the red gown of the law all the way through, as Othon seems to be. Tarrou's says, "he appeared, and was, a kindly, good-natured man" (*P* 222). In contrast with the way Othon seems in public with his family, M. Tarrou "was always very kind" to his son, but on the other hand "he wasn't a model husband... [though] he never gave rise to scandal" (*P* 222). He was obviously not one to hold himself to all the legalities, though he wouldn't make his extra-legal activities a matter to draw social interest. This easiness of character made him more likable than Othon, "he kept the middle way, that's all; he was the type of man for whom one has an affection of the mild but steady order—which is the kind that wears best" (*P* 222). This middle way is obviously not Aristotle's, who admits that in some things—like adultery and murder—there is not a mean (*NE* 1107a9–15). His likability and friendship, then, cannot be what Aristotle would say is the kind that wears best—for it is not based on virtue, but on a certain socio-cultural *techné*, the usual skills of the political class. These skills combine what is pleasant and beneficial in a way which is pleasing to most; so let us call him another version of utilitarian. Tarrou's mother, apparently, never complained of what should be called the father's injustice to her, or perhaps Tarrou himself prefers a more easy-going friendliness than Aristotle's middle way would allow. In any case, he hasn't "the least antipathy to him, only a little sadness of heart" (*P* 226). On the other hand, maybe this sadness of heart is the beginning of a recognition in Tarrou that a pleasant socio-political middle way lacks an important good, which a human life ought to instantiate, but now the father is dead and it is too late for him to come to that.

Othon, though not doing the best things, or not doing them in the best way, does do what is necessary—in regard to the law, his wife, and his children. When he takes his leave of absence from the law it is due to a quite appropriate feeling of love for his abandoned son; he wishes to accomplish some kind of communion with him which he had not accomplished in life only partly because the quarantine law separated them. He does not become feverishly objective as some plague-parted lovers—ignorant "of the way in which [the beloved] used to spend his or her days...[reproaching] themselves for having troubled too little about this in the past, and for having affected to think that, for a lover, the occupation of the loved one when they are not together could be a matter of indifference and not a source of joy" (*P* 68). He wishes to stay closer to what his beloved boy had experienced, and due to that very work and wished for communion among the quarantined, he catches the plague and dies. Tarrou, who started the civilian helping corps, also dies of it. Works of mercy become terminally expensive in this world; but perhaps we should call them works of duty, as Tarrou or Grand might. It is interesting that Tarrou, who once said of

Othon that he was "enemy number one" (*P* 134), finds Othon sharing in the voluntary activities that Tarrou himself originally set up. They die, as it were, brothers in arms, though like Paneloux and Rieux they seem to be acting in solidarity without—at least without mutually recognizing—that unity of mind which Aristotle, Kant, and Augustine consider the mark of the true solidarity. They both die, we could also say, under that dispensation voiced by Grand: one's got to love one's neighbor, though only Paneloux might have put it that way. The man of the law acts as he does in order to be closer to his son, whose death was "a grotesque parody of crucifixion." Perhaps, then, he has some unrecognized solidarity also with Paneloux, who never lets go of the cross. Tarrou dies for a reason that touches Othon's: he wishes, in a world where there are pestilences and victims, "so far as possible not to join forces with the pestilences" (*P* 229). Othon, in this respect, goes further—he wants to be with the quarantined. In the end do they not both share in Paneloux's name: *pan-eleeô*—"I have mercy on all." Is this the "solidarity of rebellion?" Or is it something more positive than that?

This solidarity, like all charity, is rooted in truth. Not, let it be noted, my truth, or Camus' truth, or Grand's or Paneloux's truth—nor the doctor's either—but the truth about the world and human beings within it. One unequivocal element of their solidarity is that their recognition of that truth requires admission of each his own failings to live in it. Paneloux confesses this in his second sermon, Grand in his letter to Jeannie, Tarrou in his abandonment of political parties and their action groups. The doctor wonders if he is a lover (*P* 68)—which is not yet an achievement of lucidity. We each have limited views of what unites us, as we have of the heavens on a dark night, but that does not mean that the truth about us is limited; it may, in fact, be infinite, and eternal; and then, is it merely a horizon of darkness, or are there lights both beautiful and direction giving?

Adele King, among others, has rightly said that "the solidarity established by rebellion [against the absurd] has, Camus claims, an ontological status midway between an historical principle and an abstract ethic... . It implies a human nature that transcends particular historical circumstances."[13] But I wonder if that is all we have here. More specifically, it seems these characters do more, and less. If rebellion is "based on the acceptance

13 King, *Camus* 38–39.

of limitations. Violence should be limited by an awareness of the value of human life; consent to the existing world should be limited by a refusal to accept injustice."[14] But these men are all acting more positively than such limiting refusals of injustice; they engage themselves in positive works of mercy (or duty) or pathological (but not consumptive) love and communion, and they engage themselves to such positive work at the risk of death, even death that is crucifixion. An ethic that transcends, but works within, its particular historical circumstance—a kingdom of ends, then; a communion of saints? a city of God? A city where we see Othon, Rieux, Tarrou, Grand, Paneloux all consciously working together, but not all from the same reason, or with the same feeling. They do not all have the same idea of justice, nor are they all working precisely for that, but perhaps this is the best city we can hope for while enclosed by plague.

4. Paneloux, Grand, Tarrou: Solidarity, Metaphysics, Regulative Principles

The priest could (and does) tell all these other men why everyone counts,[15] though not every pleasure, or every one's chosen pleasures: each one is the image of God, born for personal communion with the divine person who loves each one; he calls this salvation. For each it is a uniqueness which does not depend on wit, talent, good looks, health, helpfulness or any other virtue or accident inhering in the person; much less is it related to the possibly wild differences in one's personal algorithm and that algorithm's index of likability. What counts about each and for each is not their pleasure or pain or even their measure of an empirically imagined happiness. The worth of each one is infinitely deeper than all that; the priest knows why he has taken the position he has in the forefront of the battle. His is a love that is both rational and deeply passionate (as Augustine's was); his life is itself the activity of deeper and more constant union with the crucified. That is what love is. Rieux confesses he does not know why he does what he does. God enables the priest to have this self-knowledge, which Rieux does not have.

14 Ibid. 39.
15 We have no indication that Grand heard Paneloux's sermons; the others all make comments concerning it (or narrate the sermon itself).

God has enlightened him as to the necessity of his actions and inspired the desire to continue what we first met him doing: helping the sick neighbor whom he comes across (*P* 16). The doctor's own being does not make sense to him; Paneloux's own being does make sense to him, and he knows how Rieux could make sense to himself as well. Perhaps Rieux does not look in his eyes because he is afraid of seeing this knowledge—which he has denied himself, about himself. It is not a knowledge of metaphysics, but of a person—from whom Paneloux will not be separated. There is a doctrine, which the priest's sermons teach, but this doctrine is from that person of whom he will not let go, and he believes this doctrine. The doctor refuses to accept the priest's doctrine, but he seems to accept some of its human and moral implications, upon which the culture he is living in is built: e.g., everyone counts—perhaps this is why each one's pleasure must be considered? This must mean Cottard's as well. Rieux seems to want to do that, but he can't see any why, nor can he see any how, really; and he is rightly unable to see these—for they don't exist. Paneloux grasps the ground of solidarity among human beings which Rieux wishes to build, but Rieux himself (like the ship freighted with lovers, drifting helmlessly into the throbbing night, *P* 111) turns his eyes away.

Rieux's mother, as we have seen, enacts this love spoken of by Paneloux with everyone who comes into her presence. To notice and accept this love seems to change Tarrou, but the doctor remains in the dark, even as he seems to act (more often than not, inexplicably) in a way that rhymes in some confused way with such love. He is the picture of a person who acts as one living in a republic, without knowing he is in one, or even how he can be in one. This is unfortunate, since living in a republic is a moral or spiritual reality, not a socio-political or geographical one, so we might say his is a zombie citizenship or zombie virtue insofar as it can be called virtue. He would like each one to make his own law, he would like "for free men to be employed" (*P* 114), but he finds it difficult to gerrymander an agreement among these subjective maxims in a freedom which allows each party what it will (as we saw operating in the meeting of the medical society). This is a deep problem, and perhaps gives some more accurate insight into Rieux's choice of "chronicling" the plague. For without a frame—about the truth of which one cannot know—how can a story be told? Having no framing faith, or perhaps the framing faith of "no faith," all he *can* do is chronicle: one thing, and then another; then death. Paneloux accepts a frame, he sets his life and death in the arc of salvation history, parts of which he repeats in his sermons; the story he tells everyone they are in has a beginning, middle, and end; his vows and way of life are a commitment to that history as the real history of the world created for this purpose by a God of love. Rieux tells no story, he chronicles: this happened, then this.... Judgements may have been made, but he does not judge any.

Tarrou had once seen his life and struggles in the arc of progress to justice in the new world order, which turned out to act just as the old order had, and, seeing this, he could no longer believe that new ordering was leading to justice, to the end of history, to an order which he envisioned as an order without murder. A chronicle, then, can be seen as a form of chastened history, chastened as Tarrou was; or perhaps as afraid of committing itself—as Paneloux was not: but neither makes chronicling a method for not being wrong.[16] There may be a real story; the real story visible through the presence of Madame Rieux, for instance. Chronicling does allow, by giving the reader only one thing and then the next, that reader may read and perhaps discover her own chastening, or realize her own commitments, or lack thereof. *Camus'* myth, then, is quite distinct in its operation from *Rieux's* chronicle. For what we see in Camus' *Plague* is that mere chronicle is one way of understanding and living a modern life. Is it possible to build a real human life as mere empirical chronicle? Or is that merely a way of hiding, of defending oneself from what goes on, as a hidden narrator might be trying to do? The citizens of Oran seem to build human lives in the chronicle—without thinking about it: they are human, that is their life, so it is a real human life. Or is that merely to see equations in motion?

Is it possible to work toward some form of real solidarity in such an empiricist, materialist world? Or does one merely fall into it?—and out; a solution at moment m for the coefficient of solidarity (S). Rieux seems incapable of building solidarity, though he wishes to do so; his first failure is with his wife, of whom he is reminded at the end of the day by a dying rat; he does not understand Grand, though he does freely treat him; he cannot

16 For a more complete account of contemporary man as living in a chastened history see Chantal Delsol, *Icarus Fallen: The search for meaning in an uncertain world,* translated by Robin Dick (Wilmington, DE: ISI Books, 2003).

find explicit common ground with or understand Rambert. Though he takes up Tarrou's diary as part of his chronicle, he seems to be taken up by Tarrou into such friendship as they do manage. It is through Jean Tarrou that he seems first to come to see even the light which is his own mother; the first notes about her lightness are from him. A chronicle is "of what happens"—it is a moving finger that writes and having writ moves on—to which we all are passive. Tarrou organizes groups of men to work together to gain some control over what our sentence will be; he volunteers to organize volunteers who each voluntarily agree to the necessity of their action for the sake of a good they can all share; such is the outline—and the workings—of a republic. Other members of the town will have good done to them by the members of this republic, but they are themselves not true members, for they have not taken their share in the activity necessary for the shared good of all to be accomplished. Perhaps some do not wish for a truly human life, or any other community than the accidental collocation of algorithms. Perhaps they know not what they do—they have not time for thinking. Is that a truly human life?[17]

If it is Tarrou who takes up Rieux (by fits and starts) into his way of being and seeing as Rieux takes up Tarrou's diary—the insertions of which break the boundaries set by the doctor's intent of chronicling, we see exemplified a first instance of a sort of relation between moral kingdoms. Tarrou both sees how Rieux lives and brings Rieux up to at least viewing his kingdom, but Rieux cannot get to Tarrou's wider or deeper life on his own. Let us put it this way: while Camus' work wishes to move (and does move) from the absurd to rebellion to love, the movement from notice of the absurd to rebellion is, in a sense, a narrowing of possibilities by actuating one of several responses. Tarrou, too, revolted against the absurd in joining the communists; but he saw that this was no answer, and we saw him at the

17   Camus' novel makes us raise this question about life in the modern city. At the end of *The End of the Modern World* (Wilmington DE: ISI Books, 2001), Romano Guardini raises similar questions: "Is it possible to build a life for man or for society upon exclusively empirical grounds, a life which could endure? Could such a life foster the values and insights necessary to remain truly human? Could it even reach the goals which it seeks?" (p. 112). The example of Dr. Rieux seems to provide an answer; the answer is negative, as was that of the district medical stores depot (*P* 32).

start of the novel writing recipes for how to spend one's time in awareness of the absurd, but unwilling to act in any way that would take sides with the infection. This is why the Spanish asthmatic is his example of sanctity. His own experience has taught him this, and he also knows that the doctor's work is "a never-ending defeat" (*P* 118). His return to consciousness of the absurd, rather than some hopeful work in the direction of the (illusory) end of history, is what allows him the freedom to notice Madame Rieux's lightness. In turn, she can (and does) bring him up into her world, though he cannot, and would not, get there on his own. Similarly, Paneloux can enter Rieux's world (and freely does so), but Rieux does not and cannot (on his own) enter Paneloux's. These seem to be ontologically distinct kingdoms, in which the members of the higher are allowed into the lower of their own accord, but the lower can only be brought into the higher if they accept to be taken under the passport of that higher; one's faith makes one a resident of another kingdom, and while some kingdoms have passports allowing them into many others, several do not open to any who do not have the correct passport.

The "rights of man" were not born in 1789 with the Republic of France, nor at the dawn of the Enlightenment. Kant says that the moral law is the principle of pure practical reason, but this universality across all beings who share in reason is what gives us duties (and so gives others rights) and he is merely bringing into the light what has always been at work in us. We should note that rights are not a first principle for Kant. Still less are they a first principle if we change this Kantian beginning to "all who share in the *logos*." This latter way of speech—to speak historically—may be found elsewhere in the chronicles of mankind. The Gospel of John says nothing about rights, for in regard to God we have none, but he does say that the logos is the true light which enlightens all men, *panta anthrôpon* (Jn 1:9). Kant ascertains that the freedom to choose that all one's practical maxims accord with the categorical imperative first of all gives us duties toward all other such rational beings; from this, rights are born—not in us directly, but in every other person first. All who recognize this law are, through that recognition itself, engaging their rational activity in building the kingdom of ends: "the systematic union of different rational beings through common laws" (*FMM* 433) that each makes for himself and knows can be approved by all others. We enact our citizenship in this kingdom precisely by acting only on maxims that can be universalized;

we act against this kingdom by doing otherwise. Kant does not call this kingdom a republic, however, because he considers it possible that there is a legislator who "is subject to the will of no other" (*FMM* 434), who yet legislates in accord with the categorical imperative as do all the other members. For that being it is not an imperative constraining an otherwise oriented free will, for He has no other orientation than love. Under either title—kingdom or republic—this would be living justice, shared by all, and that within which every empirical republic—were there any—could be seen as a republic. Scipio would agree to this, we know. For our chastened contemporaries a republic is, then, not necessarily a metaphysical reality, but a regulative idea; one in which every rational being may freely participate—or not. But then, if we so live, are we not making it come to be?

We have seen that Grand, most explicitly, lives in this kingdom. That he helps his neighbor who has just attempted an action contrary to the categorical imperative (and which Kant himself discusses several times) indicates that he understands the depth of his citizenship: only the person himself can (or can try) to remove himself from this kingdom, but the neighbor's attempts do not determine Grand's citizenship, or his duties— only Grand can determine that. Cottard still is a being with practical reason, and "one's got to help one's neighbor" (*P* 19). Grand knows (as Rieux apparently doesn't) that this does not mean Grand has to help his neighbor in all of his projects—or even not stand in the way of some of them. Grand gets Cottard down. It is only licit to help in those projects which respect all other members of the kingdom—including Cottard himself. To not save Cottard from this attempt to escape his citizenship would be Grand's denial of his own citizenship; Rieux, on the other hand, encourages Rambert in his attempt to break quarantine. While Tarrou never speaks in a way which echoes these Kantian themes, we can see that he and Grand—though they seldom meet—share in this sort of citizenship. Tarrou's constant offerings to Cottard of opportunities to act (as Grand does in his small ways) as a citizen of this republic, is one way we can see their solidarity—they both act in ways that respect Cottard's personhood, and encourage him to act in respect of his own. When Grand falls ill, "Tarrou volunteered to stay with him" (*P* 239), and Rieux approves—not sending him to the hospital, though he injects him with the serum. We could hope that this is a case of the civic law being superseded by respect of the virtuous for the good, but it may merely be an inclination to try to satisfy as many inclinations in others as possible. Aristotle says that "when men are friends they have no need of Justice, while when they are just they need friendship as well" (*NE* 1155a25–27), but are all three perfect friends? More likely, Rieux is just trying to satisfy the desires of both men so far as he can. He does not think Grand will last the night. "All night Rieux was haunted by the idea of Grand's death. But the next morning he found his patient sitting up in bed, talking to Tarrou... ." Tarrou, watching through the night, is already happily sharing in Grand's new life: "'Yes, doctor,' Grand said, 'I was overhasty. But I'll make another start.'" Rieux is "completely baffled by this 'resurrection'" (*P* 239); Tarrou participates in it.

Philip Thody[18] suggests something in Joseph Grand that a reader might ordinarily not see. First of all, he embodies "the true nature of rebellion... against injustice [which] lies in the humble task which helps a man fight against it"; his work is like that of the "trade union secretary in keeping his accounts up to date." Secondly, though he seems to fail everywhere—in writing a "letter of explanation to Jeanne, in asking for an increase in salary, or in making any progress with his novel... in him, Camus' own love of ordinary humanity shows itself." The latter is certainly true. We have explored in some detail the moral significance of Grand's continuity of effort and discovered that he is the enactment of what Kant would call "practical love," which engenders in anyone who sees it both respect and what he would call "moral interest" as distinct from the passional or inclinational interests we might have in a man for his good looks, friendly conversation, or helpfulness in our particular desirous efforts. It seems that Camus' description of Grand—missing most of his teeth, wearing clothes a size too big for him, and having such a strange "pastime"—disallows that Camus' love of ordinary humanity is based on the rubbing together of the "agreeable," but must itself be based on our common "interest" in the moral.[19]

18 Philip Thody, *Albert Camus: A Study of his Work* (New York: Grove Press, 1959), p. 32 (firstly), and pp. 38, 39 (secondly).

19 See Immanuel Kant, *Critique of Judgement*: "That is agreeable which the senses find pleasing in sensation" (*KU* 205). On the other hand, "The delight which we connect with the representation of the real existence of an object is called interest" (*KU* 204). Thus we have an interest in the moral independent of its agreeability.

The feeling the novel engenders in us for him has a ground we cannot find in our relation to the equally ugly, but perhaps more successful Cottard— or even, I think, regarding the doctor. We find through this experience that the mutual recognition of autonomy in acting in accord with the moral law is an extremely important thread for weaving human solidarity—even in relation across the world of fiction to the real world. But, contra Thody, we see just as clearly that this thread is itself not necessarily twisted from the raw material of metaphysical revolt. For Grand, who lives on the only street made of greenery (rue Faidherbe) in this high desert setting, does not revolt against creation as he finds it like the doctor does; rather, he accepts what fate and the city administration have dealt him, and each day he goes forth to make what perfection he can out of the tasks he has been given and those he has taken up. We wish things to be better for him. We wish for him to finish and send that letter to Jeanne, and for her to respond. We know what his inability to finish the letter means—that love cannot ever be completed or completely spoken; that is to say, it requires eternity, and requires of us a perfection we have not got, even though we may be more talented and richer than Grand. Among other things, we have learned that love desires the constant conscious presence of the beloved, as Grand's constant return to his horsewoman: beauty within a picture of natural beauty is his exhibition of that love. He seems almost the embodiment of the Plotinian Intelligence, of which Camus had once written "there is…an indigence in relation to itself and from which it suffers and stirs."[20] What then could be the real answer in which Grand achieves the happiness which we are united in wishing him to have?

Here a nameless, equally impoverished woman might give us a suggestion. While Rambert is waiting to escape the quarantine at the house of the brothers who will let him through their guard post, he spends a lot of time with their aged mother, who goes to Mass every morning. She asks if he is afraid of infecting his wife, an eventuality he considers unlikely, though if he stays they might never meet again. She asks if she is nice, and pretty, and when Rambert affirms "'I think so.' 'Ah,' she nodded, 'that explains it.' … 'Don't you believe in God?' she asked him. On Rambert's admitting he did not, she said again that 'that explained it.' 'Yes, she added, 'you're right. You

20 *Christian Metaphysics and Neo-Platonism*, 104.

must go back to her. Or else—what would be left you?'" (*P* 183f). Without God, who, along with freedom and immortality is practically implied in every act of pure practical reason according to Kant, the human moral project is impossible, so there is nothing that can make sense except "the agreeable." Activity in accord with the rule of practical reason is "delusional," for without this trinity that work cannot even be started, much less be accomplished, *and we know it*. Rambert's world, at first, is bound within such a horizon. The old lady affirms that he is right not to believe in the moral project, which would require him not to act on the maxim of escaping the plague when under quarantine. If he does not believe in God, it is simply nonsense to act as if there is something other to live for than what is agreeable. She does not share his disbelief, but perhaps her questions make him face the small nature he has reduced himself, his beloved, and their love to: "we suit each other perfectly" (*P* 78) is not a legitimate explanation for citizens of the kingdom of ends, yet that is all he has at this point in the story. As with Grand, this old lady—a smaller, seemingly less important character—sees and acts with the deeper love, a more universal understanding of what is true of persons. She is undisturbed by the plague, and seems to have a deep-seated and serene acknowledgement, as if from a place high above the small house she shares with her sons, of how the world and its people are. She speaks from within a love that sees more in a person than Rambert can at this time; and by speaking to him, perhaps she even aids in loving that 'more' into existence in Rambert himself. When the reported deaths jump the day Rambert is scheduled to escape she says, "There's so much wickedness in the world.... So what can you expect" (*P* 184). Her comprehension shares much with Tarrou, and her hope much with Paneloux. She exhibits what Thomas Hanna called "the paradoxical greatness of" Christian faith, "that it poses the 'should' against the 'is' of this world but yet cannot bring itself to despise the 'is.'"[21] And in holding these together, the wizened lady is gentle even to the would-be sinner.

Like the old lady, Grand and Paneloux carry a verticality within themselves that enriches the horizontal world, and like hers disturbs that world in great (widespread panic) or little (harmlessly eccentric) ways—if one

21 Thomas L. Hanna, "Albert Camus and the Christian Faith," in Brée, ed., *Camus: A Collection of Critical Essays* (Englewood Cliffs, NJ: Prentice-Hall, 1962): 48–58 at 52.

does not lose attention and close the door to them. But these ways of look-ing at them are not what their own lives are about—as they show us. They seem, rather, to be partaking of the kind of life Mme Rieux also embodies; they all intimate a light more stable than any empirical chronicle can men-tion, and a love more certain than any empirical relation can found. We should notice a solidarity among them all that is not at all related to that which depends upon feeding in the same place, as could be true of cattle (*NE* 1170b13–14). Though they all are members of the same kingdom, they do not ever meet in this chronicle. Their verticality frees them from the world's weathers, its ebbs and floods of opinion and worry, its interest in the prophecies of Nostradamus or the latest thing on social media.

That Paneloux and Madame Rieux are as hand-in-glove as the explica-tion of what God's love is, and the figural presentation of God and God's love, brings into doubt Matthew Sharpe's claim that "Paneloux hypostasizes God's omnipotence at the cost of rendering his providential omnibenevo-lence wholly beyond human understanding. From a doctrine of consola-tion, Christian faith…becomes the difficult basis for a heart-rending unquestioning acceptance of the fundamental, divinely willed injustice of creation" (*Camus, Philosophe*, 123). God's omnipotence is self-limiting in the very act of creation of the natural world—which has its own laws; his love is not so limited, and like Mme Rieux's is ever-present, even if unno-ticed. There are, then, occasional miracles—Grand's resurrection, for in-stance.[22] Those occasional miracles take place within a larger one, which

---

22 Modern philosophers seem not to want to allow divine love to create either a world or a being with its own laws (or its own law-making powers); and if the divine being does so, that provides evidence against that being's love. David Hume shows the lengths to which such arguments can be taken in his *Dia-logues Concerning Natural Religion*, sections 10 and 11; one has to wonder, however, what it would mean to take his arguments seriously. See Gene Fendt, "Empiricism or Dialectical Destruction Thereof? Reading Hume's *Dialogues Concerning Natural Religion* on Evil." We have argued that Augustine takes the world and human choice within it as the most serious of divine projects: both are given their own kind of being. This does not deny the power of the divine will as Asherite Muslims fear, or as late medieval scholastic voluntarism went too far to save, since God himself created both to be that sort of thing that each is.

we pride ourselves on understanding the workings of—Creation. This pride is, when moderated by the humbling wonder that we can come so far in understanding, really not so much pride as gratitude at being able to share so far in the thought of God, as both Aristotle and Einstein said. It is not the case that we see in these characters "a metaphysical zero-sum game, between submission to God (Paneloux) and hybristic *apotheosis* (Tarrou/Rieux), with no *tertium datur*" (*Camus, Philosophe*, 137). Nor, at his end, does Tarrou seem to be considering the dilemma "either that (false) dilemma, or absurdity." Rather, touched and cared for by Madame Rieux, he says "Thank you," and that all was now well. Perhaps he did not himself have faith, but the work of art allows us to hear an old revelation come from his lips: "And all shall be well, and all manner of thing shall be well."[23]

Grand's choice of his own life, despite its personal absurdities—like having been promised that his position would be made permanent decades ago, by a man now dead—and that life's consequent limitations, and his daily reiteration of the choice to try to make something perfect within that life, has prepared him to live in solidarity with all others who live in the absurd. But unlike David Sherman, who thinks that Grand has "lofty 'metaphysical' aspirations, [a] desire, never to be realized, for at least one thing, one sentence, to capture Truth (with a capital 'T')," which he attempts "in the concrete language of literature,"[24] it seems much more plausible to consider that Grand's unending work on his horsewoman is an effort to get his love right. Perhaps that is unrealizable too, but then no rational being could begin it—except perhaps "by virtue of the absurd," which some have considered cheating. In acting as he does, Grand is fulfilling what Diotima long ago taught Socrates: that love aims to have the beautiful as its own forever (*Symp* 206a). And in this task Grand knows, as Kant pointed out, that we must begin again at every moment, for this love is an activity, not a state. And he will know his love is right when he can put in words what, and

---

23   These words were spoken to Julian of Norwich by Christ, on what she supposed was her deathbed, as she wondered why the onset of sin had not been prevented by divine wisdom. Cf. Julian of Norwich, *Showings*, translated by Edmund Colledge, OSA and James Walsh, SJ (Mahwah, NJ: Paulist Press, 1978): 224f.

24   Sherman, *Camus* 117.

how, his horsewoman is in her movement down the avenue: he aims at having the real woman consciously present, so present that she is no longer an imagined woman whose story is coming (and so might whet Rieux's appetite), but the person herself, fully present, before whom all the publisher's gentlemen will take off their hats. It is not capturing Truth, but a perfect conscious living in beauty's presence, and bringing others fully into that presence that Grand aims at. That is what it means to love one's neighbor, and so he does. So, despite living alone—as his neighbor Cottard—Grand has not, like him, "an ignorant, that is to say lonely, heart" (*P* 272). His heart is perfect; he merely has a constriction of the aorta.

5. Friendship in the Modern City?

The friendship we see enacted between Tarrou and Dr. Rieux has seemed to most readers the best form of human solidarity available in the modern city— a city without intimations of any religious, metaphysical, or even regulatively ideal nature—and so it is. But we should pay attention to how Tarrou himself labels the most holy moment of this friendship, the previously considered non-transfiguration above the city, and the baptism which follows, outside it. Above the city and the faint clatter from the houses below, Tarrou asks whether they are friends, to which Rieux responds "yes, of course, we're friends; only so far we haven't had much time to show it," to which Tarrou responds, "suppose we now take an hour off—for friendship" (*P* 221).

This exhibits perfectly Augustine's complaint about happiness in the world: they have to take time off from the world of plague. As he says, we have a constant need for fortitude (among the other virtues); for we ourselves, and all those around us are beset by weakness—the wandering concentration of which Tarrou accused himself being perhaps the least, but most basic, of these weaknesses. "So long, therefore, as we are beset by this weakness, this plague, this disease, how shall we dare say that we are safe? And if not safe, how then can we be enjoying our final beatitude?" (*DCD* 19.4) We can't be, of course; nor would Tarrou and Rieux be surprised at this, for they do not believe there can be such a thing. Let us note, however, Augustine's response to this admitted fact: If such men have true virtues, "they do not profess to be able to deliver the men who possess them from all miseries," and this being the case, they must know, at all times, that the

183

friendship and happiness they do share is unsafe, and "if not safe, how could it be happy?" (*DCD* 19.4) Only by being, in some way, outside of this world, "miserably involved in many and great evils" as it is, can they taste a pure happiness and friendship. Their hour off for friendship shows that Augustine's analysis is true: they are, for an hour, above the plagued city, and then, swimming beyond it. The scene is constructed, then, to intimate something more than our narrator's chronicle is able to say or Rieux himself is able to see: This scene seems the scene of happy love, love fulfilled and at peace, just so far is it a scene of these two "in the same rhythm, isolated from the world, at last free of the town and of the plague" (*P* 233). Insofar as they are not really free of the plague of this world's weaknesses, insofar as they are still, like us, "encompassed with evils, which we ought patiently to endure, until we come to the ineffable enjoyment of unmixed good," their happiness is, even here, "laboring toward its end rather than resting in its finished work" (*DCD* 19.4). The scene does intimate this picture of ineffable good, but it is just as clear that such a good is outside the city we live in, we are not there yet, as the scene itself presents, for "at one point… unexpectedly they found themselves caught in an ice-cold current. Their energy whipped up by this trap the sea had sprung on them, both struck out more vigorously" (*P* 233). The fulfillment of their friendship in peace is, then, an illusion—and a dangerous one, a trap. "Far be it from us, then, to fancy that while we are still engaged in this intestine war, we have already found the happiness which we seek" (*DCD* 19.4). If we admit that this kind of human solidarity is what we do seek, then life is but brave misery since such love is impossible of fulfillment—or even an hour off. Beginning is absurd, or, perhaps, begin by virtue of the absurd. Or perhaps: for a moment, waiting for his friend to dive in, Rieux looks up into "the dome of sky lit by the stars and moon" (*P* 232). This access upward, toward the eternal is still available to him, then they swim out together into the seeming infinite sea, seemingly "isolated from the world, at last free of the town and the plague" (*P* 233). Catherine Pickstock has pointed out that this modern infinite, the infinite of space, is not a symbol of eternity, but "*a substitute for eternity…which* [robs] *of life.*"[25]

25 Catherine Pickstock, *After Writing: On the Liturgical Consummation of Philosophy* (Oxford: Blackwell, 1998): xiv.

Augustine thought it "a surprising mistake" for certain philosophers to "contend that this is a happy life which is beset by these evils" (*DCD* 19.4), but it is no longer surprising, for the error is no longer seen as such by many. The modern person who considers such a problem—the problem which is the deepest element of the absurd—that each still has this desire for the unity of love to be safely happy, while she must know that everything in herself as well as in the world testifies to the presence of a plague which disallows it, considers that this is "just how things are." This, Camus has said, is "the essential passion of man torn between his urge toward unity and the clear vision he may have of the walls enclosing him" (*MS* 17). Tarrou rightly concluded that only death could free him from this torturing plague; he does not, like the Stoics whom Augustine is criticizing "make fortitude a homicide" because he sees this conclusion. He chooses life in the absurd. There are no grounds for this choice, however this desire for unity already posits an end, much as Grand's work on his novel posits an end: all work in this direction is an embodied hope, a lived hope, a dwelling in hope; the hopeless person is the one who does not attempt such love, like Cottard. He has other work; jobbings which adjust his comfort or ease in continuing his hopeless way, thus the plague makes of him "an accomplice" (*P* 176)—for it is dis-ease which he always seeks to mitigate in himself; sometimes working with some, always working contrary to others. Solidarity, friendship, and love are not among the things he hopes or attempts. Nonetheless, Tarrou keeps offering it to him; Cottard does not understand this, and so at turns is "puzzled," "offended," afraid, or considers Tarrou "a fellow one can talk to...because he's really human. He always understands" (*P* 144, 145, 174).

Tarrou's humanness is precisely in this constant offering of second chances at solidarity, suggesting that the best way of not being cut off is a clean conscience (*P* 138, 175) and sharing in Cottard's hope for a "clean sheet" and "new lease of life" after the plague. But what can that phrase really mean for Tarrou—"after the plague?" Though he wishes for the clean sheet, Cottard "wasn't interested in hearts; indeed, they were the last thing he bothered about" (*P* 251). Tarrou's vision is of a wider world: his work and hope for universal human solidarity opens him to Cottard, and requires these elements of forgiveness of sins, renewal of conscience, and constancy of heart. None of these are visible in the world around us; indeed, in the world shaped by death where we all have plague, who could think them possible? Who could reasonably begin? Cottard, fully empiricist, scoffs. His world, as his heart, is much smaller than Tarrou's, it cannot really include the man. He is carted off at the end having shot a dog.

Against Tarrou's good, though self-contradictory, nature Paneloux comes off, perhaps, as cold. While there is no scene in which these two speak to each other, the Augustine scholar surely agrees with Tarrou about the difficulty of the human condition: "So long, therefore, as we are beset by this weakness, this plague, this disease, how shall we dare to say that we are safe?…Then that virtue which goes by the name of fortitude is the plainest proof of the ills of life, for it is these ills which it is compelled to bear" (*DCD* 19:4)—always. Of course Tarrou isn't looking for a final beatitude, but it seems life offers much less even than this to one who waits and knows that only death can free him (*P* 229). "Oh happy life, which seeks the aid of death to end it!…What, then, if by some secret judgment of God you were held fast and not permitted to die, nor suffered to live without these evils?" (*DCD* 19:4). Tarrou knows (as did Augustine) that the disease against which we must constantly fight is not only in us, but infects the world, and living in this world means, for some, living under the additional burden of authority over others, for some—bishops, district attorneys, judges—have the duty of keeping order in this ward. Their use of authority is a form of care for them, as work of surgery and cauterization, of incising buboes, ordering quarantines and ensuring their enforcement are also some men's duty. Thus, "by reason of certain official positions in human society, it is necessary for us to be both loved and feared" (*Conf* 10.36.59); but if this love and fear is not grounded in justice it is nothing but a perverse and deceitful increase in the torture of the plague-stricken. It is an ineffective serum which does not rid the body of its plague, as Paneloux said, and Castel's "twisted smile" (*P* 195) seconds. I am speaking now both spiritually and physically. For such as these, their work is the work of an office, as well as of a man, therefore they may look less human (as Othon and Tarrou's father). Tarrou wishes for a world without such duties, a world in which we are all not, even at a distance, involved in the deaths of others (*P* 226–228). Paneloux is more lucid about this world where all have plague: he refuses to look over the wall—or to attempt even an hour of escape. Such "holy leisure is longed for by the love of truth; but it is the necessity of love to undertake the requisite business" (*DCD* 19.19). Tarrou and Rieux take an hour off for friendship, thus "they fabricate for themselves a happiness in this life" *(DCD* 19.4), but Paneloux's love is already fully at work in this world—working in hope, a hope that is "grace," that is, a theological virtue. It is something the doctor admits he does not have; his serums can only lengthen the suffering then. Even if they work. "Human society...compels" such duties, "not with the intention of doing harm," but in the ignorance of incompletion, in the (all too human) hope of an order that will be somewhat less miserable (*DCD* 19.6). That hardly seems beyond blasphemy, and it has not yet achieved prayer. On the other hand, "if any man uses this life with a reference to that other which he ardently loves and fervently hopes for, he may well be called even now blessed, though not in reality so much as in hope" (*DCD* 19.20).

As his sermons tried to make clear, the real recognition of love requires genuine sorrow for one's own sins against it. Because charity is a participation in the love of God, a participation in the love with which God loves human beings, charity goes out into the darkness to seek the lost, and Paneloux confesses that his first sermon had lacked this—as many of us also frequently do even if acting "appropriately" and speaking truly. But in the second, he places himself with the lost—in the darkness of the plague, walled in by quarantine, and unwilling to look out over that wall. Thus, starting where they are, he brings the truth about love in to the plague-bound, aiding them by both teaching and prohibitions concerning that love, encouraging all of us to renew our efforts of concentration upon charity in the midst of all our activities here—under plague. This requires the constancy of mind and heart we see throughout the novel in Madame Rieux. Madame Rieux and her son divide what Paneloux knows he must try to keep together, though at one time and another he fails. We must be both mother and son; we must be that human being created male and female, the symbolism of which Augustine discussed in *De Trinitate* 12.3.12–13, only Camus reverses the image. In Augustine the woman's head covering

> could suitably be used to symbolize that part of the reason
> which is diverted to the management of temporal things, signi-
> fying that the mind of man does not remain in the image of

God except in the part which adheres to the eternal ideas to contemplate.... . But through that reason which has been delegated to administer temporal affairs he may slide too much into outer things by making unrestrained advances; and in this the active reason may have the consent of her head, [which] may fail to curb her.

In Camus' imagery the woman (Madame Rieux) remains in loving contemplation while her son slides too much into outer things. Mother and son thus picture a reversal of the story of Adam and Eve, where Eve is tempted to much by certain fruits in the world, and Adam does not check her. Paneloux, if anyone, achieves the proper order and balance of meditation and work in the world. When we first meet him, helping Michel back home, "his eyes were smiling behind his big round glasses" (*P* 16). In charity, he does the good thing: contemplative love in action.

Paneloux is more lucid than Rieux or Tarrou regarding these matters, therefore his edges seem sharper to those of us sunk in mere human fellow feeling—the solidarity of which cannot be depended upon. Then there is the additional problem that such political and public matters can only be rightly undertaken if for our neighbor's good, not "to build up some sort of private superiority" looking for and hoarding up "marks of approval" (*Conf* 10.38.63). Perhaps Paneloux goes too far in correcting for this temptation when he wonders if a priest can have friends, but he sees correctly that in this world—the world where we all have plague—even friendship offers a type of temptations. For the praises of others might bring us to displace our good from that love which is justice, and from the good itself, to loving such praises for their own sake. Alternatively, fearing their disdain, we might abandon some part of the truth—a truth about our friends and fellow citizens that they need to hear, and that true love must speak, as Paneloux speaks, attempting to get Oran to hear. Thus "our daily furnace is the human tongue" (*Conf* 10.37.60f). It is doubtful that Cottard ever stepped into the church or considered such matters, but it is certain that he would find Paneloux less human than Tarrou. In what world, however, should we trust Cottard's judgment of such matters?

Paneloux believes and lives what Tarrou tries to live, but does not believe. Neither I, nor Augustine, nor the Augustine scholar can prove the reality of that most desirable good of true human love, we can merely point out how the best of men live: in a city that as yet is not visible, under a rule they all accept as just. Tarrou, in the light (which is Madame Rieux), is grateful and says everything is well. Rieux, sitting in his own darkness, considers only love's death.

QED.

BIBLIOGRAPHY

Adams, Henry. *The Education of Henry Adams*. Boston: Houghton Mifflin, 2000.

Aristotle, *Nicomachean Ethics (NE)*, trans. Martin Ostwald. Upper Saddle River: Prentice – Hall, 1999.

_____. *Poetics (Po)*, trans. Stephen Halliwell. Cambridge, MA: Harvard University Press (Loeb), 1995.

_____. *Politics (Pol)*, trans. Benjamin Jowett. In *Basic Works of Aristotle*, edited by Richard McKeon. New York: Random House, 1941.

Augustine. *Confessions (Conf)*, trans. John K. Ryan. New York: Doubleday-Image, 1960.

_____. *City of God (DCD)*, trans. Marcus Dods. New York: Modern Library, 1950.

_____. *On the Freedom of the Will (DLA)*, trans. Anna S. Benjamin and L.H. Hackstaff. New York: Macmillan, 1964.

_____. *Expositions on the Book of Psalms*, edited and condensed from the Oxford translations by A. Cleveland Coxe. *The Nicene and Post-Nicene Fathers*, Vol. 8. Grand Rapids: Eerdmans, 1983.

_____. *Soliloquies*, trans. Kim Paffenroth. Hyde Park, NY: New City Press, 2000.

_____. *The Trinity (DT)*, trans. Stephen McKenna, C.SS.R. Washington DC: The Catholic University of America Press, 1963.

Barthes, Roland. "*The Plague*: the annals of an epidemic or a novel of isolation?" in *Œuvres complètes*, ed. Eric Marty. Paris: Seuil, 2002. Vol 1: 540–545.

Bastienelli, Marco. "Wittgenstein and the Mythology in the Forms of Language," in *The Darkness of this Time: Ethics, Politics and Religion in Wittgenstein*, edited by Luigi Perissinotto. Mimesis International, 2015: 87–114.

Bastienelli, Marco. "Wittgenstein and the Mythology in the Forms of Language," in *The Darkness of this Time: Ethics, Politics and Religion in Wittgenstein,* edited by Luigi Perissinotto (Mimeisi International, 2015): 87–114. (Cf n40 p29)

Bataille, Georges. *The Accursed Share,* trans. Robert Hurley. New York: Zone Books, 1988.

Bourgault, Sophie. "Affliction, Revolt, and Love: A conversation between Camus and Weil" in *The Originality and Complexity of Albert Camus's Writings,* ed. Emmanuelle Anne Vanborne. New York: Palgrave Macmillan, 2012:125–142.

Brée, Germaine. *Camus: A Collection of Critical Essays.* Englewood Cliffs, NJ: Prentice Hall, 1962.

Buonarroti, Michelangelo. *Selected Poems, with translations from various sources.*https://archive.org/stream/selectedpoemsfro00michrich/selectedpoemsfro00michrich_djvu.txt

Camus, Albert. *The Plague* (*P*), trans. Stuart Gilbert. New York: Random House, 1975.

_____. *The Fall,* trans. Justin O'Brien. New York: Vintage, 1991.

_____. *The Rebel: An Essay on Man in Revolt (R),* trans. by Anthony Dower. New York: Knopf, 1961.

_____. *Lyrical and Critical Essays (LCE),* trans. Ellen Conroy Kennedy, ed. Philip Thody. New York: Vintage, 1970.

_____. *The Myth of Sisyphus and other essays, (MS),* trans. Justin O'Brien. New York: Vintage, 1955.

_____. *Resistance, Rebellion and Death (RRD),* trans. Justin O'Brien. New York: Vintage, 1988.

_____. *Christian Metaphysics and Neoplatonism,* translated with an introduction by Ronald D. Srigley. Columbia: University of Missouri Press, 2007.

_____. *Selected Essays and Notebook,* edited and trans. Philip Thody. Harmondsworth: Penguin, 1962–1979.

Carroll, David. "The Colonial City and the Question of Borders: Albert Camus' Allegory of Oran," in *L'Esprit Créateur,* Volume 41, Number 3 (Fall 2001): 88–104.

Cristaudo, Wayne. "The Johannine Christianity of Albert Camus," in *Culture, Theory and Critique* 52.2–3 (2011): 145–161.

Cruickshank, John. "Levels of meaning in *The Plague*," in Jesse G. Cunningham, ed., *Readings on The Plague*. San Diego: Greenhaven Press, 2001.

Dahlberg, Edward. "Can These Bones Live?" in *The Edward Dahlberg Reader*. New Directions, 1957.

Davis, Colin. "Camus's "La Peste": Sanitation, Rats, and Messy Ethics," *The Modern Language Review*, vol. 102, n. 4 (October 2007): 1008–1020.

Delsol, Chantal. *Icarus Fallen: The search for meaning in an uncertain world*, trans. Robin Dick. Wilmington, DE: ISI Books, 2003.

Engstrom, Stephen "Virtue and Vice in Aristotle and Kant," in Pavlos Kontos, ed., *Evil in Aristotle*. Cambridge: Cambridge University Press, 2018: 222–39.

_____. "Happiness and the Highest Good." *Aristotle, Kant and the Stoics*, ed. Engstrom and Whiting. Cambridge: University Press, 1996.

Fendt, Gene. *Love Song for the Life of the Mind: An essay on the purpose of comedy (Love Song)*. Washington, DC: Catholic University of America Press, 2007.

_____. "Aristotle and Tolkien: An Essay in Comparative Poetics," in *Christian Scholars Review* XLIX, 1 (Fall, 2019): 63–82.

_____. "Empiricism or Dialectical Destruction Thereof? Reading Hume's *Dialogues Concerning Natural Religion* on Evil," in *International Philosophical Quarterly* 61, 2: 139–160.

_____. *Comic Cure for Delusional Democracy*. Lanham, MD: Lexington Books, 2014.

Freud, Sigmund. *Civilization and its Discontents (CD)*, trans. James Strachey. New York: W.W. Norton, 2010.

Garfitt, Toby. "Situating Camus: The formative influences," in Hughes, ed. *Cambridge Companion to Camus*, 26–38.

Guardini, Romano. *The End of the Modern World*. Wilmington DE: ISI Books, 2001.

Hanna, Thomas L. "Albert Camus and the Christian Faith," in Germaine Brée, ed., *Camus: A Collection of Critical Essays*. Englewood Cliffs, NJ: Prentice Hall, 1962.

Henry, Patrick. "Albert Camus, Panelier, and *La Peste*," in *Literary Imagination: The Review of the Association of Literary Scholars and Critics*, vol. 5, n. 3 (2003): 383–404.

Herbert, Zbigniew. *Barbarian in the Garden*, trans. Michael March and Jaroslaw Anders. New York: Harcourt Brace Javanovich, 1986.

Hughes, Edward J., ed. *The Cambridge Companion to Camus*. Cambridge: University Press, 2007.

Hume, David. *A Treatise of Human Nature*, 2nd ed., ed. L.A. Selby-Bigge. Oxford: University Press, 1978.

Julian of Norwich. *Showings*, trans. Edmund Colledge, O.S.A. and James Walsh, S.J. Mahwah, NJ: Paulist Press, 1978.

Immanuel Kant, *Critique of Pure Reason (A…/B…)*, trans. Norman Kemp Smith. London: St. Martin's Press, 1970.

_____. *The Critique of Judgment (KU)*, trans. Werner S. Pluhar. Indianapolis: Hackett, 1987.

_____. *Critique of Practical Reason*, trans. Lewis White Beck. Indianapolis: Bobbs – Merrill, 1956.

_____. *Foundations of the Metaphysics of Morals (FMM)*, trans. Lewis White Beck. Upper Saddle River, NJ: Bobbs – Merrill, 1997.

_____. *Metaphysical Principles of Virtue*, trans. James Ellington. Indianapolis: LLA, 1964.

_____. *Religion within the Limits of Reason Alone (Rel)*, trans. Theodore M. Greene and Hoyt H. Hudson. New York: Harper Torch, 1960.

_____. "On the Common Saying: That May Be Correct in Theory, But It Is of No Use in Practice," in *Practical Philosophy*, ed. Mary J. Gregor. New York: Cambridge University Press, 1996: 273–309.

Kelly, Debra. "*Le Premier Homme* and the literature of loss," in Hughes, ed. *Cambridge Companion to Camus,* 191–202.

Keynes, John Maynard. "Economic Possibilities for our Grandchildren," in *Essays in Persuasion*. London: Macmillan and Co., 1931.

Kierkegaard, Søren. *Either/Or,* trans. David F. Swenson and Lillian Marvin Swenson. Princeton: University Press, 1959.

King, Adele. *Camus*. New York, Capricorn Books, 1971.

Kolakowski, Leszek. *God Owes us Nothing*. Chicago: University of Chicago Press, 1998.

Krapp, John. "Time and Ethics in Albert Camus's *The Plague*," (TEAC) *University of Toronto Quarterly: A Canadian Journal of the Humanities*, 68.2 (Spring, 1999): 655–76.

Kraut, Richard. *Aristotle on the Human Good.* Princeton: University Press, 1989.

Lešić-Thomas, Andrea. "The Answer Job Did Not Give: Dostoevsky's *Brat'ia Karamazovy* and Camus's *La Peste*," in *Modern Language Review* 101.3 (July 2006): 774–88.

Lévi-Valensi, Jacqueline. "Le Temps et l'espace dans l'oeuvre Romanesque de Camus: une mythologie du reel," in *Albert Camus 1980*, ed. Raymond Gay-Crosier. Gainesville: University Presses of Florida, 57–71.

Lockwood, Thornton. "Aristotle on the non-Greek Other," delivered June 10, 2020, to Society for Ancient Greek Philosophy.

Lorcin Patricia M.E. "Politics, Artistic Merit, and the Posthumous Reputation of Albert Camus," *South Central Review* 31.3 (Fall 2014): 9–26.

Margerrison, Christine. *'Ces Forces Obscures De L'Âme': Women, Race and Origins in the Writings of Albert Camus*. Leiden: Brill – Rodopi, 2008.

Marx-Scouras, Danielle. "Portraits of women, visions of Algeria," in *Cambridge Companion to Camus*, pp. 131–144.

Maze, John Robert. *Albert Camus: Plague and Terror, Priest and Atheist*. Bern: Peter Lang, 2010.

Merton, Thomas. *The Literary Essays of Thomas Merton* (Merton), ed. Brother Patrick Hart. New York: New Directions, 1981.

Mill, John Stuart. *Utilitarianism*, ed. Oskar Piest. Indianapolis: Bobbs – Merrill, 1957.

Moses, Edwin. "Functional Complexity: The Narrative Techniques of *The Plague*," in *Modern Fiction Studies* 28.3 (1974): 419–429.

Nancy, Jean-Luc. *Adoration: The Deconstruction of Christianity II*, trans. John McKeane. New York: Fordham University Press, 2013.

Newmark, Kevin. "Tongue-tied: What Camus's Fiction Couldn't Teach Us about Ethics and Politics" in Margerrison, Christine, Mark Orme, and Lissa Lincoln, eds. *Albert Camus in the 21st Century: A Reassessment of His Thinking at the Dawn of the New Millennium*. Amsterdam: Rodopi (2008): 107–120.

Nietzsche, Friedrich. *Beyond Good and Evil*, trans. Walter Kaufmann. New York: Vintage, 1966.

O'Brien, Conor Cruise. *Albert Camus: Of Europe and Africa*. New York: Viking Press, 1970.

Onimus, Jean. *Albert Camus and Christianity*, trans. Emmett Parker. University, AL: University of Alabama Press, 1970.

Palud, Aurélie. "The Complexity and Modernity of *The Plague*," in *The Originality and Complexity of Albert Camus's Writings*, Emmanuelle Anne Vanborne, ed. New York: Palgrave Macmillan, 2012: 19–33.

Pickstock, Catherine. *After Writing: On the Liturgical Consummation of Philosophy*. Oxford: Blackwell, 1998.

Picon, Gaëtan. "Limitations of *The Plague*," in Jesse G. Cunningham, ed., *Readings on The Plague*. San Diego: Greenhaven Press, 2001.

Pölzler, Thomas. "Camus on the Value of Art," in *Philosophia* 48, 1: 365–376.

_____. "Camus' Feeling of the Absurd," in *Journal of Value Inquiry* 52, 4 (2018): 477–490.

Plato. *Republic*, trans. Allan Bloom. New York: Basic Books, 1968.

Quilliot, Roger. *The Sea and Prisons: A commentary on the life and thought of Albert Camus*, trans. Emmett Parker. Tuscaloosa: University of Alabama Press, 1970.

Radulescu, Domnica. "L'amour dans *La peste*," in *Dalhousie French Studies*, vol. 33 (Winter 1995), pp. 83–95.

Rothko, Mark. *The Artist's Reality*, edited with an introduction by Christopher Rothko. New Haven: Yale University Press, 2004.

Said, Edward. *Culture and Imperialism*. New York: Alfred A, Knopf, 1993.

Sarah, Robert Cardinal. *The Day Is Now Far Spent*, trans. Michael J. Miller. San Francisco: Ignatius Press, 2019.

Sartre, Jean Paul. *Existentialism and Human Emotions*, trans. Bernard Frechtman. New York: Citadel Press, 1985.

_____. Jean-Paul Sartre, *Being and Nothingness*, trans. Hazel E. Barnes. New York: Philosophical Library, 1956.

Sessler, Tal. *Levinas and Camus: Humanism for the Twenty-First Century*. London: Continuum, 2008.

Sharpe, Matthew. *Camus, Philosophe: To Return to Our Beginnings (Camus, Philosophe)*. Leiden: Brill, 2017.

_____. "Camus and the Virtues (with and beyond Sherman)," *Philosophy Today*, (Summer 2017) 61. 3: 679–708.

_____. "The Black Side of the Sun: Camus, Theology, and the Problem of Evil," *Political Theology*, 15.2 (March 2014): 151–174.

Sherman, David. *Camus*. Malden, MA: Wiley – Blackwell, 2009.

Smith, Barbara Herrnstein. *Contingencies of Value: Alternative perspectives for critical theory*. Cambridge: Harvard University Press, 1988.

Solomon, Robert. *Dark Feelings, Grim Thoughts: Experience and Reflection in Camus and Sartre*. Oxford: University Press, 2006.

Srigley, Ronald. *Albert Camus' Critique of Modernity*. Columbia: University of Missouri Press, 2011.

Thody, Philip. *Albert Camus: A Study of his Work*. New York: Grove Press, 1959.

Thoyakkat, Sreedharan. "The World Is What Was Given, The World Is What We Make: Albert Camus' Bifocal Credo in *The Plague*," in *IUP Journal of English Studies*, vol. 4 Issue 3/4 (September 2009), 7–27.

Todd, Olivier. *Albert Camus: A Life*, trans. Benjamin Ivry. New York: Knopf, 1997.

van der Poel, Ieme. "Camus: A life lived in critical times" in Hughes, ed. *Cambridge Companion to Camus*, 13–25.

Weil, Simone. *The Need for Roots*, trans. Arthur Wills. New York: Routledge, 2002.

Woelfel, James. *Camus: A Theological Perspective*. Nashville: Abingdon Press, 1975.

Wood, Allen W. *Kant's Ethical Thought*. Cambridge: University Press, 1999.

Zaretsky, Robert D. *Albert Camus: Elements of Life*. Ithaca: Cornell University Press, 2010.